JESUS

Books by Walter Wangerin Jr.

The Book of God: The Bible as a Novel
Paul: A Novel
This Earthly Pilgrimage
Saint Julian
The Book of the Dun Cow
The Book of Sorrows
Preparing for Jesus
Reliving the Passion
Little Lamb, Who Made Thee?
The Manger Is Empty
Miz Lil and the Chronicles of Grace
Mourning into Dancing
The Orphean Passages
Ragman and Other Cries of Faith
A Miniature Cathedral and Other Poems
Measuring the Days
Whole Prayer
In the Days of the Angels
As for Me and My House
The Crying for a Vision

For Children

Swallowing the Golden Stone
Mary's First Christmas
Peter's First Easter
God, I Gotta Talk with You
The Book of God for Children
Probity Jones and the Fear-Not Angel
Thistle
Potter
In the Beginning There Was No Sky
Angels and All Children
Water, Come Down
The Bedtime Rhyme
Branta and the Golden Stone
Elisabeth and the Water Troll

JESUS

A Novel by Walter Wangerin Jr.

LION

Copyright © 2005 Walter Wangerin Jr.

The author asserts the moral right
to be identified as the author of this work

A Lion Book
an imprint of
Lion Hudson plc
Mayfield House, 256 Banbury Road,
Oxford OX2 7DH, England
www.lionhudson.com
ISBN-13: 978-0-7459-5202-4 (hardback)
ISBN-10: 0-7459-5202-X (hardback)
ISBN-13: 978-0-7459-5227-7 (export paperback)
ISBN-10: 0-7459-5227-5 (export paperback)
ISBN-13: 978-0-7459-5203-1 (paperback)
ISBN-10: 0-7459-5203-8 (paperback)

First hardback edition 2005
10 9 8 7 6 5 4 3 2 1
First paperback edition 2006
10 9 8 7 6 5 4 3 2 1 0

Acknowledgments
Watercolour illustrations by Michael Ingle

The text paper used in this book has been made from wood
independently certified as having come from sustainable forests

A catalogue record for this book is available
from the British Library

Printed and bound in Great Britain by
MPG Books, Cornwall

Walter Wangerin's website address is:
www.walterwangerinjr.org

Unto these, who are the future:

Noah
Cassindra
Emma
Maxwell
Thea
Anna
Theron

CONTENTS

Prologue 9

Book One: The Son of God 13

Part One: Mary 15

Part Two: The Beloved 55

Book Two: The Shepherd of the People 71

Part Three: Mary 73

Part Four: The Beloved 123

Part Five: Mary 155

Part Six: The Beloved 169

Part Seven: Mary 203

Book Three: The Sacrifice of the Messiah 239

Part Eight: Mary and the Beloved 241

Part Nine: The Beloved 341

Epilogue: Word 359

PROLOGUE

I am standing on the high south side of a rugged defile, a wadi which cuts a long descent through cliff-stone to empty its waters into the Dead Sea. The Salt Sea. I am not so far from the sea that I cannot see its waters off to my right. There is a hard wind blowing from north to south down the gullet of the sea, causing armies of waves to roll and rise and break into whitecaps. They crash in triumph and defeat.

It is late in the afternoon.

I spent the morning among the Essene community whose people sleep severally in caves and underground rooms and tents in this wilderness. But they gather in a large building to study and to write, and always they eat together, declaring their meals to represent and to celebrate the new world coming. I saw the tables at which they write and the ink pots and the clay jars in which they keep their scrolls. I saw their wheels and kilns and the pottery these produced. They catch water from the wadi to keep in pools, to drink, to wash. They bathe often. They baptize unto the purity of their persons.

I listened to their teachings, particularly their expectation of the end when they shall be shown to be the true Israel, and false priests and powermongers shall be dismissed and displaced.

And then I came apart to this place, the south side of a falling gorge in which I've stood for half the afternoon in my own frowning and hollow meditations. I think of nothing. I can consider no thing within my heart. My heart is empty, grieving me, causing me to breathe with something like a panic.

But suddenly, there – to my right, far off and down where the wadi meets the shore of the Great Salt Sea, but flying this way between the walls of the gorge, ascending higher and higher along its floor and filling the defile with the sound of its own wind, the wind of her great wings beating – comes an eagle.

I am standing at the very edge of her long approach! I watch her magnificent ascent, her bright adventing here, and my breathing grows deeper: she is coming straight towards me! I see the motion of her flight; she rows the wind; her wings sweep forwards and backwards low, and her neck gives a little lunge with each rowing, and there is astonishing strength in her breast and shoulders, and her beak is hooked and terrible with danger.

And then there is a moment when she is but ten feet in front of me, passing me at my level exactly; and though she does not turn her head, her single eye — yellow, fixed, sharpened by a bony brow — sees me. The eagle looks at me. She does not stop flying by. Nevertheless, it seems to me that this moment lasts and lasts, and I cannot draw a breath, and in the eagle's eye is the sun and the sky and all creation and God in the still, black centre, the pupil of the eagle's eye, and all are staring straight at me. I am no longer a secret on the face of the earth, a man sneaking from here to there whom no one notices. I am *known*! The earth and the heavens, they know me! In her eye I see that the eagle must even know my name, and by the gaping of her beak will shortly scream my name, and this terrifies me. For shall my name be screamed in judgment or in blessing? And what shall *be* my name when it resounds to the four corners of the world?

But then I realize that the eagle has flown on, higher and higher off to my left, unto the horizon of the evening, into the dying sunlight, where she seems to burn like golden fire and turn to bronze.

BOOK ONE

THE SON OF GOD

PART ONE

—

$\mathscr{M}$ARY

THE ROOM

Zechariah and his son, John, had preceded the rest of the families by ten days to the city of Jerusalem. Indeed, *all* the able-bodied priests in Palestine, and all the Levites too, arrived in the Holy City some few days ahead of the worshippers: they had to prepare themselves for their sacred service, and then to prepare – to purify – the Temple and its precincts for the remembrance of the Passover and the Feast of Unleavened Bread. More than one hundred thousand pilgrims would pour into a city whose normal population was thirty thousand. Jerusalem, swelling four times its size, required the services of all twenty-four divisions of priests and all the weekly courses of Levites, a workforce of eighteen thousand men.

Zechariah's division was the eighth, that of Abia out of the hill country of Judea. It lay closer to Jerusalem than most of the others. Nevertheless, Zechariah left home a full week earlier than priests from regions more distant than his. He had reasons. He had purposes. But, though the man was pious truly, piety was not one of those purposes.

Zechariah had grown most old. His eyes had hardened into a pearl-white and staring blindness. The last time Mary had seen him – and this a year ago – she'd suffered pity for those eyes overhung by great bushes wild and uncut; pity, too, for his shoulders, bent at right angles to his spine, driving his face forever towards the ground. She had known him old and strong, the man now old and stooped. Travel was hard on him, even when he crouched upon his little donkey and was held in place by the hand of his son. For this reason Zechariah had left early with John, who was old enough to know the way, to lead the donkey, to find both food and drink for his father, to arrange places of rest every other hour in the day. The boy had turned thirteen just eight months ago. He'd attained the age of a man.

There was yet another reason for their early departure, more pragmatic than spiritual, more familial than personal. Zechariah wanted to secure a room in one of the houses owned by the Temple. Not a house. Just a single room.

Despite his great and respectable age, the old priest was as ordinary as any other country son of Aaron. His only advantage would have to be in approaching the Temple authorities first. On this year particularly Zechariah desired his family to eat the Passover meal within the walls of the city of Jerusalem. His whole family, in a room large enough to accommodate three tables and twelve bodies.

'He was able to reserve the same room for ten years straight,' Mary said to her son as they walked among the pilgrims. 'Two years ago he lost it. Last year too we ate in a strange place. Poor Zechariah. He knows we like familiarity. Then the women have no trouble finding the oven, the dishes, cloth, water, cushions – '

Mary walked in silence awhile.

Then: 'But I don't think that's the deepest reason he wants the same room again this year.'

Mary and her husband had discussed the matter of Zechariah's tremulous intensities, how absolute he had become regarding things of small significance.

They sensed finality.

Joseph and Mary both suspected that this would be the last year the old priest would serve at the Passover. Actually, the lack of sight was not his greatest handicap. Zechariah knew by heart every inch of the generous esplanade and every gesture of his office. But now his hands shook with an uncontrollable violence. He could scarcely hold the silver tray beneath the flow of the lamb's arterial blood. Last year Joseph had been forced to grab the priest's wrist so that any blood at all might be caught on the tray.

Finalities, then: Joseph believed that Zechariah, unable and infirm, sought a little rest and a lot of sunlight in his shrinking years. 'He'll stay to home next. Man'll sit on his roof and smile.'

Mary, on the other hand, thought it likelier that Zechariah would not live to know another Passover, not in Jerusalem, not in the hill country where he dwelt, not in this world.

The silver cord will snap – So went the sentiment in the woman's mind, a mournful sort of music: *the golden bowl will break, the pitcher crack upon the fountain, and the man that once could move with the strength of the sea will, under a withering sun, sink into himself like a dry well full of dust.*

Aloud, and more than once, she said to Joseph, 'When he cannot go up to Jerusalem, he will not live at all.'

Joseph said, 'I think he'll wait till his son turns priest. Like himself. Like Elizabeth's father.'

Mary said, 'They waited nearly to death for the boy to be born in the first place. And when they received him, they received the assurance of descendants.' Mary had been present at that birth. She had seen the transfiguration of the parents, stunned by such a birth in their old age. 'For him, Joseph,' she said, 'for Zechariah, I think this is life enough, that a son has followed him into the world, not that a son must follow him into the service of priests.'

'Children are children.' The big man bit his sentences, making them short. 'But grandchildren are descendants.'

Yes, but Mary was often more than a step ahead of him. She had said *for Zechariah* because she knew her husband's mind: that for him, for Joseph the carpenter, the development of one's son was all in all the purpose and the merit of a father's life. Young Yeshi, twelve years old, had conned *his* father's craft, stood skilfully in *his* father's tradition. The boy's deft use of a plane caused Joseph to nod with silent approval, thin shavings curling before the blade, olive wood smooth as basalt behind.

But more than the craft, it was Yeshi's intellectual aptitudes that silenced the carpenter's mouth with pride. For at the age of five the child had suddenly begun to read the Aramaic words he saw everywhere in the big city of Sepphoris; and then at seven he, with an ancient rabbi in their tiny synagogue, was reading the Hebrew of the Holy Scriptures – causing Joseph's eyes to water and his nose to run. And why shouldn't the father permit himself such tender internal delights? He and Nazareth and most of his kind couldn't read a word in any language.

'He'll make his living as a carpenter,' Joseph whispered in Mary's ear while they lay abed together. 'But he'll make his name as a scribe. In Jerusalem. I'll be there. Old, crippled. Content.'

A grand company of Galilean pilgrims had been climbing the hills of Judea for half a day towards Jerusalem for the Passover, when Mary and Joseph and the boy turned aside. They departed the jubilant music and the great river of Jews going up to Jerusalem. Leading the donkey that bore their loads, they went single file up a narrow, stony path until they came to a little village as old as Moses. There they approached the house of Zechariah and Elizabeth.

It was almost a week ago that young John had seen to the old man's travel. Now these would see to hers. She would ride. They would bear their possessions on their own backs.

'Elizabeth? Elizabeth, are you ready?'

Everyone would arrive safely there. And they would celebrate the story again, and they would experience deliverance again as if it had happened just yesterday.

THE STORY

—

At three in the afternoon Mary withdrew from her work and dashed to the door of the room the women were preparing. From the south-west pinnacle of the Temple, a Levite had just begun to blow a stunning blast on his trumpet.

Mary ran out into the sun and squinted and found the diminished figure of the man standing halfway to heaven. His perch was the topmost corner of the gates of the Holy Mount. He lowered the instrument and breathed a moment, then raised his trumpet for a second blast. Long he blew it. The length of his full lungs he blew it. He caused the sound to snarl, to shake the air across the city. Beyond the city, surely. Beyond the Mount of Olives as far away as Bethany! Mary could scarcely breathe. But her elation was not so much for herself as for her son, who must, she thought, be feeling a wild joy right now – now, while he and his father were mounting the steps to the Huldah Gates of the Temple.

And then the third blast –

Mary knew the ritual. She'd heard that preternatural howling often before. But on this occasion the mother felt every part of the Passover more exquisitely than ever, hearing it through the ears and seeing it through the eyes of her son, for whom it was all new. Mary covered her mouth, devastated by the weight and the glory of the feast.

How bright must be the fire in your face, learning from your father the practices of the sacrifice. How cold the water that washes you clean. How purified your soul now entering the Temple –

When the Levite vanished from his height, Mary returned to the room and rejoined the women who were preparing for the

Passover meal. But the mother's front teeth were set together, her lips drawn back as if smiling: in her fierce imaginings she was elsewhere, entering the Huldah Gates near the bottom of the south wall of the Temple Mount. As lightly as breath she was attending her son step by step, Yeshi, who was carrying (she knew because she strove to *see* it) the sheep which Joseph had purchased that morning.

Up the interior stairway, the great stone arches overhead, the pressure of the crowds ascending with them: Joseph and John and Jesus, the youngest one rapt and the oldest watchful. In the city behind them vendors had shouted their wares: wines and spices, pepper, herbs, vegetables, pomegranate sticks, bolts of an orient cloth. The streets behind them had smelled of foods and human habitation.

But now, arriving on the esplanade in front of the Royal Portico – that forest of stupendous columns – they were met by other sounds and other odours. Here at hand were doves round-eyed in their cages; sheep bleating, goats nagging, rams staring slot-eyed, erect and strong; calves and bullocks both chewing and dropping manure: beasts for sale for sacrifice. Here, too, were tables upon which quick fingers exchanged the pilgrims' coins for coins to be spent in the Temple.

But there, out in the Court of the Gentiles, the sounds became murmurous, talking and praying and wheels of people turning in a sky-like motion. So tightly did Yeshi grip his sheep that the animal craned its head and bawled. But the boy's attentions were on his father, whom he followed through the gate of gold called 'Beautiful' into the Court of the Women, then up some fifteen steps, through the Nikanor Gate of Corinthian bronze into the Court of the Israelites.

Massive before them stood the Altar of Whole-burnt Sacrifice, the Altar of Holocausts, from which arose a white cloud of smoke. Now the scent was of a spitting, roasting meat, the fat of the offerings borne up to the fires on the altar by a continual line of priests. Now, too, the odour was coppery, humid, cloying in the nostrils: fresh blood and then a gouty, thickening blood. And the sound was song, covering the cries of the sheep; the sound was a choir of Levites accompanied by twelve reed pipes. Cut into the pavement at his feet, Jesus saw a channel through which ran a river of red blood; the blood flowed with the angle of the pavement downwards into a system of stone pipes, and through these down yet again into the Kidron Valley east and south of the Temple. So enriched was the valley by the lives of endless sacrificings, that the vines on its terraces grew greener, and the grapes of the new year fatter, than anywhere else in Judea.

'Jesus!' his father called above the music and the bleatings. 'Bring the sheep.'

Ha!

During the moment of the boy's distraction, Joseph and John had found old Zechariah; John had kissed his father, and all three had knelt together, the priest with a tray that flashed wildly on account of his shaking, Joseph with a slender knife, the haft in the palm of his hand.

Swiftly, Jesus knelt as well. Joseph wrapped an arm around the sheep, grabbed its forehooves in his left hand, drew them up to its belly, and with one clean stroke sliced open its neck and a single artery. A fountain of blood sprang forth, startling in its readiness, splashing the pavement. John took his father's wrists to still the tray and to catch the blood. The life in the sheep's eyes quietly subsided. On a huffy sigh, it breathed its last.

But then the old man had to proceed on his own, for none but priests could enter the interior court. He rose to his bended height. He turned. In order to preserve some blood in the silver tray, he pressed its edge against his chest, into the white linen, into his flesh, and blindly limped the distance. Zechariah found the stones of the altar by touching them. Then he clapped the tray against it, spotting it with some few drops of fresh blood. Even so did Zechariah signify that the Lord redeemed his people.

O Lord, I am your servant, the Levites sang:

I am your servant,
The son of your handmaid;
You've loosed all my bindings!

To you I offer
The sacrifices
Of thanksgiving —

In a twinkling (as it must have seemed to Yeshi) the little animal was dressed and flayed, its legs unbroken, its head attached, the whole of it wrapped in its own unspotted pelt.

But Mary's son was relieved of his burden now. Joseph carried the fleece-packaged meat back through the courts of the Temple and down the tunnelling stairs and out the Huldah Gates, into the streets, past the markets, through the shouting crowds, through the sweating, milling crowds and the heat of a hundred thousand bodies.

Mary, straining to see their coming, stood on the roof of the house in which the room was ready. The woman's shins against the edge of the parapet, she peered northwards, seeking the face of her boy, his hair a cap of tight curls: *Yeshi, what did it mean for you? Have you learned? Will you be able to kill the lamb when you've become a man?*

Probably not. It took most boys more than one year to learn the rituals that would define their futures.

The tables are spread and set. The room is purified. There is no leaven in this place. The whole sheep, its legs and head tucked into the cavity of its rump, has been roasted on a pomegranate spit in the clay oven, which now sits cooling in the courtyard.

There are three low tables placed at right angles to each other, forming three sides of a square; bolsters are laid on the floor along the outside edges of the tables. Mary will serve, kneeling in the centre of the square. The room is lit by lamps in the niches of its window-wall. The oil is clean, though smoke has marked the plaster above the niches. On each table three lamps of a finer clay illumine stone bowls of food, lettuce, chicory, pepperwort: the bitter herbs. Stone plates and stone-carved vessels are arranged for each of the people now entering the room. The beams of the ceiling tremble with shadow. On the walls shadows bloom and swell to fantastic shapes as members of Zechariah's family move past the flames to their places.

It's late. Most of the meals in Jerusalem have already been eaten. Outside the tiny windows, people are chattering, strolling about, kinfolk meeting kinfolk with great good cheer now that their rituals are finished. Who wants to sleep tonight?

Zechariah. He wants to sleep. Nevertheless, both he and his

relatives had to wait while he finished his Temple service, then bathed, then changed his clothes, then crept on the strength of John's arm here, to this room, to accomplish one more thing before he can allow himself to lie down on the thinnest of pallets and sleep.

John gripping his right elbow, Joseph his left, the old priest is lowered to the floor at the middle of the central table. He's the host. With a grunt he reclines on his left side, the bolster beneath the pit of his arm, his elbow crooked, his head dropping heavily upon the palm of his hand. Weary, weary Zechariah, in a darkness deeper than the night.

Elizabeth likewise requires the help of younger hands to put her safely on the carpets. Now everyone else reclines, each at his and her own plate. They draw the sleeves of their tunics up and fold them under; though they washed in larger jars when entering the room, they reach to shallow bowls and wash their hands again. They settle.

The old man cannot pour the first cup of wine. John, still at his right, does; and Mary carries the cups around.

The people turn their eyes towards Zechariah. In the hush that follows, he says, 'Blessed, blessed, you – ' He coughs sharply, swallows, blinks his blind eyes, then utters the blessing in short phrases and a voice like gravel. ' – king of the universe... who chose us... from every people... and exalted us among... every tongue... and sanctified us by your commandments.'

With ceremony, everyone drinks. A second cup of wine is poured and served and swallowed. 'We are Pharaoh's slaves in Egypt,' Zechariah says slowly, an ancient man uttering words of the most ancient age. 'The Lord our God... brought us forth... a mighty hand. An outstretched arm. Or we would still be... slaves...'

Old Zechariah reaches slowly, shakingly, towards a stone plate and the round, flat bread upon it. He lifts the bread, holds it in a trembling hand. 'Blessed you are, O Lord,' he says, 'who bringest forth bread from the earth.' He cracks the bread. He cracks it again and again until there are pieces enough for everyone. One into his own mouth. Pieces of bread all around. Then they begin to eat. Portions of the roasted meat, at least as large as a good sized nut. Finger-bunches of the bitter herbs dipped in the *harosheth*, a vinegary paste of mashed fruit and crushed nuts.

Mary serves Yeshi last. At twelve, he is the youngest present, placed at the end of the table to Mary's right as she serves. His mother gazes at him but cannot see into his eyes. The boy keeps his rusty lashes lowered, a freckled hand beneath his chin, its fingers curled into his mouth. Mary longs to murmur his name, to draw his looking up that she might read the meaning there. She wants to say, *Eat, Yeshi! This is one meal you can't leave uneaten, dreaming.* He is, after all, still a boy and still in her keeping. But she holds her peace, rises, and returns to her own place to nibble a little before the second cup of wine must be poured and served.

And when it is, when everyone is looking at Yeshi and waiting for him to continue the ritual, his mother grows fretful. He has nipped a little meat, has her son. He has touched a lettuce leaf to the mash and laid it against his lips. But he has not yet raised his head. *Yeshi!* She yearns to alert him – no, to scold him, truth be told.

But Zechariah, cocking an ear to the room around him, says, 'Jesus? Son of Joseph?'

And that's enough.

The boy looks up, startled, his eyes going wide with apology. Then Mary's unspoken rebuke straightway warms into pity.

'Why – ' her Yeshi mutters. His skin grows dark with embarrassment. He gathers his legs beneath him, sits up on his heels, and speaks with clarity, saying: 'Why is this night different from all other nights?'

Zechariah nods, his eyebrows sweeping up and down: the youngest has asked the question; the oldest now may answer at length.

We were slaves of the Pharaoh of Egypt. But the Lord would not bring our parents only out of Egypt. Behold, we and our children and the children of our children were slaves of the Pharaoh in Egypt!

Oh, sing it, ancient Zechariah. Sing it like Joshua. Or if you must, cry it out as your namesake did, the prophet Zechariah the son of Iddo. Make it real again, and say:

He sent Moses his servant,
And Aaron his chosen,
To work his signs among them,
Miracles in the land of Ham.

O sweet priest, tell the story for us all, for every generation yet to come:

He covered the land in darkness;
He bloodied their waters;
Their cities he fouled with slippery frogs;
He opened his mouth and uttered swarms of flies,
Drove hail like raindrops down from heaven,
Stripping their vines and blasting their figs;
He howled a black sirocco of locusts,
Then smote the firstborn in the land –
He led his people golden-shod from Egypt.
Not a foot of them stumbled on stone,
For he remembered his promise to Abraham.
The Lord led Israel forth with joy,
With timbrels and singing,
To this land,
To this land of milk and honey –

Finally, priest, before you're done, speak the reason for which the Lord has undertaken the saving of Israel:

To the end
   that we should keep his statutes,
To the end
   that we should observe his laws…

Zechariah's frozen eyes are shining. He makes neither a sob nor a sound of his weeping. And he has completed all his eating. Others make sure that nothing remains except the bones of the sheep and the hide, which will be tanned when Joseph is home again. But Zechariah is finished.

There will be a third cup of wine and a long prayer of thanksgiving and boisterous *Hallel* psalms and a fourth cup yet before the people rise up. Someone will beg God (as has many another person tonight) to redeem the land from Roman powers. This has been a piece of the Passover for the last century.

But Mary's son, his thin mouth closed, a muscle pulsing at the corner of his jaw, still leans towards Zechariah. Yeshi hasn't moved since the priest, his oldest living relative, began the story. And he wears now the expression of an ecstatic, one who experiences a tale so intensely he seems to leave his body and enter the telling as if it were itself a world, and the only true world after all.

Mary frowns. She doesn't understand the boy's bedazzlement. He *knows* this story. It isn't new. He's read it himself in the Books of Moses, quoting passages in Hebrew for her and translating them for her sake: *How I bore you out on eagles' wings and brought you to myself.* Why is the child so lost in the mysteries tonight?

Already when he was two years old Mary was telling him tales of Egypt and the Exodus while he lay on his pallet and stared at the ceiling.

And always (she remembers this with a start, since Yeshi is suddenly twelve, no longer an infant) – always she closed their evening's ritual by praying the night-time prayer she'd taken from one of the Psalms:

'Father,' they said, Mary's cheek against her babe's, the baby lisping along with his mother: 'Father, into your hands I commend my spirit.'

And then, as if they two were the whole congregation of Israel, they said, 'Amen.'

But Yeshi leans forward to the old priest's ear and whispers a question made over-long by qualifiers: 'What did you say God said Moses should say to Pharaoh about the kinship of the Children of Israel back to himself? What did God call them?'

And Zechariah whispered in return, smiling for perhaps the first time during that week: 'God called Israel *My son*. God said to Moses, *And you shall say to Pharaoh, "Thus says the Lord, Israel is my firstborn son, and I say to you, 'Let my son go that he may serve me.'"'*

FATHERS
AND THE FATHER
—

'Have you seen him? Please! Have you seen my child? D'you know where he is?'

In the latter part of the afternoon a rainsquall had blown up from the west. Pilgrims one day's journey from Jerusalem had dashed for shelter. They'd crouched on the lee side of the rocks and hills, had pulled their robes up over their heads, and tried to hold the larger skins of their tents against the wind.

'Yeshi!' Mary had screamed. It was compulsive. Mother-fear. Foolish. Of course the boy couldn't hear her under the roar and the stinging pellets of the rainstorm. She'd hoped he had sense enough to join another family. But the boy was coatless! Mary had been carrying his robe ever since dawn when she had snatched it from the tent before Joseph struck it and folded the goat-skins.

He's with John, Mary had thought at the time. Then she busied herself with breakfast, with helping Zechariah and Elizabeth to dress, with packing everyone's things for the trip back home again.

It was still the morning when Mary and Joseph made the detour to Zechariah's house: four going one way, two coming back to the ridge road and its long line of travellers. Young John, free to enjoy himself for the first time in three weeks, planned to go home in his own good time. Before them he was wandering among the crowds. With Yeshi – so Mary had assumed. And Yeshi would find them at the end of this first day of travel – surely in time for his supper.

But then the afternoon sun was extinguished, and a furious wind tore dust from the hillsides, and a black cloud draped the sky in darkness, and rain whacked them in their faces – and suddenly Mary was terrified for her son.

'Yeshi! Where are – '

Snap-BOOM!

A crack of lightning gave Mary a stuttering vision of raindrops fixed in their falling, a vision too of Joseph's broad back bent over several women who, like chicks, peeped round his shoulders. Her husband was protecting strangers, but not their son!

Where was Jesus?

Even later when the air was still misted – when all at once a hard bar of red sunlight broke between the cloud and the horizon – Mary begged Joseph to return to Jerusalem, searching all the way they'd come that day, while she herself ran forward from one family to the next.

'Have you seen my child?' Mary was crying. 'My son? Jesus? Small for his age. About my size. Tight curls, reddish brown hair, more brown than red, no, but dark brown, I'd say, yes, dark brown, oh dear – '

Mary could not restrain herself. She flew from family to family like a bee among the blossoms. The faces of strangers swung round, mindlessly chomping their suppers, offering nothing but ignorance, infuriating the woman: 'Oh, you *raca*! Jackals! Fools!'

But when she found people she recognized, poor Mary paused. For these were willing to listen.

'Mary? Mary, what's the matter?' they asked.

And they knew her Yeshi. And they bit their lips in sympathy, uttering prayers for the safety of the boy. Neighbours from Nazareth, cousins of her father, familiar faces and kindness – all of these caused honest sobbings suddenly to rise in her throat. Mary allowed them to see her fears.

By now the red bar had sunk into the earth, leaving behind a bank of fanned coals. The faces of her neighbours glowed in the ruddy light.

Ah, but none of them had seen Jesus on the way.

'Not at noontime?'

'No.'

'Not even this morning? Please: when we started out from Jerusalem?'

'No.'

'With John, surely! John the son of Zechariah! I know they wanted to walk together.'

Well, various cousins had seen *John*, yes. In fact, he had travelled with them awhile: a big-footed fellow, right? Hands so large he could break an axle between them? Yes. But Jesus wasn't with John. They were sorry, Mary. And they had to set up their tents for the night. And the ground was everywhere wet. The wind had caused an unnatural cold. This was more difficult than usual. They were truly sorry. But it was suppertime –

O God, are you watching over my son?

Mary reversed herself and ran back in the direction Joseph had taken. All around her were the murmurings of people fixing their food, people feeding their animals, arranging the night: contentment. Families untroubled. She flew by them all. Her feet were freezing from the rain, her fingers numbed as much by the cold as by fear. She yanked her skirts up between her legs and tucked them into the band at her waist and ran. She ran.

When, in the dying light of the day, she came upon her husband, Mary lost control. She yowled in astonishment. Why, she could *hit* the man! He was erecting the tent for the night.

'What do you think you're doing?' she cried.

'We need the shelter, Mim,' he said, kneeling, hooking a cord around a peg already pounded into the ground. He glanced up at her. 'And you need the drying out.'

'What I need is to find my son! Who knows what's happened to him? No one's seen him the whole day long.'

'Nay, but Jesus is twelve, Mim. He's levelheaded and canny. It'll be completely dark in a – '

'What're you saying? What're you thinking? You'd leave the baby alone?'

'Now, now, sweet Miriam – '

'Where was he when the storm hit? D'you know? Did he start out late? What if he's lying alone on the road?'

With maddening slowness the man rose up and faced her. 'He can make a fire quicker and cleaner than most men, Mary. Please. Calm down – '

'*Don't* tell me to calm down! This is *not* a time for being calm – '

'But, Mary – '

'Cold men! Unemotional men! It's a time for the heart, Joseph! For doing! For *loving!*'

'But the lad knows wood. He knows tools – '

'Pack up the tent!'

'What? Mim, what'll it serve – '

'Don't you "Mim" me!'

Suddenly she bent down and began to snap cords from the pegs. The hood of her robe fell back; her wet hair whirled like snakes-tails and stuck to her forehead.

'Wait. Mary, wait.'

Joseph reached to touch her, perhaps to comfort her. But she jerked away and glared at him.

'You do what you want to do,' she said, pointing at him. 'As for me, I'm gone searching. I'm already gone, walking the whole road back to Jerusalem.'

Joseph's eyes said, *Now?*

Mary refused the question. She chose rather to see a blinking plough-ox in his face. She groaned an 'Oh!' of frustration and began to march south.

But: 'Mary!' Joseph called. And: 'Stop there!' he boomed with such command that she stopped in spite of herself.

'If we're going back,' he continued, 'you'll ride the beast and I will walk.'

He would walk.

She would ride.

It meant as well that the man would take the tent and all the rest of their possessions on his back all over again. But Mary kept the robe her son should have been wearing.

If she ate anything in Jerusalem the following day, Mary couldn't remember it. Nor could she remember sleeping the next night either. *Two* nights lost to wakefulness and worry. Two dawns torn asunder by the crowing of roosters all over Jerusalem.

The city, reduced to its more squalid population, filthy with the damage and trash of an eight days' invasion, had become for Mary an alien place. She could scarcely understand the southern dialect of the poorer people; and the rich made her feel rude and useless.

They walked the back streets.

'Have you seen – ' Joseph would ask in narrow doorways which opened upon small courtyards and four-room houses in which two families and all their livestock lived. 'Have you seen – ' he questioned three families and four in cramped shelters, and then he would describe their lad to frowning men, the heads of their households, while women slapped barley dough behind them, and children jammed the doorway. 'He's twelve years old,' Joseph would say in speech eternally slow. 'His skin, his face and his arms are covered with reddish freckles. He has a hard bunch of kinked hair. Like a cap on his head. His eyes light brown – '

'An alert, a *sparkling* brown,' Mary interrupted, 'but surprisingly light in his eyes, almost luminous...'

But no. No. No one had seen such a boy.

Besides: who could pick one face out of the great herds of pilgrims who overran their city? Careless people, the poor declaimed. Trampling property, drinking the water, plugging the drains?

'Go away. Leave us alone.'

Yeshi, sweet Yeshi: where are you now?

Mary was growing gaunt with worry. Her jaw hurt from gritting it. Her joints trembled.

They had searched all down the central valley, the smiths' bazaar, the butchers' street, the row of little bakeries, every workman's shop on both the market streets. They had questioned sweepers driving filth into the Valley of Hinnom – *Gehenna*, where fires burned continually. They'd approached tailors at the city gates, those who pressed oil on the Mount of Olives, even the tanners in their stinking quarters outside the city walls.

'If he's dead,' Mary said, wrapping her arms around herself, 'I will die too.'

But they had been talking to people too much like themselves, the poor, or so it seemed to Joseph, who, when he heard the despair in Mary's words, decided to make some decisions of his own. 'Miriam,' he said, putting his hand at the small of her back, 'go back to the tent. Wait in the tent. I'm going to the king's house. The guards keep a sharp eye over everyone.'

Bold, bold Joseph knew nothing of weaponry, nothing of the language of the powerful or of the bribings of their soldiers. What he did know, however, was the violence with which a poor man might be troubled. But his wife had spoken a wish to die, and he believed the moods of his wife. He, Joseph, would broach the house of the king.

He was thinking of the magnificent palace which Herod the Great had built along the west wall of Jerusalem. In fact, the slow-spoken carpenter was wrong. No longer did a king dwell in that grand compound. When Herod died twelve years before, Rome took it over, calling it the 'praetorium'. Roman soldiers were garrisoned in its barracks. And rather than a king, it was the Roman governor who inhabited its several hundred apartments when he came from Caesarea with a splendid retinue and four cohorts of soldiers to control the multitudes during the Jewish festivals.

But Joseph would ever remember the fortress as it had been when furious Herod crept among its gardens and slept on beds of silver feet.

Now he walked across the public square east of the praetorium. He skirted the orators' platform – the *bema* where the governor sat to render judgments – and approached the gate in the wall once meant to protect a vicious royal family.

The gate stood open. Joseph, swallowing with difficulty, peered inside. What gardens, pools, groves, canals! Yes, but how empty the verdure was. Joseph didn't know that when the pilgrims left Jerusalem, so did the governor and the greatest part of his armies. To the Galilean carpenter this stillness seemed ominous, as though something lay in wait. Never in his life had he seen waters so flat or lawns so cropped.

All at once he heard, 'Move!' He felt a sharp poke in his kidney, and little Mary pushed past him, straight through the gate and inside.

She, too, registered the silence. Immediately. Well, no trouble here! Mary would call, would curse, would find someone in this luxuriant, improvident place and demand a word of him –

But then a gross voice behind her growled, '*Ave, mulier!*'

Not Joseph's, to be sure. This was a foreign language.

Mary turned. The man who had spoken was sitting on his heels, grinning: a young centurion, by the helmet in his hands. Two guardsmen flanked him, each of them weaponed, leaning against the wall.

'*Mulier*,' the centurion said again, '*quem quaeris?*'

He was milky-eyed, his skin as white as the moonlight, a great scar across his cheek and upper lip, causing the lip to look like two pieces badly attached. Mary could see a pink tongue flicking inside when he talked.

She said, 'Please! Please, we are from Nazareth. Galilee. Our son is lost. Jesus – is lost.'

'Ahhh doo nut,' the centurion spoke, nodding and gesticulating, 'shpick yoor lang-widge.'

'Oh, you do, you do!' Mary cried. She went down on her knees, her eyes level with the sitting man.

'*Mulier*,' he said, pointing at her.

'Joseph, he means me,' Mary laughed breathlessly. 'He means "woman".'

'*Quem*,' the man said. The man said, "Wot – ?"'

'What!' she repeated.

'*Quaeris*: seech. Seark – ?'

'Search for! Seek! You mean "seek"! You want to know what we're looking for! Oh, you good, good man!'

Still on her knees, she stumped closer to the soldier and seized one of his hands.

The carpenter cleared his throat. The woman's eyes were dancing with tears.

'A boy!' she cried. 'My son. Jesus. I – I call him Yeshi!'

Mary jumped up and patted the air in order to indicate his height, his gender, his beauty.

'Bouy,' the soldier rumbled in return. 'Boo-y. Boy! *Puer! Puerum tuum quaeris!*'

'Oh, Joseph, he understands!'

But the centurion was no longer grinning his slit-lipped grin. Rather, he was shaking his head and standing up. '*Quia nescio puerum istum, quem dicitis.*' His tone was formal. His face was apologetic. Mary's heart tightened all over again.

But the centurion nodded to Joseph and beckoned him to follow. The two men stepped out the gate, Mary watching with fear and yearning. The soldier raised his arm and pointed across the square, down an avenue of wealthy mansions, over the valley and towards the Temple.

'*Custodia,*' he said. '*Custodia templi,*' and he demonstrated the sense of it, marching back and forth like one who kept watch, like a –

'Guard!' Mary cried, coming up behind. '*Templi*: temple! He means the Temple guards! The Levites! Police! Oh, Joseph! – why didn't we think of this ourselves?'

How little the poor expect from the powerful! In this world neither one considers the other.

Already Mary was running. But quickly she returned and knelt before the centurion in gratitude – then dashed off again across the public square.

They had, of course, already sought their son on the Temple Mount. It was the first place they'd gone in Jerusalem, praying prayers of a parents' panic. But the Court of the Gentiles alone covers thirty-five acres, more than three times the size of the entire village of Nazareth! And it hadn't occurred to them to approach the Levites appointed to guard that place.

By the time they were climbing the monumental stairs from the Tyropeon Valley up to the southwest gate of the Temple precincts, Joseph was bearing Mary's weight upon the crook of his arm. The height was exhausting.

And 'Yes!' said the very first Levitical guard whom they approached.

They were in the Royal Portico on the south side of the esplanade. This cheerful, chubby Levite pointed diagonally to the porches of Solomon at the eastern edge of the mount and babbled happily: 'Such eyes as you describe? Such a tight, curly field of hair? You bet I've seen that kid, though by his talk I'd've sworn him fourteen or fifteen. He's there. Just there, inside those columns, against the back wall – '

Mary sprinted, choking on joy. Oh, she'd throw her arms around the boy and cover his face with kisses. Yes! She'd embarrass him with motherlove, and didn't she have the right? Yes!

She raced between columns seven times as high as herself, then dashed to the back of the portico –

There!

There sat Yeshi! – her golden boy!

But... there sat Yeshi... unconcerned. Listening to one of a number of Pharisees seated on cushions around him. Yeshi was healthy. Yeshi was clean. Yeshi was calm. And Yeshi was... *unconcerned*!

The Pharisee doing the talking, the smarmy one, that elitist all full of his learned self – he afforded the approaching mother of that boy not so much as a how-do-you-do, not even a pause in his lisping rhetoric. And her *son*, mind you, leaning forward as if these words were vastly more important than three days of sleeplessness and a mother's hungry desperation; her son, when he noticed her staring at him, offered but a glance, a nod, and the mere flap of his hand for all the greeting he had it in him to give!

No, it was not joy: it was a perfect anger now choking Mary's throat.

'Do you have any idea – ' she started to say, but her stance outside this group didn't grant her advantage enough. She picked up her skirts and stalked straight to the centre, men or no men, teachers or beggars!

'Madam,' the Pharisee said, 'what – ?' Sure, *now* the mule would pause since Mary had given him pause! The horse! He had a gap between his two front teeth, and *all* the front teeth splayed out of his mouth like a goat's!

But Mary turned to her blinking son. She planted her left fist on the jut of her hip. She aimed a finger at His Majesty and let him have it.

'Three days, boy! Three long days your father and I are looking high and low for you. In the hills! In every street of the city! And worried to death that maybe someone has knocked you in the head and you're lying in a ditch. How could you? Jesus, how *could* you have treated us so miserably? Irresponsible pup, what do you think we are? Bones for the burning?'

The lad kept sitting.

'Mama?' he said as if he'd been slapped and didn't know the reason why.

'And look at little king Jesus now!' Mary seethed. 'So full of himself he won't rise up before the woman who birthed him!'

Jesus did begin to stand. 'Mother,' he said again, this time with reproach.

The boy's voice is changing, thought Mary. *Lowering. Man-like.*

And then, at his full height and in cold tones, Jesus said, 'Woman!'

Suddenly it seemed they weren't related at all. Mary lost her martial posture. Standing, Yeshi's gaze was level with hers, and his brow was a bending thing. Growth! This, too, was new; or else she hadn't been paying attention. She felt as if she should drop her eyes. She didn't. But she frowned as if looking into the sun.

'Why,' Jesus asked, 'would you even *look* for me?'

He waited.

What? – the boy was expecting an answer? Didn't it show? Wasn't motherlove the very blood that heated her face?

Then, in dead earnest, Jesus asked a second question: 'Didn't you know that I *have* to be in my Father's house?'

His Father's house: he wasn't referring to Joseph. *Ah, Yeshi, how much do you know already? How much has it been given you to know?*

'Admirable!' cried the young Pharisee who'd been speaking before. He, too, rose up.

'Admirable, Jesus. You know the prophets better than all the boys I'm given daily to teach. For the Holy One through Hosea said, *Out of Egypt I called my son.* It is altogether right, thou son of Israel, to call the Temple the house of your "Father". Admirable.'

Joseph, bulking biggest in that company, bunched his cheeks in a smile of kindness. He raised his workman's hand and said, 'God bless you, rabbi,' to the young Pharisee whose phylacteries looked new, whose cheekbones were smooth, whose chin whiskers were soft, still striving to sprout. 'God bless you for seeing to my son. And for praising him.'

'Call me Eleazar,' the Pharisee said in return. A glad spray shooting from the gap in his teeth. 'Your boy deserves the praise. His questions show a natural bent for sacred matters. Why, his questions make *me* wiser than I am. Bring him back. Let me teach him. I'll make a way for him. I promise, I'll not forget this youth, this Jesus.'

Mary's mind was racing. She was suffering an internal twist of guilt. There was a duty she had been long neglecting, altogether too long. It was time to fulfil it. Not here. They would have the quiet and the privacy while the little family was returning alone to Nazareth.

Moreover, if ever she should lose him again, it must not be before her son is well apprised of his origins.

TWO NATIVITIES

Such a wedding, Yeshi — such a hurry-up wedding, I had to wear my mother's veil. No time to sew my own.

And who walked as the groomsman? My father. The only groomsman Joseph had. No one else in the village knew what we were doing. Not that we were keeping secrets. Just that my big husband was in a giddy fit to get it done – and he as round-eyed as a dove. So then, who was the bridesmaid? My mother. All in the family.

It was my little mama who washed me, oiled me, fought my frizzy hair into a bush of glory, dressed me. And all the while Joseph is in the courtyard, grinning at the livestock and tugging his beard and waiting – having only just announced that very same morning – waking us up, you understand, in order to announce – that today was our wedding day!

This is the man who never hurries. This is the man by whom the sun decides to rise and set. This is the man who keeps all the laws. All the laws, Yeshi – except one law, on the day of our wedding.

For we were already betrothed. We'd been betrothed nearly a year. Promised, you see. Married in the eyes of God and under the law. But then I could not hide from Joseph the fact that I was pregnant. Not by him. Not by him, Joseph. So the law said Joseph could divorce me.

When he came pounding on our door that morning, I thought he'd come to keep that law. But no. This good man – oh, Yeshi, he came to say, 'Today is our marrying day!'

They were sitting near the well which, so said the ancient stories, the patriarch Jacob himself had dug two thousand years ago. Joseph was in the town of Sychar trading for food for the rest of the journey. Jesus had drawn a little water for his mother and himself. As they drank the moment became intimate. Mary then, though she gave a casual tone to the telling, began to discharge her duty.

She said, ' "My Father's house." ' She reached to wipe a smudge from his chin. 'That's what you called the Temple. And that billy-goat Pharisee teaching you – he thought you were talking as an Israelite called out of Egypt.' Mary paused and gazed a moment at her well-knit son. 'But I know my boy. I know how he talks. You meant it personally, didn't you? "My Father's house." You were skipping Joseph, weren't you? Going straight to God. Jesus: the Son of God.'

Yeshi had grimaced when his mother was wiping his chin. Now he looked steadfastly into her eyes. *Luminous*, Mary thought. He seemed to be reading the words in her heart even before she uttered them.

'Please, Yeshi, I have you with me some little while yet. While I do, allow me still to teach you.

'I have a round, unvarnished story to tell you, child: how it is you came to me in the first place, and who you are, and why you are right to call the Lord God, the Holy One, your Father.'

What am I now? By common counting, a woman who's lived the half of her life. Look at my hands. These calluses come from the loom, and roughness from clay, and redness from fire and lye.

But I was young once. A maid, my father used to say with great groaning. For I was strong as a donkey, faster than boys, good at games, unhappy with my exploding hair. When we were children, we all of us played and raced and whirled the sling like little King David, laughing. The boys and I, you couldn't have told us one from the other.

But, Yeshi. There came the season when my body got a mind of its own and chose womanhood. Parts of me started to soften; parts of me started to harden and to swell; all of me stopped growing, leaving me short while the boys kept sprouting. Papa stopped groaning and started to smile. Mama said she had things

I should learn. At night they discussed marriage. I was of age. Even if you don't want to count the years, the years count you. I was of age.

One morning my father came to me puffing his cheeks.

'None of the young ones fancy you,' he said.

'So,' said my papa, suddenly breaking into smiles, 'we have arranged for you to marry an older man, a good, reliable man.'

Joseph the carpenter could have lifted ten of me in one of his strong arms. Joseph the carpenter came to our house and blushed when he said: 'Yes. Ahem. A lovely sort.'

Truly, it was the blush that made me like him. I surprised myself. Me, I was going to outshine any man my father would bring, out-think him, outrun him, out-talk him. Talk the poor dope dizzy! But this man, this Joseph, actually listened to me. And nodded, paid attention, never interrupted. Never, in fact, felt the need to talk at all.

Well, and in the months to come his huge hand touched me only on my elbow by the tips of his fingers only. That made me like him. And on the day of our betrothal he wept and smiled together, big drips at the end of his nose. That, too: I liked him.

But love him? Oh, Yeshi, what made me love him was that, never minding I was pregnant, Joseph refused the rules and all the law, and married me anyway, married me as I was.

The angel Gabriel came to me.

Came down from the throne of God. Dropped like lightning, like a pillar of fire that hit the ground while still affixed in heaven. I was standing on the ridge over Nazareth, and I couldn't move.

The lightning spoke, which was its thunder: REJOICE, O FAVOURED ONE, THE LORD IS WITH YOU!

I sat flat-down afraid.

Rejoice? Who beats me up with 'Rejoice'?

But then the pillar of fire resolved itself into the figure of a man starlike, sparkling, who spoke more near my natural hearing.

'DON'T BE AFRAID, MARY; THE LORD HOLDS YOU IN HIS HIGHEST REGARD AND SENDS ME TO TELL YOU: WOMAN, YOU ARE ABOUT TO CONCEIVE. YOU WILL BEAR A CHILD. YOU WILL CALL HIS NAME JESUS. SO GREAT WILL BE THE BOY YOU BEAR, THAT

EVEN THE ANGELS WILL CALL HIM "THE SON OF THE MOST HIGH"!'

Gabriel's voice was a waterfall. You too, Yeshi my son, you will hear that voice one day: like the music that made the mountains.

But even if my messenger was an angel, he didn't make sense.

'How can this be?' I said, getting to my feet. 'How can I have a child while I'm still a virgin? I have never yet lain with a man.'

Gabriel said, 'THE HOLY SPIRIT WILL COME UPON YOU' – no, not said; he was singing it now like the wind at the mouth of the cave – 'THE POWER OF THE MOST HIGH WILL OVERSHADOW YOU, SO THE CHILD TO BE BORN OF YOU WILL BE CALLED HOLY! THE SON OF GOD!'

I didn't understand this 'overshadow'. Like a cloud, maybe? Neither do I have a memory of anything like 'overshadow' happening to me. But it must have worked.

'YOU KNOW THAT YOUR KINSWOMAN ELIZABETH,' the angel said, 'IS LONG PAST THE CHANGE. NEVERTHELESS, SHE HAS BEEN PREGNANT FOR SIX MONTHS NOW. MARY: WITH GOD, NOTHING WILL BE IMPOSSIBLE.'

Elizabeth? And Zechariah? Oh, my! – just like Abraham and Sarah, whose belly in old age swelled with the gift of the Almighty!

And me?

Yeshi, I looked straight into the showering light of the angel and said 'Yes' to you. 'Yes' to your borning. To everything God intended to do, intends even yet to do. In the presence of that lightning-crack of a messenger, I cried, 'I am the servant of the Lord. Let it happen to me according to your word.'

Well, so, what did I do then? I ran. I was a very good runner in those days.

To Mama I ran with news about Elizabeth. 'She's going to have a baby!'

Mama, of course, did not believe me. I said I heard it from an angel. She said she'd have to see it for herself. I said, 'Come on!' and took off.

If she was going to follow me, she'd better hurry because I was on my way, not even looking back –

Like the sparrow I flew south and south, then east on the stony trail to Zechariah's village.

And the moment I opened the door into her courtyard, old Elizabeth rose up and clapped her hands and laughed. I had only just begun to greet her — 'I came to tell you' — when she grabbed her belly and gasped in wide-eyed astonishment.

'Mary,' she cried, 'blessed are you among women! Blessed is the fruit of your womb!'

How did she know? How could she know?

Oh, Yeshi: her tummy big as a melon, Elizabeth waddled over and took my hands and bent and kissed me, causing me to tingle.

'As soon as you spoke,' she said, 'my baby jumped. He jumped for joy that you are here, the mother of our Lord!'

And that too! She knew who you were to be!

Her giggles, the wrinkles all over her face: they were like timbrels, and I couldn't help it. I began to clap. I shuffled my feet. I danced! And I — me, Yeshi, your foolish mama: I started to sing.

'My soul proclaims you great!' I sang to our God. Elizabeth, that old lady! She danced as well.

Well, and my words weren't mine at all. They fell on me like rain:

My soul proclaims you great, my Lord;
My spirit laughs in you, my Saviour!
 Your name be glorified!

You raised me from my low estate;
The world will call her fortunate
 Who in your shadow lies.

You have unbent your righteous arm,
Scattered the rich, sent proud, proud hearts
 Stricken and empty away.

You've swept the mighty from their thrones;
But the poor, the poor and the hungry ones,
 You've filled with good, my Lord;

You've served your servant Israel,
And, recalling all things merciful,
  Serve us forevermore.

And then it was less than two weeks later that I got the news of you. Announced to me this time by my own body. My breasts grew tender. The pretty tunic my mother had made for me, soft as lamb's wool, remember? When it touched my nipples, it scratched like burlap! I thought I'd jump out of my skin.

And my mother – who, yes, had come not only to control her flighty daughter, but also to be Elizabeth's midwife – stared at me from the corner of her eye. 'Signs of a baby,' she said. She frowned. This did not make her happy. 'What have you been doing?' she said.

Dear Elizabeth didn't frown. She winked and smiled at me. I was so thankful that someone knew and believed and could befriend me and for a while could distract my mother from her suspicions.

That marvellous old woman, Elizabeth! Three months later she bore a red, squash-faced, slickery infant into the world. I watched. I helped. My mother was a mighty force. 'Don't push,' she said, her hands adjusting flesh and bone inside Elizabeth who was squatting on the birthing stool. Then 'Push!' she said with such assurance that Elizabeth did exactly as she was told. 'Push, sister! Like God with the whole world coming, push!' I held the lamp that scorched the knife that sizzled the cord when the baby came, cut and closed the wound at once. And when he did come, oh, how that baby bellowed! And the biggest little hands and feet ever I saw on a newborn.

Mama pressed her forehead down hard on Elizabeth's stomach until the afterbirth came out into her hands.

'Of course,' said the old men sitting with Zechariah in the courtyard, listening to the baby bawling. 'Of course you will name him "Zechariah".'

And the women in Elizabeth's room said, 'Ah, tiny Zechariah! Your abba has finally gotten glory!'

But Elizabeth said, 'Not "Zechariah".' We'll call the baby John.'

'Hush,' the women said. 'His father will name him, and we

know what name Zechariah wants for his only son.'

But in the other room the old priest was already writing on clay in a clear script these words: 'His name is John.'

'John? Why John? Who is John, after all?'

'John,' Zechariah said. An angel had named him so, he said, even before the baby was conceived.

'What angel?'

Oh, Yeshi, you should have seen the looks on all those faces, eyebrows up, mouths pinched as if constipated.

But Elizabeth — she winked at me. We both knew what angel Zechariah was talking about.

Joseph, however, did not wink at me. He did not smile. It might have been my mother told him. It might have been he saw the puffiness in my face and my waist.

He knew I was pregnant, and it was not by him.

Oh, Yeshi, he didn't even speak to me. I saw how his countenance fell. I saw the tears brim in his eyes.

'Joseph, it's fine, it's fine.' I pleaded with him. I tried to take his hand. 'Everything is legal and fine.'

But he drove his hand into his robe and shook his head and went away to his own house. And that, I thought, was the end of that. Let shame come down upon my head. Let all the world reject me. My betrothed, he was not wrong to put me away.

But this man! This carpenter who has maybe twelve words in his head, wood and angles and measurements else. At sunrise the very next day he came tumbling down the path to my father's house and pounded on our door and raised us all like God at the end of the world.

For the angel Gabriel (he said) had visited him in a dream and had explained about God and me and the thing you were to be.

'Today is the day, sweet Miriam!' my great bear roared through the lattice to my room. 'Today is our marrying day!'

Six months later we were travelling south, Joseph and I, because the Roman governor of Syria wanted an official list of all the Jews in Judea. A new thing in a new way: we were about to pay tax monies to the empire.

And now it was you, my beautiful Yeshi, who was the melon

inside of me. I have been strong, but I've never been big. You know this. I carried you high beneath my ribs and straight out in front. I could hardly breathe.

Joseph lifted me to the back of our little donkey. Dogs are bigger than that donkey was. I had to hoist my feet. I tucked my hands beneath my belly to ease the pressure. Such a weight on my bladder were you, that we stopped every hour, and every hour I watered another farmer's field. I looked around at the edges of those fields for giant fennel and gathered the leaves to let them dry before my pains should come. Then, back on the donkey. Joseph kept a balancing hand at my shoulders as we went the ridge road south. Well: we had to go to Bethlehem because my husband is a descendant of King David. Bethlehem's where David was born. The Romans wanted us in the cities of our ancestors.

Late in the afternoon of the fourth day, we passed through Jerusalem.

At nightfall, just as we entered the gates of Bethlehem, the donkey stumbled – and my water broke. The donkey turned its head towards me because of the odour, I think, more than the wet. She knew. And immediately you wanted out. My stomach muscles hitched and gripped so hard that I bowed my head and cried, 'Joseph! Oh, Joseph!'

'Mim?'

'The baby's coming!'

'Wait!' he said. 'Wait. We need a place for the baby. Wait!'

The dear ox! He went lumbering off, leaving me in the gate of the village, then straightway rushed back, blushing, and pulled the donkey after him. He beat on the doors of houses and inns. 'A baby,' he roared. He terrified children and law-abiding citizens. 'Coming!' he cried. 'We need a room!'

But people shut their doors in his face. Or never opened them at all. And Joseph was too obedient to beg any further.

My back had gone into cramping so severe, I could scarcely speak. 'Any courtyard will do!' I whispered. 'They can't deny a birth!'

But he tried another house with pounding. And another.

And you pressed against my lowest parts, and I couldn't help it: I let go a terrible scream, and Joseph began to bubble in confusion. He dropped the bridle. And then the donkey – all on her own – trotted down behind an inn two stories high, down into darkness and a little cave below, then back through the cave to an alcove where the travellers' animals were tethered.

Joseph came running, woofing, begging forgiveness. Ah, Yeshi, that blunt carpenter who had the tenderness to adopt you –

– I scolded him.

I said this place was as good as any. Lift me down! Light the lantern! Lay me on clean straw. Build a back-rest behind me. Joseph (I said) I'm drawing my tunic up behind my back. Crush the fennel leaves. Mix them in oil and a little wine. No! No, not to rub on me! I'll drink it! To make my labour go faster.

Thank you. Thank you.

Pull back my robe. Joseph, look at me! This nakedness is no shame. And there's no midwife here but you. Pull fresh cloth from our bundles. A winding cloth. Now tear my tunic and twist it into a narrow twine. Bring your knife. Run its blade through the lantern flame.

Now, now, now, Joseph, rub my back. No! The lower part. Harder! Oh, it hurts!

Can you sing, my husband? Have you ever sung a gentle song?

Ha! EEE-Yow! Here it comes. Lift my shoulders. Here the poor baby comes. Ahhh! – but not yet. He shouldn't come yet. He'll tear me if he comes. Joseph, put your hand here. Here, Joseph! Your palm against his head! Hold it, hold it, hold the baby back. Wait!

O Lord God, look down on your son! Let all my openings ease. Wait… wait. OK! Now! Slowly. Ahhhhhh! Ha! Let the little one slowly into this world. OK. Yes. Yes. Yes. Ahhhh –

Oh, Yeshi! Oh, little baby – yes, yes, cry. Make a spoon of your tongue. Cry the wideness and the pain of the world. Cry as hard as you want to.

Joseph? Tie the linen-twine around the cord at his belly. Yes. Right. Now, take your knife. Heat it in the flame. Cut the cord. Shhh. It won't hurt him. Or me. Cut it.

Ah-hah! Hah!

No, Joseph. Nothing to fear. Only one other something to come out. The animals know it. The afterbirth. They'll eat it, if you're not careful.

Bury it. I want you to bury it.

So, so, so. Yeshi, baby, here you are.

Now, my husband, wash the boy. And wrap him. Wrap him as tightly as was my womb tight. Wrap a good world, the sweet world of our Creator, around him.

And give him to me. I'll put him to my breast.

Oh, Joseph: what a wonderful ox of a midwife! Jesus is pink with health. And he's smiling at his papa, his wonderful abba. Do you see it? Can you see?

Angels in legions sang when you were born, my beautiful Yeshi! At midnight they spiralled down from the heavens, every one a whirling star, ten thousand voices in a skyborne choir.

'Glory,' they sang, and I felt the bedrock tremble. The animals stamped backward. The mules, the horses and donkeys raised their heads against their tethers and rolled their eyes.

'Glory to God in the highest!' the hosts of heaven thundered.

Joseph had washed me and packed for me a pallet of the freshest straw. You he laid in the stone enclosure manger. Then the angels sheeted the night with such brilliance outside that your tender brow lifted; you fought your soft eyes open and peered around, seeking the source of the music and finally waving your hands as if to catch the stars in them!

'Glory to God in the highest,' proclaimed the storm of the Lord, 'and on earth, peace!'

Soon a troop of ruffian shepherds crept into the cave to gaze at you. Gabriel had been back, announcing the good news even to these, the lowest in Judea, houseless, coinless, unpropertied: 'Where is this Saviour?' they asked Joseph as they came widdershins in. 'Where is this Christ the Lord?'

Joseph took no offence at their intrusion. He nodded welcome and pointed at you. Ach, Yeshi, but what a stink they brought with them! Even our donkey sneezed.

But the angels, that great wheel of the sky's slow turning: on your birthday, they made a morning of midnight. No warriors these! Nor hurt nor harm in the tempest of their voices. They were a wind of the Creator. They uttered the sublimest desire of God, the thing yet to be accomplished in you. In you, Yeshi, the only begotten Son of God Almighty:

'Glory to God in the highest, and on earth peace to the people with whom he is pleased.'

'It is right,' Mary said, 'that you call God your father. Nor should I wonder that you've come to know this on your own. I'm sorry. I should have told you these things long before. Only – ' Mary fell quiet a moment. She lowered her eyes slightly, perhaps in apology, then raised them and turned towards to Joseph who walked behind her while Jesus walked in front.

'Only, I've been worried for this abba of yours,' she said. 'He gave you a lineage. He gave fatherhood a face. He's opened a place for you in his house. In Nazareth. And I didn't want to trouble Joseph.'

'Well,' said Joseph, 'but you've troubled me the more by trusting me the less.'

By now the little family was climbing the steep slopes north of the Esdraelon Valley towards Nazareth. True to his character, Joseph had not interrupted Mary's long story. He'd been content to listen – until this moment when she reached her reason for silence regarding the sacred nature of the birth of their son.

Here Joseph was compelled to speak.

'Mary. I follow you in most everything,' he said. Joseph stopped. Mother and son stopped as well and turned to him; and though she yearned suddenly to explain herself, Mary said nothing. His tone had taken that commanding quality she could not disobey. Besides, he had called her 'Mary'. Not 'Mim'. Not 'Miriam'. He was in earnest.

'But in this you're wrong,' he said finally. 'It don't trouble me to hear the truth. Nor to speak it either. So Jesus isn't my blood son. So this don't trouble me. It's my life. A man can't do better than this, to raise up the boy of God. And of my wife.'

Joseph gazed so intently at Jesus – and Jesus so brightly back at him – that Mary suddenly felt as if she were an intruder on intimacies.

'Your mother's tale's both true and good,' Joseph said softly. 'But she didn't finish it. You got to hear the whole.'

Mary made a whining in her soul. *I was going to tell him*, she thought. But she held her peace.

'When we went to the temple for her purification,' Joseph said, 'came a white-haired gentleman up to us. A prophet, I don't doubt. Said you were salvation, my lad. "Salvation": a puzzlement to me. But the rest was clear: said y'were set for the fall and the rising of many in Israel. The *fall*, boy. And that you'd be a sign the people'd speak against.

'And when King Herod heard you were born, well, that bloody old fighter went looking for you. Was going to murder you. This is part of the story. Only by the warning of the angel did we save your skin.

'It'll not be easy, Jesus — whatever you're meant to do. Nor for your mother either, seeing that the white-haired prophet also said a sword would pierce her too: "Pierce through your own soul". Take care of her, Jesus. You take care of your mother. And do not plan too much on pleasures in your life.'

DEPARTURES

—

All these things Mary kept, pondering them in her heart, bearing her memories with astonishing clarity even unto the end; yes, and bearing the growing load of her experience in obedience, but in a fractious obedience as times continued, and in bitterness too and downright fury – until the day she opened the load and gave it piecemeal away by telling it to one who would neither defame her nor ever dishonour the story by editing the fleshiness right out of it.

As Mary in wholeness lived the tale, so must the tale in wholeness be told again among the peoples.

Zechariah died during the date harvest five months later. Within six weeks of the Passover the old priest had slipped into a blind silence. He sat awhile in the summer sun, as Joseph had thought he might. But then he ceased to eat, even from the hand of his old wife. Finally, with an interminable sigh, the spirit left Zechariah and he was dead.

Less than a year later, Elizabeth followed her husband. Their son gathered her up in his arms and bore her to the tomb. He, with his large hands and his severe expression, laid her on a ledge nearby the bones of his father. And then, not halfway through his fourteenth year, John the son of Zechariah vanished.

Mary heard no word of the lad, neither from his neighbours nor from relatives. In time she stopped asking after him.

In time, too, she turned to sorrow more immediate.

Joseph was building an upper storey on a stone house in Sepphoris, about an hour's walk north of Nazareth. He and Jesus would leave before sunrise, descend the Nazareth Ridge into a valley, cross that, and ascend again an acropolis into the city itself. Once or twice Mary went with them in order to sell her own handiwork, articles of finely woven woollen clothing, in one of the marketplaces there. (And once she went to attend a wedding there.) But for the most part, her men went alone, returning as the sun set, when they would wash and sit and eat the supper she had prepared. Daily Joseph carried to and fro the more precious of his tools in a leather bag. Jesus carried two wooden tablets hinged together so that they might close to preserve the wax on their inner surfaces. In his scrip Jesus also kept several styluses because a young, educated rabbi in Sepphoris was teaching him how to write.

Yeshi spent the mornings with his father, bearing lumber and building the upper storey. In the heat of the day, however, he bent over his tablets in a synagogue, copying letters and words from the book of Isaiah. This work he often brought home to show his mother before pressing the wax smooth again. And he would read what he had written: *My servants shall eat, but you shall go hungry; my servants shall drink, but you shall be thirsty; my servants shall rejoice, but you shall be put to shame. My servants will sing for gladness of heart, but you shall cry out for pain of heart...*

During the fourth week of their trips into Sepphoris – no, Mary is more precise than that: at noon of the twenty-fifth day, not counting the sabbaths, Jesus came racing along the dirt road of the little village and bursting into the tiny courtyard of their house with such grim determination that Mary wanted to laugh.

'All of a sudden my Yeshi is old? So serious! Did he just read of the floods of Noah?'

Jesus stood still, gazing at her with his mouth closed, catching his breath through flaring nostrils. His nose was angular, the wings of it chiselled.

'Yeshi?' Mary said. 'You have something to show me?'

He shook his head. He did not speak.

Mary took a step towards him, intending to brush his cheek with her knuckles. She reached towards him, but the round fixity of his stare halted the gesture. 'It's the middle of the day,' Mary said softly. 'You should not be home.' Then, sharply: 'Why *are* you home?'

Yeshi's chest was heaving. He was past catching his breath. Some emotion drove his breathing now and not the run that brought him here. But he did not speak. He didn't open his mouth, nor did he turn his eyes away from her.

'You *tell* me, Jesus.' Mary heard a note of scolding enter her voice. There was no controlling it. Her tone rose up a register: 'Why are you home at the wrong time?' The longer he stared at her unspeaking, the more his mother wanted to slap the silence off his blunt face.

'This isn't funny any more. Something's wrong. You're killing me, boy – '

Jesus swallowed. He began to blink. He said, 'Papa fell – '

'No!' Mary cried. 'No, don't say it!'

She ran to him. She grabbed his arms and flung him around and pushed him. 'Go back,' she yelled. 'You go back and help your father and come home with him at the right time and I will have supper ready for all three of us then and it will all be fine. Go.' She pushed him again, roughly.

He stumbled a step towards the door, then caught himself and stood still.

She hit him. With an open hand Mary hit the back of his head. 'What are you waiting for? Get out of here! Do what I – O my Lord!' she wailed. 'O my God!'

The woman crumpled to the ground. Jesus bowed his head. His shoulders sagged as though his mother's shrieks were a nearly impossible weight. Then he turned and knelt slowly down before her. He wrapped his arms around Mary and drew her howling mouth, her flowing eyes against his breast. He rocked her.

'Papa fell,' Jesus said when his mother's grief had turned to sobbings. 'He was on a ladder. Just four feet off the ground. Plastering the lower part of the upper storey. Papa fell. Backwards. His neck hit the edge of the mixing tub. And. Broke. Ah, Mama. Papa only just fell down.'

PART TWO

=

THE BELOVED

A VOICE

——

It is just at this point that I begin my own eyewitness account of Jesus of Nazareth.

I saw him first when he came to the Jordan River to be baptized by John the son of Zechariah. I was in those days a disciple of the one whom people called 'the Baptizer'.

Before he was anything else to me, this John bar-Zechariah was a Voice. Not the velvet voice of a courtier, nor the lisp of old wealth, nor the crushed mumbling of the peasant. John's was the loud, singular, absolutely self-assured voice of the God-struck prophet. It caught hold of me and brought me from the city into the wilderness of Judea.

Prepare the way of the Lord! Even so did John's message invade Jerusalem: *Make his paths straight!* He never came to the city himself. He never wore soft clothing or moved in populations of the comfortable. John was lean, crooked as a stick, as hard and gnarly as the olive tree. He preached at crossroads far from the Temple, in the wastelands of the beasts, under the carrion birds, on the banks of the Jordan. Yet his *Repent!* assailed Jerusalem, for those who heard him directly brought it back with them, and the effect of the Voice showed in their faces and in their behaviours: *Repent, for the kingdom of heaven is at hand!* And, repenting as they had been bidden, they were baptized by John in the Jordan River for the forgiveness of their sins.

I need say this much about myself, and then no more: that I was one of those who looked for the consolation of Israel. In me the yearning was unspeakable. It had drawn me to the Holy City in the first place, where I listened to various teachers, prayed daily in the Temple, begged heaven for light, for sight, for seeing, for knowing, for…

But as in the days when Samuel was a boy, so it was for me: the word of the Lord was rare, and there was no frequent vision.

How then could I not respond to this latter-day prophet? The yearning that drew me first to Jerusalem now drove me out into the Judean wilderness in search of God.

The man was like Elijah. His person and this rigorous territory were suited for one another. So it seemed to me. Declining eastwards towards the Jordan – or else yet farther down to the Dead Sea in which the Jordan buried itself – the whole land was rocky, chalky, desolate. For man and beast, passage was distressed by the vast dramatic scarps and deep canyons and by tremendous limestone cliffs.

In the rainy season a thin grass sprouted on the plateaus, and shepherds led their flocks up there; then the grass withered under the sun and little else grew in the wilderness, except near the river or where springs broke from the stony earth. Here and there in the lowest wadis an acacia tree survived. Serpents and lizards and insects, else. And John, the son of Zechariah.

And when I found the prophet, there was no resisting after that. He moved. He walked constantly, often at the speed of hurtle. Even when he stopped, his arms flew and his knees bounced, and the Voice arose like a rush of birds. People at a distance heard him quite as well as those nearby.

'Repent!'

Repent, indeed! It was his primary theme. And his continual motion lent it urgency. 'The kingdom of heaven,' he announced as if he'd never announced it before, 'is at hand.' And then the *kingdom of heaven* seemed to be the very clouds massing in the west, about to break on the higher hills: BOOM!

I breathed the quicker, hearing him. Everything in me wanted to assure him of my own heartful repentance.

But my bare assurance would never have been enough. For he shut my mouth with the further word: 'Bear the fruit that befits repentance.'

John stopped and turned. We all stopped. Swinging his arms, his hands like shovels, he began to elaborate his image: 'Even now the axe is at the roots of the trees. Those that don't bear fruit will be cut down and burned in fire.'

Now there was in all of us an urgency equal to the prophet's.

'But how? What fruit?' someone grew bold enough to ask: 'What should we *do*?'

John was not an angry man, though his manner was abrupt. His face was riven and ditched, his hair and eyebrows bleached from heat, the light and the dryness. Rather, John was a man of compelling urgency. And absolute conviction. And very little time. That's it: John was in a hurry.

What should we do?

He answered, 'If you have two coats, give one to the one who has none. If you have food, feed the hungry.'

The authority of his command was in the man himself, in his way of life; for he wore the cloak of the nomad, woven of camel's hair. He refused foods of refinement, eating straight from the land: locusts, wild honey, water.

'Teacher,' began a round, sweating fellow, 'I am – ' But then the man saw all the faces turned towards him. He blushed and closed his mouth.

'You are?' John barked. 'Say it! Name yourself!'

'I,' the man said miserably, standing central in the crowd, 'I am a tax collector.'

'A tax collector?'

'Yes.' He seemed to shrink into himself. 'Yes,' he whispered. 'Could you – Would – I mean, what is the fruit that I should bear? What should I do?'

John stepped towards the tax collector. 'Why are you nervous?' he said, reducing the moist fellow yet further. 'Are you afraid of me? Of these?' – indicating the crowd.

'No.' The poor man could scarcely speak. 'Not afraid,' he murmured. 'Ashamed.'

Immediately John raised his eyes to the people around. 'This is it,' he declared. 'This is right. This is the beginning of repentance! And who would withhold baptism from so low a suitor?'

To the man, he said: 'When you collect the tax, collect no *more* than the tax, no little something for yourself.'

The sweating man bowed slightly.

John said, 'It isn't the knowing that's difficult, is it? Come. I will baptize you.'

John turned and started at a quick pace to descend a marly path to the Jordan. His feet were huge, camel's feet untroubled by rough terrain. Veins coursed visibly down his calves.

We followed him, calling out our stations in life and begging John's direction.

'Sir? I am a soldier. What about me?'

John didn't so much as glance at him. 'Stop robbing folks. Cease your violence,' he said. 'Neither sword nor force should give you the advantage. Be happy with your wages.'

Approaching the Jordan, we left the hard, unyielding clay and entered a swampy greenery, willows, canes, reeds, poplar trees. Jackals and leopards prowled this thicket. We fell into something like a double line behind the prophet.

Then, before the rest of us broke from the buzzing vegetation, we heard John yell: 'What are you doing here? Who warned you, you brood of vipers, to flee the wrath that is to come?'

Soon enough I came into sunlight and saw the objects of John's fury. Comfortable on the backs of their mules, dressed in the whitest, lightest linen, smiling benignly upon this ruined stick of a prophet, was a five-man delegation, two of their mounts drinking water from the Jordan. These were priests and Levites, representatives of some of the most powerful families in Jerusalem.

'Greetings from the House of Kathros,' a bland, angular priest intoned, ignoring John's more explosive greeting: *You brood of vipers*. This priest distinguished himself by means of a blue stripe that ran down his tunic from the shoulder to the hem. He was grey and urbane, as smooth as John was rocky. His turban was wrapped with dramatic bulk and pinned with an amethyst.

'What do you want?' John snapped. 'To repent? To be baptized? I've come to this place to baptize.'

'No need,' the priest assured the prophet. 'We are – just *as* we are – saved from the judgment.'

'What does that mean?'

'That we live within the covenant of Abraham. We are the children of Abraham.'

'A cold, dense-headed boast, because – ' Suddenly John bent down and grabbed a stone in either hand, then stood erect and cracked them together, saying: 'Because God is able from these stones (*crack!*) to raise up children of Abraham!'

'My, my,' the priest on his mule remarked, smiling. 'It is just as they've said of you, that you speak with a certain force. I approve of passion. But just for our little business here, John, son of a priest yourself, I beg a more reasonable discussion. Can you manage reason, John?'

John turned his back on the mounted priest, dropped the stones, and walked from the river into the crowd, which parted as he came.

'Whence your commission, Baptizer?' the well-washed, oiled and well-dressed priest called. 'What gives you the right to baptize?'

There was palpable threat in the challenge. The family of Kathros lived in one of the most magnificent mansions on Zion. For generations they had produced the spices and the incense used in Temple ritual, which monopoly had rewarded the name with wealth and influence and a cruel, unchecked privilege.

Nevertheless, John kept moving through the crowd until he found the rotund tax collector. 'Come with me,' he said, taking this man's hand. Then, to the grey priest: 'I'll tell you who I am not. I am not the Messiah.'

'Good to know. We've had enough such claims to fill a village with messiahs. So, then: what else empowers you? Are you Elijah come back to earth again?'

It was hard to tell whether the question was spoken in scorn or in earnest.

John was drawing the tax collector out of the crowd and into the Jordan, an arduous task, since the deeper they went, the more fearfully, the more tightly did the fat man cling to him. 'No,' said John.

The priest urged his mule towards the water's edge. 'Are you the prophet Moses promised?'

'No.'

'Sir, grant me the civility of your attention! Mine is not an insignificant matter! What gives you the authority to cry the end upon us? And whence your right to baptize?'

The river's current chewed at the tax collector's waist. Yet John wrapped an arm around his back, placed a huge hand over his face, and crying, 'I baptize you with water,' threw the fellow backwards, down, completely under the water. There was a moment of perfect silence, John's face bending over the quieting surface.

Then, with astonishing strength, he hauled the big man up into the air, water streaming from his shoulders, his clothing stuck to the bulges of his body, something like laughter blowing from his mouth.

And John was crying again in that nagging, unbeautiful Voice, perhaps for all the Jews to hear, certainly for the tax collector and the delegation from Jerusalem – and, please God, also for me: 'I baptize with water. But after me comes another so much mightier than I that I'm not worthy to latch his sandals. He will baptize you with the Holy Spirit and with fire! Even now his winnowing fork is in his hand to gather the wheat into his granary. But the chaff he will burn with unquenchable fire.'

THIS QUESTION: 'WHAT ARE YOU LOOKING FOR?'

—

During my days with John I saw Jesus of Nazareth on three separate occasions. Each remains bright in my memory. Each dropped its root in me, though we did not speak until the third.

The first occasion is memorable primarily because John's behaviour changed in the encounter. I noticed a short, glittering man among the crowds because he stood still, neither speaking nor moving. People pushed past him. They clamoured for John's attention. They swooned both ashore and in the water. John continued baptizing them, all of them, his Voice an insistent cry for repentance. But for hours that afternoon this one figure stood singular, waiting. Otherwise, he seemed unremarkable to me: lightly built, his hair and beard curled close to his head and cheek. Patience in his eye, to be sure; but a face uncluttered, clean.

Nevertheless, when evening descended and the crowds were departing; when the disciples had gathered kindling and begun a small fire for our supper and John, coming up out of the Jordan, raised his eyes and saw the man standing alone, he dropped to his knees in shallow water. Both men were shadows to me, each a silhouette with shape but without features; yet John's posture was bent in a humility I had never before witnessed in that stern stick.

'You,' John whispered.

'It is I.'

'How long?'

'Eighteen years since my first Passover.'

'But I knew you from the womb. Why have you come to me now?'

'To be baptized.'

'No. Please. I should be baptized by you.'

'John, baptize me.'

'You have no need!'

'Come, it is proper for us to fulfil all righteousness.'

The shadow of John then rose to standing, while the shadow of the other walked into the water. Together they went farther and farther out into the water. I lost sight of them.

Suddenly, a brilliant rip of lightning sundered the night, horizon to horizon, an arcing light that blinded me.

Immediately there followed a great calamity of thunder. Then all was silent. All was dark. The storm that I expected never came.

At supper we discussed that strike of lightning because it was so naked, unaccompanied by wind or rain or bluster.

I didn't see John again until the next day.

There were exactly forty days and forty nights between the first and the second occasions of my seeing him, Jesus from Nazareth, a relative of John's, as it turned out.

I thought that their kinship contained the cause for the Baptizer's behaviour in the presence of Jesus, so I let the matter slip from my mind.

But on the forty-first day, while we were walking near the Dead Sea, John touched my shoulder and pointed eastwards, to the long descent of a limestone escarpment.

'Look,' he said.

I did. I followed the prophet's finger and finally picked out the distant motion of someone coming in our direction, walking down the more gradual slopes, but leaping, his cloak billowing, climbing hand and leg where the grade fell steeply away.

'That,' John continued, 'is the Lamb of God who takes away the sin of the world.' A fathomless declaration, and his tone lent a terrible devotion to the words.

'A lamb?' But the traveller was moving lean as an antelope. 'Who takes away sin?'

'He is the one I meant when I said, "After me comes another

so much mightier than I that I'm not worthy to latch his sandals."
He is Jesus of Nazareth, whom I baptized.'

Yes, of course. I remembered him then. 'The night the
lightning scored the sky,' I said.

'It was no lightning. When Jesus came up out of the water, the
firmament itself split open – '

John spoke softly. The nagging quality of his mightier cry was
swallowed up in awe. 'I saw,' he murmured, gazing at the man
approaching now on smoother ground, 'the Spirit of God drop
from heaven like a dove and alight on him: a fearsome, flashing,
commanding dove – and a voice in heaven thundered, *You are my
beloved Son. With you I am well pleased.* Immediately the dove came
between us, driving him across the Jordan and far into the night.'

Forty days and forty nights since he left.

What I saw when the man arrived before us, quietly asking for
bread and water, for a clean pallet and a place to sleep until the
morning – what I saw harrowed my soul.

Jesus was tired almost beyond recognition. He had lost meat in
his temples and cheeks, his head a skull-like apparition. His neck
and his wrists were thin to breaking, his stomach an empty
shovel. He shook with weakness.

'Soup,' I whispered. 'I'll give him thin broth before the bread.'

Yet it was not the ravages of his body that most unsettled me.
It was the calm – no, the serene – horror in his eyes. What had
he seen? What could have caused such endless wells of knowing
in his vision?

And upon the wing of abominations shall come one who makes desolate –

The words of Daniel arose in my mind. Had Daniel seen what
this man saw? There were both desolations and calm
compassions in this Jesus of Nazareth.

Who he was, what he had become: this hectored me the rest
of the day and all night, too. I didn't sleep. I was being chewed
between opposing jaws, one of terrors, one of an absolutely
pellucid peace.

At some time in the darkness, Jesus must have departed our
small band. He wasn't there at breakfast. Strangely, his absence
only intensified my restlessness, as if there were a blank spot in my
sight and I was missing half the world on account of it. I didn't eat
breakfast. Nor could I drink; water tasted like metal to me.

Morning and afternoon, John baptized. I served. Perhaps I appeared unchanged to the others; if so, I was playing at being myself rather than truly existing in the present.

And then, towards evening, came the third occasion of my meeting Jesus.

Exactly as he had yesterday, John touched my shoulder and pointed, saying, 'Look.'

There was Jesus, walking erect and in good health, passing by us at some little distance.

Again, as yesterday, John said, 'The Lamb of God,' and I felt a stab of panic: *he's leaving! I may not see him again.*

Straightway I left John. Without a word. My heart seemed bound by strings to this… this impossibility, this man Jesus. And even as I moved to follow him, there came to me a sense of fearful delight. Whatever it was he was, I was in for it.

I heard footsteps just behind me. For an instant I thought John might be coming to draw me back. Not John, though – it was another of the disciples, Andrew, a wild look in his eye.

Still wordlessly, we strode side by side behind the Nazarene for half an hour. The sun began to set, striking the sky with golden fire.

Suddenly Jesus stopped and turned to us. We stopped too.

Although he moved in health, his face remained gaunt.

'What are you looking for?' he asked.

'Rabbi,' I said, astonishing myself with a strong inclination to weep: 'Where are you staying?' – *because where else in the world would I want to stay but by you?*

And he spoke the fulfilment upon the both of us, upon Andrew and me, by answering: 'Come and see.'

We went and saw and stayed with him that night and a thousand nights thereafter.

ENGAGING THE ENEMY

What follows is as accurate an account of 'the time between' as I can gather, not having been there to see it myself. To state the matter clearly: no one was there except Jesus and the Adversary. And he never told us the tale wholly, in a single sitting.

On the other hand, at three separate times in the years to come he made pointed, aggrieved references to these darksome forty days.

First: after he had fed more than five thousand people fully – the full congregation, and *to* the full – upon a mere five loaves and two fishes, many of them rushed at him crying, 'We'll make you our Bread-King! We'll love you more than we love the Emperor!' Jesus murmured in my hearing: 'This is Satan, as once in the wilderness, multiplied in five thousand faces, seducing me.'

Second: when members of his own family, misbelieving him, urged Jesus to go to Jerusalem, there to 'give evidence of your marvellous claims by working wonders before the public', Jesus said: 'This is Satan, as once in the wilderness, tempting me, tempting me now by the tuggings of my own kin.'

Finally, in his darkening days, when death awaited him, the Lord's deep soul wanted to cry out, *Catch me, Father! Father, save me from this hour!* he said instead, 'Father, glorify your name' – and to me my dear one, haggard, also said: 'Now he tempts me to tempt the Father and so to give over all my sorrows. This is Satan, as once in the wilderness, abiding in my own mind.'

Of such slight indications as these have I pieced together the following report: Jesus, in the forty days and forty nights before his ministry began, engaged the Enemy of Life and Love on behalf of the people of this world; Jesus went alone into the groves of the Devil.

'You are my beloved Son…'

Immediately after the thunder had uttered those words in Heaven, that predacious dove drove Jesus over the Jordan and into the wilderness, where it left him solitary among the rounded hills. Days passed, and he did not eat. A week, two weeks in which his sleep grew fitful for the lack of food. He would have acknowledged the sabbaths, except that all his days were sabbath days in this wordless place, a long, debilitating rest. Three weeks. Four weeks. The intense heat had early burned his skin; since then it had developed a nearly Nubian darkness. The close cap of his curls allowed his sweat to evaporate with greatest efficiency – a small gift for which he thanked the Father.

Near the end of his sixth week in the wilderness, Jesus awoke one afternoon to a cooling breeze and a light, pattering rainfall. He had been lying on his side. Now, blindly, he turned his face heavenward and opened his mouth. Sweet drops ran down his tongue. He swallowed. All his body received the rain as a washing by ten thousand tiny hands. He was becoming clean.

'If you are – ' a merciful voice began. Jesus opened his eyes. A short distance away he saw a column of shadow rising skywards as if from stoves below the earth, smudging the heavens and dropping a gentle rain. Sitting within the shadow, his face rimed in an ancient light, was the figure of a man more beautiful than any angel, in form and proportion breathtaking. What mortal could look on him and not fall in love?

'If you are the Son of God,' he said to Jesus, his voice soft as the night dew, 'command these stones to become loaves of bread.'

The sable figure smiled. It was a smile of earnest, thoughtful compassion. The effect of this smile on Jesus was to twist his stomach with so sharp a cramp, that the falling rain warmed into the caressing tears of a sweet self-pity.

Already there were stones heaped up like loaves between them.

But Jesus spent his energies on gathering his limbs together, pushing himself like a young cub to his hands and knees, then, by one foot and the next, standing up in order to confront the Tempter.

'It is written, "No one lives by bread alone."' His own voice was a cough of dust. 'But by every word that comes from the mouth of God.'

In a twinkling the wilderness vanished, and Jesus, without shifting a muscle, found himself standing at a dizzy height upon that wing of the Temple which the Levites mounted for blowing the trumpet. Below was the Tyropeon Valley and a marketplace swarming with infinitesimal humanity.

Neither had the column of darkness changed. It stood the same distance from him as before; and Satan sat therein.

'If you are the Son of God,' he who is the dragon said, 'pitch your body headlong down. Fear nothing. Prove everything, for it is written, "He shall give his angels charge over you. In their hands they will bear you up, lest you strike your foot against a stone."'

When Jesus spoke this time, the physical effort unbalanced his stance, and something within him seemed drawn to the drop, fascinated.

His battle was interior. The words, therefore, cost him all his virtue and all his strength:

'It is written,' he whispered, '"You shall not tempt the Lord your God."'

Immediately that struggle ceased. Jesus collapsed backwards – and this time found himself sitting in a chair, a royal throne carved all of obsidian and set upon the mountain no mortal ever sees, but whence all mortals may be seen, all their kingdoms, all their nations. This is the cosmic mountain which dwarfs Olympus and Ararat. It is established on no earthly ground but on the firmament of the glory of human desirings.

The column of the Devil's darkness, that dismal cloud, was visibly expanding, embracing Jerusalem and Judea and Arabia, Mesopotamia, Asia, both the Greek- and the Parthian-speaking peoples. In a moment it would swallow Rome and the Indus and the circle of the Sea and all the earth entirely.

And the soul of the Saviour felt as though it were swelling too, great to bursting, a terrible, murderous pregnancy.

'All these,' said the Devil, Satan, the ancient Serpent, 'will I give you, if only you fall to your knees and worship me.'

Jesus rose from the throne. In a tremendous roar he cried,

'Satan, begone! For it is written, "Worship the Lord your God; serve him, serve him, serve only him!"'

Then the Devil departed, and it seemed to Jesus that the stony ground rushed up to strike him bodily, as though to break all his bones. And the land was as dry as it had been before; and he was unspeakably thirsty, for he had seen the horror at the core of wickedness – who had only left for a little while, waiting a more opportune time.

To me once, gazing at his mother as she stirred a stew in the distance, Jesus said, 'What the Ancient Liar did to Eve at the beginning of things, he did to me. The Mother of All was a mighty woman. She thought to outface the Serpent. She thought to brazen it through as though she were herself equal to evil.'

Jesus cocked his head, minutely to study his own mother, her brisk, self-confident gestures, the presumption, now calling people to supper, that none would disobey; all would hear and come.

'Eve chose to argue with the Enemy. She herself, alone,' said Jesus. 'It was a good intent. It was a proud overestimation and a monumental failure. Every child of Eve thereafter has died because of that failure. And so must I.'

I got up, obeying Mary's call.

The rest of our company arose as well and brought bowls to her, into which she ladled stew.

Only her son did not move. Neither did he shift his eyes from her. Nothing, absolutely nothing about her person escaped his scrutiny.

BOOK TWO

THE
SHEPHERD
OF THE
PEOPLE

PART THREE

MARY

A HOMECOMING

The big city Sepphoris, built afresh by Herod Antipas while Jesus spent both his boyhood and his youth nearby, sucked produce from the folk of the countryside. It demanded their crafts, their livelihoods, their independence. Wood, stone, water – every kind of food and almost every kind of good – were consumed by the city, spreading blight like a bitter ash around itself to all the places where these necessities no longer served the villagers.

The city was a concentration of wealth and power and human want. It required quantities of bread. Therefore, the farmers who used to divide their annual labours among several crops and various domestic animals (for, though one crop might fail in a year, other crops would see the family through); the farmers who used to allow a third of their fields to lie fallow for renewal, who led their herds and flocks to graze on unsown pastureland, the same farmers now were forced to plant one crop only, and that on every available foot of land. If *that* crop failed, the family failed as well, and whole villages besides.

At the same time, all the farmers, the peasants, the vintners, hunters, herdsmen, shepherds: everyone was beaten down by the taxes the authorities in the city demanded for the maintenance of their more splendid lives. One couldn't travel, except he was taxed. One couldn't sell his goods, except he was taxed in kind – yes, and with coin as well. One couldn't live on the land in Galilee, except he was taxed. Fully one-third to one-half of a poor man's production was lost in taxes to the city, to the Herodians, to Rome.

In consequence, farmers sold out to the priesthood. They

began to work as tenants for men they seldom met and never loved – on land their ancestors had ploughed before them. Or they moved their families into single rooms in the city, earning a living as day-labourers during the harvest, eating stones and serpents the rest of the year.

Or they turned to begging.

Or else they became bandits and insurgents, roaming the countryside in gangs whom the peasants did not altogether blame.

The poorest sold themselves into slavery.

Or sold their children in order that neither should die.

The rich, thereby, enriched themselves, buying human lives, buying all the little plots in order to create singular estates over which they placed stewards to manage land and labourers and production in their absence.

In consequence, too, the village of Nazareth languished. Its houses were crudely built of fieldstones and mud, thatched roofs. In places the thatching covered entrances into natural caves. The roads in Nazareth were never more than gravel paths, not one of which was straight. Nothing was paved. No public buildings existed here. Nothing marble, nothing artful, neither mosaics nor frescoes. The synagogue offered the largest gathering space, and it was but the size of two houses joined, one room the whole of its interior and, like every other enclosure in Nazareth, a floor of dirt.

Once wine had been pressed and strained, fermented and stored in Nazareth. Once the grain had been ground here. Once a rough pottery was produced. Once there was a carpenter. None of these activities remained. They had all gone to Sepphoris. Except the carpenter. He perished poor. His son saw to the trade awhile, but then he too departed and travelled south into Judea.

But on his slow return a decade later, this carpenter's son was making a name for himself.

What? – could success be coming back to Nazareth?

Then Mary was everywhere in the village. She carried small honey cakes as gifts to the elders, washed the clothes of the old, patched rips, swept courtyards, hauled water and charcoal. And everywhere the widow went, she managed to mention that her son was coming home. Her educated child! No, not a child at all (she laughed at herself) – a man. A rabbi! Worthy of some attention, she mused, since a report had reached their kith and kin that he was teaching in synagogues with an astonishing authority. In Aenon. Yes, and in Salim, in Capernaum and Nain and Japhia and Simonias.

More marvellously: this teacher bid fair to be a prophet. Mighty works were ascribed to him! Healings!

'What if – ' Mary said. 'Wouldn't it be a splendid thing – for *Nazareth*, I mean – if this son of our village were invited to read and to speak on the sabbath? In our own little synagogue? We could celebrate the return – and after sundown have a banquet!'

Mary was most gratified – and not much surprised – when no one objected. In unison Nazareth agreed. There was so little to elevate the folk who had remained in the village and nothing to justify a downright pride. Of *course* Jesus the son of Joseph should read; and everyone, absolutely everyone, expressed a hunger to hear his teaching.

'Surely, we've sat in shadow long enough,' the people said, especially younger men made bitter by their narrow prospects and their poverty. 'It's high time the Lord God shined on us. Read the Hebrew? Teach us? Oh, Mary, we hope he'll do more than that. Let him *stay* in his proper home and give us reason to smile again.'

The synagogues of larger communities never lacked for readers. Someone was always available to declaim the appointed portions of Torah. In fact there were often two or three who read from the Prophets next, translating the Hebrew, then teaching the people.

In the village of Nazareth, however, there had been no one to read the Scriptures since their ancient rabbi died two years ago. None had come to take his place. Moreover, the rough building in which Nazareth gathered to worship had doubled as the rabbi's home, the home of his children too, until they preceded him in death. Presently the *Hazzan* and his wife lived here, a man prepared to assist at worship whenever the opportunity arose. Before the sabbath he swept the place, repaired and polished the benches, trimmed the lamps, and always protected the scrolls from weather and insects and vermin. Sometimes a rabbi might travel south from Sepphoris to speak and teach when the people gathered. But for the most part, sabbath gathering was composed of the recitations and prayers, the Shema, the Ten Commandments, the eighteen benedictions, and a private, murmured praying. It was a people's service, as it ought to be; common folk intoned the various prescriptions. But no Torah was translated. No teaching upon the Prophets. And only those Psalms certain old men had by heart.

No: Mary was not surprised when Nazareth agreed so enthusiastically to receive her son and to receive his teaching. But the people's immediate, complete conviction that this was a homecoming for good: why, Mary had scarcely permitted herself to dream such a wonderful thing.

She begged heaven for that favour, truly; but her prayer knew a truth regarding the man that no one else in Nazareth knew. Therefore, she prayed: 'It is sure that he will ever remain before you, Father. But let it be that my son – and your name – may also remain here, in this place, from new moon to new moon and from sabbath to sabbath.'

Things remain the same. Yes, and things change, too.

For all her giddy expectations, Mary was strangely, girlishly restrained when Jesus did finally arrive in town late that afternoon. Several men came walking with him. And Nazareth recognized its son immediately: curling hair, a close curling beard; eyes made glittering by constant motion, by his watchful attention to everything around him. The graceful tread, the body light and lean and accurate – yes! Except that he had lost his youthful freckling, this was the one, all right, Jesus, as we remember him!

Old men came forward and kissed him on both his cheeks; young men beamed and bowed and burst into volumes of questions, hopes and dreams and needs and solutions. The children, watching their elders, stood in wonder, then ran laughing away. Grandmothers took his measure by a needle eye and found him likely enough. Families, wives, showered him with invitations: to bless a particular infant, to see a particular calf, to teach a shrewd child Hebrew, to come and eat a sumptuous meal, if not tonight, then surely tomorrow.

Two women pulled scarves over their heads and slipped from the village eastwards, unnoticed by all save Mary, who stayed back from the merriment, watching it all from the doorway of her house. Anna was one of these, daughter of the ailing, sightless Bithiah, Anna herself a widow since Abbas had died. Whether it was shame that veiled the women's features, or whether secrecy, they hunched and travelled quickly. This much was known: both were mothers of sons so resentful of the crushing of their lives, they'd joined a band of brigands who waylaid the wealthy on the highways to Sepphoris. And Mary knew this too: these two, Anna and her companion, were blameless, both humble and just. Perhaps, she thought, they'd found the argument to bring their young men home again – even as hers was coming now.

For look how the entire village had abandoned itself to hope, becoming a parade! Boisterous, clapping, no one hesitating, everyone grinning, people reaching to touch the precious promise of their fulfilment. He had come! Their soaring son was home again! And the heavens themselves shed approval on the event, for the descending sun covered Nazareth in a honeyed light, and every glad face glowed.

Yes, but Mary had recognized from the beginning the unvarying direction of his progress through the town. To her. To the house of his youth. And the closer he came in the midst of the moiling crowd, the harder her poor heart beat. She put her hand upon her lips, her eyes widening with a speechless love and with a sharp stab of uncertainty. How many years since he had left her? And though messages had come regarding him, no message *from* him had been sent directly to her. Ah, God! – and there was no precedent for such a relationship as theirs. All was new. All was as old as Jehovah.

Halfway up the road at the end of which was Mary, waiting, the people suddenly parted. Jesus lifted his shining eyes and looked at her. A whimper caused her breast to heave; but she suppressed the sound. *Yeshi? Is it you? Are you my Yeshi still?*

Jesus turned and spoke to the crowd. He didn't raise his voice. She heard only a word or two. They made no sense to her. But even if the woman could have heard full sentences, they wouldn't have made sense either: her mind was in a whirl of waitfulness.

Then Jesus turned again and proceeded towards the house

alone. All others fell back and separated, his companions being led to several different homes for food and for the night.

Mary remained fixed, even as the man approached her and put forth his hand and cupped her chin a moment. Next he took her hand and drew it from her mouth to his own.

She whispered cautiously: 'Yeshi?'

He answered: 'Mother.'

And the woman broke into tears. A great boo-hooing, a shaking of her head, and a rubbing of her eyes – while Jesus stood still, her hand to his cheek, and twinkled upon her, which caused even greater bouts of boo-hooing. Mary was a very storm of happiness.

Then, just as suddenly, she caught up a rag and blew her nose and pinched her lips and frowned. 'Come in,' she said. She coughed. She grabbed his hand and fairly yanked him after her, chattering, 'Come in, come in, wash up. Change clothes. I've made a lentil soup. Some fresh honey cakes. Oh, and in the back room? On the pallet I've unrolled for your bed tonight? You'll find a tunic there. I took a chance it would fit you. But I look at you now and I know: it will fit you, Yeshi. You haven't grown an inch. Nothing at all like Joseph, you. And the tunic: I wove it from the top to the bottom without a seam.'

Later that night, they lay down to sleep, and Jesus caused his mother to shudder with an ineffable love. For she heard him recite the prayer she'd taught him long, long ago.

In tone as trusting as childhood, Jesus said: 'Father, into your hands I commend my spirit.' And immediately he was asleep.

It rained in the night. Mary appreciated its whispering sweep across the thatch.

May he live while the sun endures, and as long as the moon, my Lord. May he be like rain that falls on the mown grass, like showers that water the earth.

Things remain the same. Things change. And the bewilderment is: they do so both at once.

The little house-synagogue was filled to the walls with men, the oldest sitting on polished benches, the younger ones standing, all of them breathing an odd humidity into the room. Behind a reed screen in the back of the room stood several women. Age and honour granted them place inside the synagogue. *Honour?* – that would be for the widow Mary, seeing it was her son soon to read and to teach. But Anna, one of those who'd slipped from the village yesterday, was also here, a look of painful uncertainty upon her face.

'Ah, sister,' whispered Mary, touching the woman's shoulder. 'I know the feeling.' They were widows together, since both Joseph and Abbas had died.

At every little window, at the doors thrown open, within the muddy courtyard, on all the puddled ground around the house, the rest of Nazareth was huddling close, if not exactly to understand the language of the proceedings within, at least to feel themselves participants in the occasion. The air was moist. The sky still threatened rain. No one minded. Whenever before had such a wonder come to Nazareth?

Hear, O Israel!

A round-chested grandfather stood proudly intoning the Shema. This they did hear out of doors.

Hear, O Israel: the Lord our God, the Lord is one! And you shall love the Lord your God with all your heart, and with all your soul, and with all your might.

Then back and forth, in vigorous antiphony, the congregation and the booming grandfather recited the Ten Commandments.

The people said: 'The Lord our God made a covenant with us at Horeb, with us, even us, who are all of us here alive today.' It was noted with a fine satisfaction that Jesus spoke the words along with the rest of them.

The old man chanted: *The Lord talked with you face to face on the mount, out of the midst of the fire. And he said, I am the Lord your God, who brought you out of the land of Egypt, out of the house of bondage. And he said:*

The people responded: 'You shall have no other gods before me.'
And he said:

'You shall make for yourself no graven image.'
And he said:

'You shall not take the name of the Lord your God in vain.'
And he said:

'Observe the sabbath and keep it holy.'
And he said:

'Honour your father and your mother.'
And he said:
'You shall not kill.'
And he said:
'You shall not commit adultery.'
And he said:
'You shall not steal.'
And he said:
'You shall not bear false witness against your neighbour.'
And he said:
'You shall not covet your neighbour's wife, nor shall you desire your neighbour's house or field, his manservant or his maidservant, his ox, his ass, or anything that is your neighbour's.'

These words the Lord spoke with a loud voice to your whole assembly at the mountain, the stentorian grandfather concluded: *out of the fire, out of the cloud, out of thick darkness; and he added no more.*

That man sat down and folded his arms across his chest. Another arose and repeated the benedictions. A third led the congregation in the repetition of a psalm.

And then, to a sudden and perfect silence, the *Hazzan* drew forth the scroll of the prophet Isaiah from its leather sheath and brought it to Jesus. This beloved son of Nazareth received the book with respect, stood up, placed it on a small table and, rolling through the extended manuscript, found a passage closer to its ending than its beginning.

In a voice of such articulate clarity that even the people outside could hear and understand the words, Jesus read:

'The Spirit of the Lord is upon me, because he has anointed me to bring good news to the poor. He has sent me to proclaim freedom to the captives, recovery of sight to the blind, release to those oppressed – to proclaim the year of the Lord's favour.'

Jesus closed the scroll and returned it to the assistant. He sat down, settling his hands upon his thighs, palms up.

Every eye was fixed upon him; and outside, every head was bowed in a concentration of listening.

Jesus said: 'Today this Scripture has been fulfilled in your hearing.'

There was a moment of astonished silence, then the place erupted in whoops and howls and peals of joy.

'In *our* hearing!'

'Yes, yes, even as he was reading. Didn't you feel it?'

'The man is ours! A prophet has come to Nazareth!'

'No longer will the pompous mock us with "What good can come from Nazareth"!'

'Marvels! Wonderful works! He'll heal the blind – '

'Old Bithiah will see the lilies again before she dies!'

'Yes, and the faces of her grandchildren, hallelujah!'

'Praise to you, O God! Your powerful Spirit in our midst!'

'And we *are* the oppressed!' cried the young men, shamelessly weeping, so deep was their relief. 'It is time, it is time that the favour of the Lord God fell on *us*.'

In all the excitement the reed screen was bumped and collapsed. Mary saw the wild emotion, the revelry of the men. She saw too her son, sitting unmoved among them, nothing like triumph in his face, his hands upturned on his thighs.

'Oh, no,' she murmured to herself. Her soul turned sober. 'O God: no!' She wanted to run out of the house; but her eyes and her heart could not be torn from her son.

The rain began to fall outside. It caused laughter at first – one more sign of God's grace and favour – and then a quietness which entered the synagogue and returned the people to a listening attitude. Of course: their reader had not yet turned the reading into a teaching.

'Teach us, Jesus.'

Men produced a genial chuckle. Young men crouched, preparing to pay attention.

But wordlessly that glittering eye moved back and forth across the congregation. The mouth remained composed.

Then he spoke a cold articularity: 'What is the matter with you people?'

What? What did he say?

'Arrogant. Self-absorbed,' Jesus continued with so little emphasis, the meaning of the words came but slowly to people's awareness. 'You stumble on pride like the man who stumbles on his laces – '

Pride? – the thoughts of the young men: *The proud are in cities, not in Nazareth.*

Almost mildly, Jesus taught: 'I say, "The prophecy is fulfilled," and you shout your joy. You become exultant. You beat each other on the back with glad congratulations. Nazareth, Nazareth, what makes you think the doctor must come to cure his own and his own only?'

The faces of the young men began to darken: *What's wrong with that? Why shouldn't he do in his hometown what he's done in other places?*

A thick, bare-armed fellow standing by a window, the side of his face trickling raindrops, said: 'The doctor that healed in Capernaum can lose nothing by healing here as well.'

'Truly,' said Jesus, looking at him; then again, to the rest of the congregation, 'the prophet will never be accepted in his own hometown.'

What? Aren't we accepting him? Don't we approve of what —

'You approve of what you think I can do for you!' Jesus completed the unspoken sentiment, then uttered a judgment with calm precision: 'Small minds are never the minds of compassion, nor are they minds beloved of God. The mind of God embraces nations. Nazareth, you cannot stop at your doorstep! You cannot love your own blood only!'

The fellow at the window took a step forward and began to tie a band around his head, pulling back his long, beautiful hair. 'Why do you blame us?' he growled.

Mary heard Anna gasp beside her. 'No!' she whispered: 'Jesus, don't do it!' Mary stared at the woman, resentment rising in her throat – but then she realized that Anna was fearful for *her* son, Anna's boy, whose name was Jesus too. Ah, yes: the man at the window! Mary hadn't recognized him. That wonderful fall of hair, those ready muscles: he'd changed since last she saw him, before he turned his bitterness into thievery.

'Whose side are you on?' the powerful son of Anna and Abbas demanded. 'You speak for Sepphoris? *We* are the taxed, man! We are tormented by the high and the mighty. We are being killed all the day *long* like sheep to be slaughtered.'

'Please, Jesus,' Anna whined, patting her hands together. 'Let it go.'

An older man stood and raised his arms in a placating gesture. 'Jesus, son of Abbas, Jesus, son of Joseph,' he affected a familiar laugh – *Heh, heh!* 'No need to cause a fuss here. No need for accusations. You're one of us, boy. Little Yeshi, no bigger than a hiccup. You played at sticks outside my house. I showed you how to make a fishhook. We're plain folks. Blame us, my boy, and you blame yourself.'

Mary's son sat composed, altogether his own person. 'Listen to the truth,' he said, still in the rabbi's tone of teaching, 'and understand the precedent of God the Father. There were many widows in Elijah's home country when the heavens were shut up and famine shrivelled the land. Yet that prophet was sent to none of them. He was sent to a widow outside his blood, beyond his people's doorstep, at Zarephath in Sidon.'

'Enough!' spat Jesus, Abbas's son. He balled his fists, his face a forest of anger. 'Get out of here, you arrogant prig!'

'Let it go, let it go,' his mother repeated. And Mary felt the very same yearning: *Yeshi! For God's sake, let it go!*

Other men were standing now, shaking with indignation. 'Are you saying we don't know God?' they yelled. 'Are you saying God won't listen to us? Who do you think you are? You turned your back on us once, as if we were beneath you. Now you return to insult us to our faces?'

Jesus stood up, shorter than most of those before him.

With the same rabbinic persistence, yet with remarkable clarity, he continued the lesson: 'And there were many lepers in the villages of the prophet Elisha, some of whom he knew when they played at sticks as children; and some, perhaps, of his own blood...' Suddenly – with a single word – Jesus shattered the air in the synagogue: 'NEVERTHELESS!' – stunning the congregation by his authority: 'none of them was cleansed! It was only Naaman, a Syrian, whom Elisha healed.'

Nevertheless!

While the people were staggered and mute with fury, Jesus moved lightly through them and out the door.

Then, for the second time that morning, the room erupted: howls of outrage. Men poured out the doors, a mob intent on driving this son of the Devil from their village, to the brow of a hill, to a bluff where they might pitch him headlong down – if they could find him.

For, by a native mobility – athletic, light, and utterly confident – Mary's son had avoided them all and left the town on his own terms.

His mother saw the feint and the departure: northwards, into the valley his father and he had traversed so long ago. *O God,* she moved her lips silently. *Almighty God, the child has changed. Who is he now? Have you ripped him from his mother's arms as once you did from his mother's womb?*

Mary stood still a moment, ignored by neighbours who were making a spittle-moist hissing of their outrage.

Suddenly she turned and went into her house and gathered some things in a leather bag, a little clothing, a little food.

'No!' she said out loud. 'You can't have him yet.'

ARREST

'What you say and what you do not say.' Mary spoke to her son unsmiling, half in admonition: 'What you do and what you do not do,' she said, 'could get you killed – '

After leaving Nazareth, Jesus skirted Sepphoris, he and his companions. They travelled northwesterly, up and down several ridges, slowly across the rich Valley of Asochis, pausing in villages this day and the next so that Jesus might speak and teach and tell stories in his unruffled manner – arriving finally in a village called Jotapata, where they found shelter and stayed awhile.

It took Mary the better part of a week to find them. But Jesus' movements were hardly secret. He left a trail of genuine wonderment wherever he went. And in the end Mary was led directly to her perplexing son when she spotted, then followed one of the companions she'd seen with him in Nazareth. His name, the young man's name… was Philip! And she would have called out to him, except that he was walking so swiftly, he and another man whom Mary didn't recognize. Philip was in the lead; Philip seemed consumed by his own conversation, gesticulating, pointing ahead of them.

Mary picked up her pace in order to keep them in sight.

Just as they turned onto a road that wound uphill – to a gate through the town wall – Mary heard the unfamiliar man repeat a most familiar phrase. It was that familiarity, not the strength of his voice, that caused her to understand the words even at a distance and to take offence: 'Can anything good,' the stranger said, 'come out of Nazareth?'

Mary paused to send that man a fiery look – but only succeeded in losing them through the town gate. She gathered her robe and ran. Shortly, a sound of a rapid knocking among a jumble of whitewashed houses signalled their location. Mary found them just entering a courtyard door. Before it closed she followed them inside and saw her son sitting on a low stone wall. Motherhood rose up as heat and happiness in her face.

But if he noticed her, he didn't acknowledge it.

Instead, he turned his bright gaze on the man who had insulted Nazareth.

'Well, look who's here,' said Jesus, inviting everyone to scrutinize the fellow: 'Meet Nathanael, an Israelite indeed, in whom there is no guile.'

Nathanael frowned. 'I've never met you before,' he said. 'Someone told you about me, right?'

'No,' Jesus said, his gaze steady and direct. 'But even before Philip found you, I saw you. I saw you under the fig tree.'

The young man's eyes widened. 'Rabbi,' he whispered. 'Son of God. King of Israel – '

A most credulous fellow, thought Mary. She looked towards the son that *still* hadn't looked towards her, and awaited the word that would restore mother wit to this bug-eyed Nathanael.

But Jesus uttered nothing of the kind. Balanced, unemphatic, with astonishing intimacy, he said: 'Do you believe because I told you I saw you under the fig tree? Nathanael, you'll see greater things than these. You will see heaven opened, and the angels of God ascending and descending upon the Son of man.'

It was in the silence that followed this moment that Mary thought it time to trim her son to standards more grounded and less celestial.

'So, Yeshi,' she said, exerting her maternal authority and seizing the talk in the courtyard: 'Under that robe,' she said, 'does there sit a boy still well-behaved?' She stepped towards him in the tiny courtyard, causing others to shuffle out of her way. 'And does this boy, whose genius is nothing less than divine, also remember to honour his mother? Tell me. Under that robe, are you wearing the tunic I made for you?'

In the evening, while Jesus and his companions were eating food she had prepared, Mary took the opportunity to caution her son.

'What you say and what you do not say – ' she said, trying to keep her voice down. 'Choose these things carefully, Yeshi. Your words fly like bolts; they can shatter or salve the soul. I've known this since you were twelve, and now I see the consequences more clearly than ever.'

He chewed raisins with a slow closure of his jaw, the corner muscle tensing beneath his beard. He didn't look at her, but he was listening. He lay on his side, on his open robe, on a patch of grassy ground outside the walls of the town. He cradled his head on the palm of his hand. She crouched close to his ear.

'What you do and what you do not do, as good as your doing is for the people, will have consequences for you as well. Mortal consequences. I think of this all the time. Your deeds could get you killed.'

Jesus filled his mouth with raisins and chewed. Though she was quiet a moment, offering him the chance to answer her, to fuss at her, he didn't.

She went on: 'What you know and what you do not know.' She paused. Then: 'It's possible that you don't know everything.'

Jesus was about thirty years old, his tight hair a darker brown than when he was a child, though it still was something ruddy, as if there were fires banked within it. Of his fierce childhood freckling, several lingered on his upper eyelids, granting weight and a certain starriness to his gaze. Mary was in her midforties. Both were slight of bone, though Mary had more meat on her person than did her son; and her hair, peppery, shot with grey, was as unmanageable as when she was the girl that beat the boys at races. Even bound by scarves and hoods, it exploded off her forehead. Her forehead: there were two deep lines above her nose where the eyebrows fisted together. Her forehead bore her worry.

'What you know and what you do not know,' she repeated her sharp thesis. 'This is what you do not know: that cousin John, the son of Zechariah, no longer moves about the Jordan as a free man.'

Jesus stopped chewing and looked at Mary.

'Yes,' said Mary, sad to bring sad news. 'He was preaching against Herod Antipas. Naming him by name. Blaming his evil deeds, but attacking especially the fact that he divorced his first wife – and she the daughter of the Nabatean king! – in order to marry the wife of his brother Philip – forcing a divorce between them too. Herod married Herodias, and John raised such a public criticism, that Herod sent soldiers to arrest him and take him in chains to the fortress Machaerus, east of the Dead Sea. There John sits in prison.'

Sad news.

Without a word Jesus rose up and walked away. Nor did Mary lift her face. She heard his motion; she heard, too, the tread of one other man who followed him away. Nevertheless, she continued to talk as if Jesus still were near and still were listening: 'What you say and what you do not say... can get you killed,' she said, her heart bucking against her ribs. She reached for her son's robe and began to fold it. 'What would I do if you were imprisoned? What would I do then?'

The folded robe she pressed against her breast.

'And yes, there is one other piece of news. A fortunate circumstance, really, since we are only two miles from Cana. We are invited to a wedding there, you and I. I think you can bring your friends.'

A WEDDING

―

The mother of the bride was Joanna. She and Mary had been friends since they'd met in a Sepphoris marketplace about fifteen years ago. Mary, the more mature, was selling finely woven woollen clothing; Joanna, young and vibrant, was buying; and the sheer boldness of the older woman – setting up a shop in the presence of male opprobrium – caught Joanna's fancy. She'd come to the market with several maidservants, looking for wedding garments, as a matter of fact – but for herself. Joanna at fourteen was about to marry a man of stature, Chuza, who managed several estates of Herod Antipas in the rich Valley of Asochis. He was a native of the Kingdom of Nabatea in the Negeb, south of the Dead Sea; but he honoured Jewish practices, and both his wealth and his piety persuaded Joanna's family to accept his offers.

In the space of an afternoon the women's friendship had been fixed forever. Mary's natural delight, her scandalous energy, caused Joanna to babble in a sort of hectic happiness; moreover, having no garment ready-made for the bride, Mary promised to weave one of finest linen for her particularly, and was straightway invited to spend the rest of the day at Joanna's house.

It was to that house an older Mary went after Jesus left Nazareth, assuming he'd stopped in Sepphoris. Now, of course, it was the house of Joanna's parents, since Chuza had taken his wife to his own home in Cana, close to the Herodian estates; yet it had always been a house of welcome for the weaver of fine clothing, despite her poverty – and marvellously, Joanna was there to greet Mary this time, too. She was visiting her parents in order to purchase in Sepphoris what she could not get in Cana, adornments for *her* daughter's wedding.

So swiftly do we grow older, Mary thought.

Here, then, in the same house, Mary heard of John's imprisonment. Chuza, distressed by Herod's decision to divorce the daughter of the king of the country of his birth, had told Joanna. Joanna told Mary. Mary told Jesus.

And then Cana. And then, the wedding.

Pretty little dark-skinned girl! Bathed by the women, her mother and the widow Mary overseeing everything.

Solemn girl, her skin anointed with a rich mixture of olive oil and cassia and cinnamon. Her clothing infused with myrrh, a sachet of powdered myrrh hanging lightly between her breasts. Oh, how Joanna's daughter shined when she was brought into the late afternoon sun, her cheeks, well-oiled, rimmed with a golden light.

Chuza was a wealthy man. His was a large house of dressed stone. Waiting outside the courtyard door was a carriage adorned with purple bunting and polished stones, the cushions stuffed with the down of the geese of Egypt. A handsome grey mule stood in its traces, waiting.

Laughing, maidservants lifted Chuza's daughter, Joanna's girl into the carriage. He himself reached up to crown her with a wreath, then he stepped back and began to beat his palms together in a weepy, emotional applause.

Mary herself was moved to see the love in this father's eyes. She began to clap as well. The carriage moved into the narrow streets. Everyone in the courtyard followed, clapping.

Such a beautiful dark-skinned girl! The warm flush of joy darkened her sober face, and her white teeth flashed, and her hair hung loose for she was a virgin – and her raven hair descended to her shoulders like rain on Gilead. And her thrilling scent went forth upon the breezes.

A woman walking behind the carriage threw back her head and sang:

Awake, O north wind! South wind, come,
And whirl across my garden!

Take my fragrance far abroad,
  A savour for my lover,
  Bring hither, winds, my lover!

A young man kicked his heels and clapped and answered her:

I'll come into the garden, bride,
  And eat my golden honey;
I'll gather myrrh and every spice,
  When all the winds are ready
  And all your portals open.

Then everyone took up a chorus and danced in the street both before the carriage and behind it:

And then we'll eat!
And then we'll drink!
And all grow drunk on loving!

Pipes blew music to the singing. Tambourines shook and slapped a rhythm for the flying feet. The marriage procession so filled the narrow streets that there was no passing it backwards; all was swept before it.

From their roofs people threw roasted wheat at the bride. From their doorways they spilled wine and oil in the path of the mule. Even the teachers and all their students poured out of their rooms to raise their arms and dance ahead of the smiling bride, to dance companionship for her giddy father. Men's fringes flew like horse tails snapping. Children dashed among the stamping legs. Torches were lit to lighten the evening darkness, and the shadows themselves got up and danced.

In the midst of these celebrations, Mary remembered Joseph and the simplicity of their wedding half a life ago. Dear Joseph, that great bear! Willing, loving, and beloved. Ah, there was a sweetness to the remembering. It formed within her a room of quiet contentment, though no one near would notice the quietness, for now it was Mary herself who threw back her head and began to sing:

Where has your dashing lover gone,
  O beautiful, black-skinned bride?
  Do you know where he turned aside,
That we might retrieve your vagabond?

Somewhat uphill of the bridal procession, winding downwards, Mary saw the first torches of the second procession.

'The bridegroom!' she cried, and she raised a delighted ululation.

Mary of the clarion voice: for an instant the people around her paused, everyone looking and, in that instant, everyone hearing a choral music descending:

You've ravished my heart, O sister, my bride!
You've ravished my heart with a glance of your eyes!

How sweet is your love, O sister, my bride!
And sweeter your loving than spices and wine!

Hoots of laughter encircled the bride. She covered her face in both hands. The pipes and the tambourines and the mule and the dancers all moved faster now, hurrying to meet the bridegroom, when both processions would form one grand cavalcade on its way to the bridegroom's house.

But your garden is locked, O sister! O bride!
Your fountain is sealed! Your waters untried –

Those in front of the bride's carriage fell away and the groom himself came striding ahead of his procession. They met at a crossing of the streets.

Pensive little black-skinned girl! Measure the brow of your beloved, weigh the gravity of his smile, seek the candour of his eye. What are you thinking, wistful girl, as you watch your bridegroom bow to your father? He bows to you – and what do you see? What strength in the arm that takes the bridle? – is it so? And what certitude in the step that leads your mule up the street, while everyone falls in step behind the both of you? Is it so?

Mary saw Jesus among the men behind the groom. She didn't move close to him, but she watched his face – and so it was that this wedding day found its fullness for her, for her Yeshi was grinning for joy.

All the women sang the verse that Mary had sung. Maybe it was the verse itself, or the answer to follow it. Maybe it was the exuberance of the celebrants, the glad abandon with which they sang, maybe the plain and ancient business of human communion, of weddings and marriages: whatever caused it, when the women began to sing, Jesus looked first at them and then at the bride and the groom before him, then raised his arms and began to dance. Yeshi danced!

> *Where has your dashing lover gone,*
>   *O beautiful, black-skinned bride?*
>   *Do you know where he turned aside,*
> *That we might retrieve your vagabond?*

One voice, one woman's soaring, sensual voice sang the response to its perfect ending:

> *My lover's come down – come down to his garden,*
>   *To lie on beds of spices,*
>   *To browse among my lilies.*
> *My lover is mine and I am my lover's:*
>   *He browses among my lilies.*

And so, in the dark and under the glow of torches, they arrived at the house of the groom, and went in.

The wedding had begun on a Wednesday. After the groom had formally introduced his bride to their new house, he led her down into the largest room of his father's quarters, where she sat down beneath the *chuppah*, a canopy most festively decorated, and ten men boomed the marital blessings in a ragged concert. In the same room, the groom took his place at the head of the table, and the feasting began.

That was five days ago. This was Sunday.

Still the *chuppah* stood in the feast room, unfaded, unsagging and squared at the corners. Still the bride would sit therein for a portion of each day's festivities (though she and the groom had been spending nights together, causing her clothing and her manner to change since Wednesday). And still the guests returned to the groom's house to recline, to sing, to tell stories and riddles, to eat and to drink great quantities of wine. By tradition, the wedding banquet was a seven-day affair. By tradition, too, each meal concluded with a special blessing for the bridegroom. By habit and personal inclination, revellers stayed late into the night.

Therefore, though the food continued in good supply (the groom's father had purchased a whole cow), in the middle of the feast on Sunday evening – before the blessing of the bridegroom, after every shop was closed – the wine ran out.

This was more troubling than the mere lack of a liquid. This could shame the household of the groom, for honour is always greater than possessions; possessions are given away for the *sake* of honour.

It was while she sat with Joanna and the other women that Mary heard of this embarrassment. A servant brought the news privately, wondering whether Joanna's husband might have sufficient wine in his own storerooms. Joanna refused even to respond, for such a solution would only have heaped shame upon shame. The *groom's* family was responsible for the wedding feast, not the bride's. All financial negotiations had been completed *before* the betrothal. No, Chuza would not haul his wine over here, because Chuza would never know that it might have been requested –

And if Mary had anything to say about it, Chuza would not even know that the wine had run out in the first place.

She said to the servant, 'Wait here. Don't do anything. Don't go back to the steward. Don't say anything to anyone else!'

Women did not eat with the men at feasts like these. Therefore Mary contrived to seem to serve. She found an empty wine cup and filled it with vinegar. This she carried into the dining room, going directly to the place where Jesus was reclining. She knelt opposite him and offered the cup. He had to take it in his hand. Its bottom was not flat, but pointed, and he had no sconce in which to set it.

Mary narrowed her eye and looked significantly at Jesus.

'It's full,' she whispered.

'I can see that,' he said.

'But you can't drink it,' she whispered.

'Why not?'

'Smell it.'

He did and frowned. 'It's vinegar,' he said.

'That's why you can't drink it,' she said, never moving her eyes from his.

Jesus lifted his graceful eyebrows. Mary loved every part of her son. Every part to her was lovely. 'Then why,' he said, 'did you bring it to me?'

'I didn't want to draw attention. But you have to know, this is all that's left of the wine. Sour stuff. Undrinkable. The wine, Yeshi, is gone.' Mary peered steadily at him.

A moment elapsed.

Finally, Jesus drew a breath and spoke: 'Woman,' he said, 'what concern is this to you or to me? My time has not arrived.'

Mary lifted a forefinger and touched it to the side of her nose. She nodded once, then rose and returned to the other room.

'OK,' she said to the servant, who was shifting from foot to foot. 'OK: whatever my son tells you to do, do it.'

Then she peeped around the wall and watched.

Jesus tilted the vinegar cup this way and that, gazing at it, his mouth closed, the jaw muscle pulsing. Then he drew up his legs and began to stand.

'Go!' Mary commanded the servant. 'Follow him!'

Jesus walked out into the vestibule through which the guests had entered the banquet room. It was there that the family kept six stone jars for ritual washings. The servant hurried after him. So did three of Jesus' companions, uninvited. Mary sighed at the ease with which others could move into the sphere of her son.

Jesus said something to the servant, who returned to the back room, perplexed.

'What did he say?' Mary demanded.

'To fill the jars with water. "To the brim."'

'Well?'

'Ma'am, each one of them holds something between twenty and thirty gallons.'

'*Well?*'

The fire in this woman's eyes drove the servant on through the women's room – and soon there were ten men passing back and forth with pitchers of water.

During these rushings to and fro, Jesus surprised Mary by appearing in the room of the women.

'Empty this,' he said, handing her the cup she'd given him.

Mary poured the vinegar into a basin.

'Wash it.'

When finally the servant announced that the stone jars were full, Jesus retrieved the clean cup and gave it to the servant. 'Fill this,' he said, 'and take it to the steward of the feast.'

Jesus followed the servant to the banquet table and reclined. The servant continued into the vestibule and returned with the dripping cup; he took it to the steward's post in the corner of the room, bowed, and held it out.

The steward frowned. The servant shrugged. The steward took the cup and sipped. Then sipped again. Then drank the whole draught down.

He rose and bustled to the groom, whispered something, then bustled to the back room. The groom was slow in getting up. The steward beckoned vigorously.

Perhaps he thought he was being secretive, then; but excitement raised his voice to the pitch of a cowherd: 'Where did you get this? Were you hiding it? I've never tasted such a vintage! Everyone else serves the good wine first and the poor stuff after folks have addled their brains. Why did you save the best for last?'

This was a sign. And the Master's companions began to believe in him.

But Mary giggled inside her soul: *I knew he would do it.*

SIGNS AND WONDERS

On the morning of the day the wedding ended, a royal official arrived from Capernaum. This man, also in Herod's service, knew Chuza. To Chuza's house, therefore, he came – he and an entourage of slaves, soldiers, clients, drivers, scribes.

'Where,' he asked his friend, 'is the man called Jesus of Nazareth?'

'Right here,' said Chuza, beaming. 'You've come to the right place, and you didn't even know it. Ha, ha! The prophet was kind enough to stay the night in my house, he and his mother.'

'Oh, God is good!'

'Come in. Let my menservants wash your feet and bring you something to eat – '

'No! No, thank you. A blessed invitation, truly – but I've something to beg of your guest, and it can't wait.'

Indeed, the official from Capernaum was haggard as much from worry as from the trip. He kept blinking. His hair was knotted, unkempt. It was clear he'd pushed himself, travelling through the night. A trade road from the Sea of Galilee past Cana to the port at Acco was well maintained, yet he had wearied the soldiers who travelled with him to protect him from bandits.

Chuza said, 'Of course, friend. Wait here. I'll fetch the man for you.'

Jesus was asleep. But his was always a feathery rest. At his mother's touch he wakened and was immediately alert.

'There is a man from Capernaum anxious to see you.'

Mary followed Jesus, and Jesus followed Chuza into the

gardens of his courtyard, where the royal official was pacing back and forth.

'Jesus of Nazareth!' he cried and, despite his rank, fell to his knees. 'Please, sir! Oh, please! Come with me to Capernaum. At once. I've a chariot for you and a driver too. I'll bring you back when we're done. But come!'

Without haste, Jesus sank down to his own knees until the two were face to face.

Chuza's eyebrows shot up. He clapped a hand over his mouth, as if he might bark with laughter at the sight.

The official, too, was taken aback: 'But, but – ' he tried to protest, blinking furiously. 'But, you – '

Jesus, looking level at the supplicant, said, 'You're telling me your solution, not your problem.' He put his hands on either side of the other man's face and caressed the eyebrows with his thumbs until the blinking stopped. 'In clear and careful words, sir, tell me the problem.'

The official kept his eyes closed a moment. When he opened them again, he could hold Jesus' gaze.

'My son is sick with a killing fever. When I left him yesterday, the physicians had given up. Everyone has given up. His mother, my wife, Susanna – O sir, she already mourns for the boy. But I heard that you were here in Cana, that you are a prophet of God, and God listens to his prophets. Please! Come! Beg God to heal my son.'

'You see?' said Jesus, still calming the man by touching his temples. 'It was the problem I needed to know, not your solution.'

Jesus looked up at the people around him, Chuza, Joanna, Mary, a gardener, two soldiers from Capernaum, a disciple. 'Unless you see signs and wonders, you will not believe.'

Jesus rose. He took the other's hand and helped him, too, to stand. 'No,' he said. 'Your solution isn't necessary. I needn't go with you. Go home. I promise you, your son will live.'

Although he was dishevelled now and looked of little consequence, in Capernaum this official wielded the power of Herod Antipas: he let out fishing rights, fish-processing rights, fish transport and merchandising rights to nearly every broker, worker and merchant in the area.

He gazed at Jesus for a full minute, astonishment making him immobile. He whispered, 'You did not – '

Jesus smiled and said, 'I have no need to. It's me you seek. It's only me.'

Suddenly: 'I believe you,' the man said. He bowed to Chuza, and he left.

AN ITINERANT

—

Jesus was a wanderer, a walker wherever he went. His staff in his hand, his knees punching the front of his robe, he strode the lesser paths, never hurrying. At every small village he turned aside and spent time with the villagers. A day or two, five days, the sabbath. He ate with them, slept wherever they offered the shelter, talked. Taught. Healed.

'Do you dance, sir?'

'Dance? When there's good reason for dancing.'

'My wife says that our little boy laughed today.'

'That's a reason.'

'Well, and six days ago he, my boy, I mean – our firstborn son, if it please the Lord – was circumcised.'

'A wonderful reason! What about music?'

'Leah! Leah, come and sing for us! Clap your hands! Sing something fast!'

Those who invited him into their houses were of every station in life: tenant farmers *and* their masters; the unlettered blacksmith *and* the scribe; centurions, tax collectors, goatherds; the widow, the grandmother, the child, the rabbi, the priest. Jesus accepted their invitations without regard for the power they did or did not have. He dealt with them all the same. That peculiar freedom of his caused a paradox of feeling within most breasts: he seemed at once sweetly accessible and altogether unknowable. For he came easily and easily held conversation with anyone; but he lacked all the signs by which people interpreted one another: he could not be placed into any single category, neither of class nor profession, nor sect, nor party, nor humour, nor creed. He didn't fit.

He loved the poor. He grieved with the landless and the dispossessed. He held their children close to his breast and kissed the crowns of their dirty heads. Never did he enter the greatest, richest cities of Galilee, Sepphoris or Tiberias. Yet he slept as readily on a wooden bed inlaid with ivory as on a pallet of straw. And while he ate dried figs with the peasant, he would as cheerfully eat beef with the tax collector. There were priests in Jerusalem who refused to walk near the houses of Gentiles, for fear of stepping on their dried, uncircumcised spit. Yet this Jesus of Nazareth willingly spent the entire sabbath with Roman soldiers and Tyrian merchants.

'Listen to this: he talked to Rahab.'

'Rahab! Nobody talks to Rahab any more.'

'I know.'

'I don't let my children pass her house. Make them take the other lane.'

'I *know*. But he talked to her when she'd sneaked down to the well. Noontime, the heat of the day.'

'Talked to the Man-killer?'

'Asked her for a drink of water.'

'A drink of water!'

'Can you imagine?'

'Well, then he knew nothing of that widow's curse: five down and one to go – if she can get that sad beggar to marry her, but she's losing her wily ways, is what I say.'

'No, but that's the wonder of the thing!'

'What?'

'That he *did* know about Rahab. Knew about each husband in turn.'

'The fool. Looks like we got a number six in the bin.'

'No, no, you don't understand. The wonder is that no one *told* him about Rahab. Neither had he met her before. Just bumped into her at the well, and *he* it was told *her* all the things she'd ever done – get it? And then she came running back to town shamelessly, all shamelessly, and beside that, happy! And I'm telling you: Rahab sounded like Miriam beating her timbrels at the sea, singing, carrying on, causing the rabbi himself to start dancing in the street. Oh, that Rahab! Still has some moves in her. Even I had to go on back to the well to meet that fellow, because she said she thought he was the Messiah.'

'The Messiah? What's his name?'

'Jesus. From Nazareth.'

'Ach! Sister, you've been snookered. Nothing good ever came from Nazareth – '

Enigmatic, unfathomable, utterly free of polite conventions: in spite of the mystery – or, perhaps, because of it – this Jesus caused both love and trouble in the hearts of the people who encountered him. His mother watched the effect of his presence upon others, how the young, both male and female, would begin to gaze at him the way a bride will gaze at her groom upon his first arriving. In their eyes was a sort of astonished fulfilment: *This is it! This is what I've been waiting for.* Their faces radiated gladness, life, and purpose. A future! – which is hope. Whether Jesus recognized the adoration or not, he treated them quite the same as he had before, kindly, equably, calling them each by name, as wholly present to one as to any other, full of the knowledge of that one, though none might know *him* altogether.

But Mary saw in other people signs of being troubled – no, threatened – by her son. If Jesus said yes, they said no. If he affirmed something, they considered it a moral outrage. When, on a sabbath, he and several followers walked the wheat fields, plucking kernels, rubbing them clean and eating them, these people condemned him for breaking the laws prohibiting work on the sabbath – and the ferocity of their complaint suggested they thought he was destroying truth itself. What power they imputed to her son! It was a measure of his effect upon the hearts of those who met him, striking life into some, and in others the fear of disaster.

Village to village Jesus wandered, lifting his long staff like a lance, lithe and tireless in his progressions. Earlier, when he had arrived in Nazareth, Mary was gratified to see that he carried a leather bag of tools, exactly as Joseph had done. By the time he left Cana, Nathanael was carrying the tools; yet it was Jesus who used them when he saw the need. And he saw the need in Capernaum.

Among the young who adored her son, some always left the villages of their births and followed him to the next village, and then the next. But one or two of these would soon begin to drag their feet. The farther they went from their homes, the more anxious they became. Even fifteen miles away, the world can seem an alien, dangerous place.

'Master, can I ask you something?'
  'Your name is not Elisha, is it?'
  'What? No. I told you my name.'
  'Yes, yes. Your name is Grass.'
  'No. Why would you call me Grass?'
  'What is it you want to ask me?'
  'Well, OK. I want to follow you. Truly. I will follow you to – '
  'Your name isn't Ruth either, is it?'
  'Master? I… I'm a man. Not a woman.'
  'True. A very young man.'
  'Why are you – '
  'Hush. What is it you want to ask me?'
  'I. Will. I will follow you. Only, would you let me first go say farewell to my family back home?'

And Jesus said to the young man: 'No one who puts his hand to the plough and looks back is fit for the kingdom of God.'

Even fifteen and sixteen miles away – not yet a full day's journey, walking – the world can seem an alien place. One by one, some turned and went back to their families.

But a few had chosen rightly. Home for these became a movable thing: no longer a shelter of wood and stone, but the wings of a person. A prophet and a teacher. Jesus. And the souls that stayed he called disciples. Philip was among these. Nathanael. Andrew. Thomas, a twin. And I. And, yes, Joanna too, the wife of Chuza, bringing with her both money to support us and her husband's blessing. She came, in fact, *for* him, who stayed behind to manage the estates.

Well, Joanna had loved Mary for more than half her life and was ever glad to be with her. But first in the wedding, and then in his response to the royal official from Capernaum, Joanna had discovered in Jesus a figure of such indisputable sufficiency and freedom that in his presence she felt like Sheba in the presence of King Solomon. Alert, relaxed, the son of her sister Mary was beholden to no one, yet was open to everyone, offering each a steadfast eye and a listening ear – and this by his own sole choosing.

Moreover, as their wanderings brought the small group closer to Capernaum, people began to flow out of that little fishing village, seeking 'Jesus of Nazareth. Where is he?'

They wanted to see him, perhaps to touch him.

'He healed Susanna's boy!' they said. 'All the way from Cana! Even before his father got home the fever broke. And this is the truth! His father confirms it over and over: that the boy was healed at the very hour when Jesus *said* he was healed!'

And Mary, glad for Joanna's company: she, too, travelled with her son, though no 'disciple', as far as she was concerned. When he was young she had been the teacher. She told him the stories. She taught him to pray. She nursed him on pure Jewish milk. More than anyone else, she'd been intimate with the baby, the boy, the youth. And now the man: though glad of them, she was not overwhelmed by the wonders he performed. Who else had pressed him into service? None but Mary. And already in Cana she knew that the official's son would be healed at a simple word from her Yeshi.

It delighted her that Jesus was coming into his own – and that she was there to see it happen. But *his* manner, his reaction to these wondrous beginnings, confused her. He did not match the satisfaction in her. There seemed in him no new emotion; no bending gratitude to God, his Father; no excitement of purpose; and surely no soaring glory.

Her son, in the moments when he sank into himself, moments his mother had long ago learned to notice and to read: her son, her Yeshi, seemed rather more melancholy than fulfilled.

A CARPENTER IN TOWN

—

'A story!' Jesus called, and the room fell silent.

'A sower went out to sow his seed,' he said. Though few farmers lived in Capernaum, fishermen dealt regularly with sowers to the west; they traded for flax, with which to make and to repair their nets. Therefore, when Jesus said, 'A sower went out to sow his seed,' his audience saw the sack strapped over the farmer's shoulder, saw the ploughed and pulverized earth, saw the seed flung out in hemispheres before the sower's going, and saw behind him two of his sons, raking the soil to cover the seeds.

'Some of the seed fell along the path,' Jesus said. 'Other seed fell on rocky ground, where the soil is thin and the stones are warm by morning. Yet other seed fell where thorn seeds waited.

'But much of the seed fell on soil ploughed and rich and ready. 'What happened to the seed?'

Jesus had grown up among farmers. His father had fashioned and fixed their ploughs. His friends had hoed the fields and reaped more barley than wheat – until Sepphoris demanded more wheat than barley. Jesus *thought* in the images of the earth and the weather and green things growing and golden things cut down to be ground to flour.

Presently he was sitting in a room used as a synagogue on the sabbath. It was in fact the sabbath. And those who sat before him were absorbed in his words, persuaded by his manner of self-confident authority: *What happened to the seed?*

'Well, that which fell on the path was the first to fail. By the evening birds flocked down and pecked it up. They pecked the hard path clean.

'The seed that fell on rocky ground lived longer. But its life was quick and quickly over. For it sprang up fast in soil so thin. But soil so thin allows no root, and when the warm sun turned to burning, baking the rocks, the young wheat withered before it matured.

'The seed that fell where the thorn seed lay grew up – grew, in fact, to a pale maturity. Yes, and the thorn seed grew up with it, aggressively, sucking the moisture, choking its growth. In the end it could yield no grain at all.

'But that which fell on the ploughed ground brought forth grain thirtyfold and sixtyfold and a hundredfold.

'Those who have ears,' Jesus cried, 'let them hear!'

Suddenly a man flew forward through the room as if struck at the back of his head. He sprawled in the dirt. His body twisted horribly, but he wasn't trying to get up.

'Ahhh,' the man growled, driving his jawbone into the packed earth as if to gnaw it. 'What do you!' he howled. 'What do you have to do with us, you! Jesus of Nazareth!'

The congregation sat fixed. Surely they knew the man. But no one moved to help him. He had been as calm and as interested as anyone else, until this moment.

'Jesus of Nazareth! Have you come to destroy us?' the man howled, the spittle darkening the earth, his teeth grinding grit, blood rimming his nostrils.

Jesus gazed at the madman with a steadfast eye.

Coiling like a serpent, the man raised his head and upper torso from the ground and glared at Jesus.

'I know who you are! I know! I know who you are – ' dust and saliva making a mud around his mouth: *'The Holy One of God!'*

'Shut up,' Jesus said in an even tone. 'Demon, come out of that man.'

The man recoiled from Jesus. He doubled backwards, whacked his skull to the ground, and shook violently – then, exhaling an endless, visible sigh, the poor man slumped and lay still.

Jesus rose and went to him. He knelt. He unwound the hem of his robe and wiped the dirty slaver from his face.

A sort of thrill ran through the room. 'What a word! What

authority!' men exclaimed. 'This – this prophet commands the unclean spirits with power and they obey! Did you see how the demon came out of Reuben like smoke?'

'Wonderful, wonderful!' A big man pushed forward through the moiling crowd. 'I never saw a deed more wonderful.' This massy, blunt-fingered fellow approached the place where Jesus was kneeling and looked down, nodding. 'There's something about you, sir,' he said, pointing at Jesus. 'Something... I don't know. You must know it.' His voice took on a dreaming quality: 'Something. So. Pure.'

The big man caught himself and shuffled. 'Ha ha! What do I know, right? Ha ha! OK! What do you want me to do? Here,' he said. He set his big feet apart, bent down, and scooped up little Reuben before Jesus could say a thing.

'Where should I take him? How about my place?' Clearly, he was speaking to Jesus, preparing to obey the teacher's response. But it wasn't Jesus who answered him.

'Put me down, you drooling horse!'

Little Reuben. He wasn't as damaged as one might have thought.

'You sure?' the big man said. 'You got a pulled muscle somewhere? A cramp?'

Reuben started to kick his legs and swing his arms. 'Yes, I'm sure!'

'You know, if some demon snapped *me* around like a witching stick, I'd've pulled a muscle or two.'

Reuben howled, 'Simon, you are crushing me!'

And Simon set him, bump, on his bottom on the ground. Reuben jumped up, slapping himself. 'A demon within me, a lummox without. And it's the lummox that gives me my bruises!'

Simon winked. 'But you like me anyway, right?' He elbowed Reuben, grinning. 'Tell the teacher that you like me.'

Reuben, little indeed, couldn't help himself. Simon's ribbing charmed him. To Jesus he said, 'Nah. Simon's not so bad, once you get to know him.'

'Ha, ha, ha!' Simon boomed. He grabbed Reuben in both his hands and kissed the small man on his forehead.

'Drool,' Reuben muttered, rubbing his forehead and walking away.

'So,' said Simon to Jesus. 'You want to come to my house awhile?'

Simon's invitation, though jovial, contained a purpose more serious than simple hospitality.

His wife's mother lay on a boxlike bed in a small, windowless room. A fish-oil lamp illumined her face: eyes half lidded, skin slick with sweat, mouth open, her lips rimed and cracked.

Simon hovered in the doorway while Jesus stood above the woman. He gazed long upon her sightless eyes. There was no haste in this healer. There seemed in him an infinity of patience. *Something. So. Pure.*

The lamp shined upward on Jesus' face, catching his jaw, the rims of his nostrils, the bone above his eyes.

Suddenly Simon understood what had fascinated and confused him in the synagogue, that this teacher, this particular healer, appeared to take into himself the condition of the one he gazed upon.

Softly, Jesus murmured, 'The stronger destroys the house of the strong.' And then the command: 'Sickness, begone.'

The woman's eyes began to flutter. Her mouth closed. She drew a shuddering breath through her nose – then sneezed. It was a wet, spasmodic, 'Ker-*chooo-hoo-hoo!*' drawing her up into a sitting position. And she was well.

Jesus offered his hand. Simon's mother-in-law took it and stood up. Then – as if she'd only come into the room to wipe her nose – she went out and began to serve them.

'Simon,' she said as she passed him, 'what's the matter with you? You look a little peaky.'

By sunset of that same day, the lanes and the alleys outside of Simon's house were absolutely packed with people. The word had rushed through the village and out into the countryside. Friends brought friends who were sick or infirm; parents brought their wounded children; cripples appeared of their own accord; blind folk followed the sound of the crowds –

And Jesus moved among them all, walking on the balls of his feet, laying his hands upon this one, that one, causing one to weep and one to shout.

They had, O God – they had been healed.

And demons flew out of the mouths of many, crying, *You are the Son of God!*

And Jesus rebuked the demons in return: *Silence, by my condemnation! I strike you now and forever dumb!* – because they knew as Satan knew that Jesus was the Christ.

In the days that followed, Jesus carried his tools down to the lakeshore; there he rebuilt and resocketed the mast of a twenty-six-foot fishing boat; he installed new thwarts in another; he refashioned oarlocks, the handles of tillers – and generally made the fishermen glad that a carpenter had come to town.

FOLLOW

—

'Blessed are the poor in spirit,' Jesus called in his clear, coherent voice, 'for theirs is the kingdom of heaven!

'Blessed are those who mourn, for they shall be comforted!'

When the air was still and the crowds, too, motionless, the teacher's voice could descend from a mount to the valley below without abatement, and every word was heard, and no one did not hear them.

'Blessed are the meek,' Jesus taught the people, 'for they shall inherit the earth.

'Blessed are those who hunger and thirst for righteousness, for they shall be satisfied.'

He would sit on an outcropping rock, lilies, myrtle, capers, dandelions scattered around him, birds alive in the pure blue air, his disciples sitting closest, villagers, pilgrims, strangers, whole families assembled in the natural theatre of an upland glen; and all the audience would feel a certain dignity, as if each one had been invited by this remarkable and well-known rabbi.

'Blessed are the merciful, for they shall obtain mercy.

'Blessed are the pure in heart, for they shall see God.

'Blessed are the peacemakers, for they shall be called children of God.

'Blessed are those who are persecuted for righteousness' sake, for theirs is the kingdom of heaven.

'And blessed,' Jesus cried out, 'are you when people revile you and persecute you and utter all kinds of evil against you falsely on my account. Rejoice and be glad, for your reward is great in heaven, for so people persecuted the prophets who were before you.'

Jesus would teach the people near the towns where fish was dredged in salt in order to preserve it and send it as far abroad as Rome for food.

'You are the salt of the earth! But if salt has lost its savour, how can the saltness be restored? It's good for nothing any more. It might as well be thrown out and trodden underfoot.

'You are the light of the world. A city set on a hill cannot be hid.' Perhaps he remembered Nazareth on its high ridge. Perhaps he remembered Jerusalem. 'Nor do people light a lamp and put it under a bushel. They put it on a stand to lighten the whole house. Let your light so shine that everyone may see your good works and give glory to your Father who is in heaven.'

In the fields after harvest; on the broad plain, himself standing on a hillock; on rooftops in the evenings, when people sought the cool breezes, Jesus taught:

'You have heard that it was said to our ancestors, *an eye for an eye and a tooth for a tooth*. But I say to you, do not resist those who do evil. If anyone strikes you on the right cheek, give him the left one too. If anyone sues you for your coat, give him your cloak as well. And if anyone forces you to go one mile, go two. Give to those who beg from you, and do not refuse those who want to borrow.

'You have heard that it was said to our ancestors, *you shall love your neighbour and hate your enemy*. But I say to you, love your enemies. Pray for those who persecute you, and you will be the children of your Father who is in heaven; for he makes his sun rise on the evil and on the good. He sends rain on the just and on the unjust. For if you love those who love you, what reward have you? Don't even the treacherous do the same? And if you greet only your family and friends, what more are you doing than others? Don't the Gentiles do the same? You, therefore, must be perfect, even as your heavenly Father is perfect.'

There came the morning when Jesus was teaching near Capernaum, on the shore of the Sea of Galilee, his back to the water. The longer he taught, the greater grew the multitudes, some folk standing so far inland that they pressed forward to hear his words. Those nearest Jesus were pushed forward – and soon it seemed the teacher himself would be driven into the water.

Some distance north two boats had been anchored at the water's edge; four fishermen were washing their nets, one of these a huge man, his stomach as big as a sitz bath, his arms like masts.

'Simon!' Jesus called.

The man jumped up and pointed to himself. 'What? Me?'

'You, Simon, son of John! Bring your boat. Let me aboard, then put out a ways and steady her awhile.'

Simon was a waterspout. Simon was leviathan, boiling with joy through the water. In no time Jesus was sitting in the back of his boat, facing the shore, while the fisherman held two oars wide, touching the surface whenever the stern would wander left or right.

Jesus called to all the people ashore: 'Do not lay up for yourselves treasures on earth, where the moth and rust consume it and thieves break in to steal. But lay up for yourselves treasure in heaven, where neither the moth nor rust nor thieves can ruin a thing. For where your treasure is, there will your heart be also.

'Never be anxious about your life, what you will eat, what you'll drink, nor about your body, what you'll wear. Isn't life more than food, and the body more than clothing? Look at the birds of the air: they don't sow or reap or gather into barns; yet your heavenly Father feeds them. Aren't you worth more than they? And which of you by being anxious can add six months to your life? And why do you worry about what you will wear? Look at the lilies of the field, how they grow. They don't toil or spin; yet I tell you, even Solomon in all his glory was not arrayed like one of these. Well: if God so clothes the grass of the field, which is alive today and tomorrow is thrown into the oven, will he not much more clothe you, O you of such little faith? Therefore, don't be anxious, saying, 'What'll we eat? What'll we drink? What'll we wear?' Your heavenly Father knows you need them all. But seek first his kingdom and his righteousness, and all these things will be yours as well.'

When Jesus was finished teaching, he turned to his boatman and regarded him a moment. Simon smiled at first. Then he cleared his throat and began to blush. 'What?'

'All right, Simon,' Jesus said. 'Let's go get your brother and the nets. I want you to put out into deep water, to drop your nets and catch some fish.'

Simon blinked. Then he laughed. 'Ha ha! You don't mean it, right? You don't make mistakes, right? Ha ha! We just spent the whole night fishing. Caught nothing. If – '

'I mean it, Simon,' Jesus said.

Simon blinked again. 'Um. Yes. Well, hey! – of course, of *course*!' He grabbed the oars and heaved his body backward. 'You say it, I do it,' he boomed. 'That's the long and the short of it, right?'

As Simon rowed them around a stone jetty, the crowds withdrew. Andrew, watching as they came, stood up and smiled.

The brothers didn't hoist the sail. Andrew and Simon together pulled the long oars, sending their boat across a placid water. Jesus sat in the bow, his lashes lowered, feeling the weather, tasting the sea.

At a word from Simon, Andrew began to let out the line of trammel nets with their floats and weights. Simon rowed slowly to keep the line from tangling. Under normal conditions, it could take an hour before the nets had all been released – and then the fisherman would wait all night while fish entrapped themselves. 'All night' because in daylight fish could see and avoid the nets.

But these were not normal conditions.

Within fifteen minutes, when not more than a fourth of the nets were in the water, the line went taut. Andrew barked in surprise and wound it around a knob on the gunnel. The boat, caught on the line, slewed and wallowed in the water. The line-side drew down – and the brothers both began to chatter.

'Simon!'

'What the – ?'

'Simon, the nets!'

'Did we hook on something?'

'The nets – they're full!'

'Full of what?'

'Of *fish*!'

'Already?'

'Help me! I can't – I can't pull them in. The nets are tearing!'

Simon with astonishing dexterity leaped to Andrew and felt the line and knew the enormous weight of the catch below.

'Yo! James! Hie-ya, hie-ya, JOHN!' he yelled. 'Come out as fast as you can!'

He whirled and looked at Jesus in the bow: Jesus, who continued offering his half-lidded face to the wind and the sunlight, not so much as turning to notice the fishermen distressed behind him.

From that moment Simon worked the net and the boat in a desperate silence, frowning. James and John approached in the second boat, took up the far end of the net-line, gathered it in even as Andrew and Simon gathered their own end in, both boats dragging low in the water for the load of fish they were taking in.

Suddenly Simon left the line, clambered over the thwarts towards Jesus, and crouched on his knees.

Jesus turned.

'Please, Lord, please,' Simon begged.

Jesus lifted his eyebrows.

And Simon wailed in genuine misery: 'Go away from me. I shouldn't look on you! Ah, Lord! I'm nothing but a sinful man!'

His partners, fish spilling all around them, were transfixed by Simon's cry. All three stopped work and watched Jesus – this 'Lord', as their friend had called him.

And Jesus returned the look to Andrew, James, and John, each in his turn.

Then he laid his hand on Simon's neck: 'Hush, don't be afraid,' he said with that lucid articulation. 'Follow me. From now on your fishing will be for the souls of those who walk dry land.'

When the boats returned to the shore, the four of them did just that. They left their fathers, their nets, their livelihoods, their villages, and they followed Jesus, Simon hugging every member of his new family – bruising Mary, rib and spleen.

HOME AGAIN, ALONE

There were times when, looking upon her son, Mary experienced the tranquillity which God had invested in the blues and azures, the aquamarines and the more tender greens of creation: sea, wheat and sky.

Come unto me, all you who labour and are heavy laden, and I will give you rest.

His manner of looking at individuals, even while he was teaching the multitudes, made all the world seem generous and thoughtful to her. His motion *through* these multitudes – touching to heal, touching to elevate and encourage, receiving the reaching arms and hands of the myriads – seemed ever to establish a centre in otherwise messy populations. A centre in the wheel of villages and fields, of rocks and rivers and hills. A centre in her life. A centre in the universe.

'If you will,' pleads a man deformed by leprosy, 'you can make me clean.' And Jesus, visibly moved by the man's condition, touches him and answers, 'I will. Be clean.'

He, his person, was lovely in her sight, his lips drawn lightly together as if he were in continual thought, his even brow, his rusted lashes, two starlike freckles on his upper lids, causing in his glances a celestial flashing – but what she saw was not lovelier than his mind, swift and gracious and capable.

'Lord, that story!' says Simon. 'Seeds and sowers and stuff. I don't get it.'

'You don't understand the parable? How will you understand all the parables?

'Simon: the sower sows the word. And these are the ones like the hardened

path: when they hear, Satan comes and takes away the words which might have been sown in them. And these are the ones like the rocky ground: when they hear the word they receive it with immediate joy; but since they have no root in themselves, when the heat of tribulations and persecutions arises because of the word, that word withers and they fall away. And in those among the thorns the word may root, may grow, but the cares of the world, delight in riches, desires for other things all choke the word, and it proves unfruitful in the end. But those like the good soil hear the word, accept it, and bear fruit, thirtyfold and sixtyfold and a hundredfold.'

As they travelled from village to village in Galilee, Mary maintained her maternal watch, feeding, as it were, upon her son. He was something like nourishment. Like sunlight. He was the health in her, both the reason and the design of her life.

Therefore, when his complexion grew pale from weariness, the effect in his mother was seismic.

'Leave him alone!' she would scold the disciples when they pestered him late into the night. 'The man needs his sleep! If you love him you will go away from him – now!'

But then Jesus, rather than thanking her, rather than supporting her efforts on his behalf, would fix *her* with the admonitory eye, quietly scolding her in return: 'Woman.'

Ach! What was she supposed to do? She was his mother, after all. God had put him in *her* care. She could not, she would not, shirk the responsibility.

Therefore, when she saw the slight crossing of his eyes after days and days of human service, she drew Simon out of her son's earshot and asked *him* to ask the others to step back from Jesus awhile. Likewise she enlisted Joanna and Susanna (who also travelled with them now) in a plan so to comfort the disciples of an evening that they would all find slumber an easy friend.

Regularly thereafter Jesus would rise up in the night and leave the group. He'd go off into the hills alone, not returning till the dawn. And Mary smiled secretly. She congratulated herself upon her motherly cunning. It was only later she discovered that Jesus never slept during his hours of solitude. He prayed.

Late one afternoon, after an especially tumultuous day among the infirm, the mad and the ruined, Mary noticed three men from Perea winding their way – with Andrew! – towards Jesus, clearly intent on speaking to him. Andrew surely should have known better! And these three had been watching long enough to realize how exhausting such work must be. Jesus had just dropped on his robe, casting his elbow over his eyes, perhaps to sleep!

Mary grabbed the hem of her skirt and rushed forward.

'Andrew!' she called. 'Andrew, wait! Let me – ah: let me get something for your guests to eat. Aren't you hungry? Wouldn't you like a – '

'Woman, *desist*!'

Jesus. He was standing. He was glaring at her. Her heart failed, and she suddenly felt like sobbing. Desist? He said 'desist'? Why does he speak to his mother with such a stern formality?

Mary sat down right where she was and pulled her robe over her head.

One of the men from Perea was saying, 'John, the prophet who baptizes, sent us to you. Even in prison he has heard of the things you do. He doesn't think there is much time any more. He wants to know: Are you the one who is to come? Or should we look for another?'

Jesus answered them: 'Go and tell that good man what you've seen. The blind receive their sight, the lame walk, lepers are cleansed, the deaf hear, the dead are raised up, the poor have good news preached to them.

'And blessed,' Jesus said, 'are those who take no offence in me!'

There was a pause, and then the shuffling of various farewells. Mary lifted the hood. Andrew was embracing the men. Disciples of cousin John. Of course. They turned and began to walk away.

Immediately Jesus raised his voice and Mary covered her face again. There was an edge to his tone which she could not altogether interpret; but the pitch suggested that he was talking to many more people than to her alone.

'Is there anyone who blames John for his challenge? Anyone? What did you all go out into the wilderness to see? A reed shaken in the wind? A man clothed in soft clothing? Ha! Those who live in luxury prowl around the courts of kings! So what did you go out to see? A prophet? Yes, I tell you, and more than a prophet! If you are willing to accept it, this is he of whom it is written, *Behold, I send my messenger before your face, who shall prepare your way.* I tell you, among those born of women no one is greater than John!'

Jesus paused. When he spoke again, the edge was gone, and Mary wondered what she might make of his final comment, whether there might be salve for her in it. He said, 'Yet he who is least in the kingdom of God is greater than John.'

Mary heard echoes of her own hymn, sung in splendid excitement thirty years ago: *The low estate of his handmaiden,* and, *He who is mighty has done great things for me* –

To Mary it seemed that Jesus had said: 'Yet she who is least in the kingdom of God is greater than John.'

She. Mary.

Could it be?

On the following day Jesus was teaching in a house of some size, in a room large enough to hold about twenty-five people, though they had to stand shoulder to shoulder. Likewise the courtyard was filled with people, and people crowded even around the walls outside, listening at the little windows. There were visitors here from as far away as Jerusalem, students and teachers, Pharisees.

Most of his disciples had found places within the house. Joanna knew the owner. She, too, was within.

Mary stood without. Her son's teaching was reduced for her to a mere murmurous music, though the rise and fall of the melody was comforting.

After nearly two hours, she lifted her eyes and saw three men and a woman carrying a fifth person on a stiff bed between two poles. They kept peering into the house, evidently at a loss for what to do. Their faces were sad.

The woman noticed Mary.

'My son,' she said, stroking the figure bent upon his stretcher. 'He's paralysed. We thought Jesus of Nazareth might be willing to heal him, but – ' she indicated the press of the crowd surrounding the house. 'We can't get in to see him.'

'And my son,' Mary began, 'is the one inside.' Oh, how that mother loved her poor, twisted child! Ha! This sisterhood of loving, this maternal kinship, became a sudden force in Mary. She decided to act. 'Come,' she said. 'Follow me.'

She led them to the alley-side of the house, where stairs mounted to the roof.

'I know the rooms inside. Take the poor boy up to the roof. I'll show you the spot over Jesus. You have two stout poles. Drive them through the plaster. Tear out the sticks, the mud and straw. Make a big hole, and lower your son before my son. He will heal him. And please: when your boy stands up again, would you tell Jesus that his mother is waiting outside? That she would like to talk with him?'

Maybe if someone else makes the request – ?

While the men began to batter at the roof, Mary hurried around to the courtyard door. She lowered her head and by a bully willfulness pushed her way through to the door of the room where Jesus was teaching.

She watched the ceiling crack and drop by clumps, causing good people to press backwards harder than ever.

She saw heads crane upwards, and the stretcher coming down on ropes, and Jesus in the open space alone, a perfectly happy grin on his face.

Hoo-hoo! Look how the widow has caused her son to *grin*!

'Take heart, my son,' said Jesus to the paralysed boy, 'your sins are all forgiven.'

Abruptly, 'What?' someone in front of Mary whispered. 'What did he say?'

Another: 'That the young man's sins are forgiven.'

'That's blasphemy! No one but God forgives sins.'

'Is somebody back there bothered?' Jesus called. The two whisperers closed their mouths and scowled. He was looking at them, the fringes of whose robes were long and the tassels well-worked. 'What bothers you?' Jesus asked, mildly enough, and: 'What do you think? Is it easier to say to the paralysed, 'Your sins are forgiven,' or else to say, 'Get up and walk'?'

No one answered. Everyone held still.

'Well, then,' said Jesus, 'so that you may know the Son of man has the authority on earth to forgive sins' – he said to the boy on the ground before him – 'Son, get up. Pick up your bed and go home.'

The boy turned over to his knees and stood and reached for the poles of his stretcher – and his mother above broke into tears.

'Thank you, thank you,' she wept, her face and shoulders visible through the hole in the ceiling. 'You healed my boy!' The whole house, watching her, felt a new flush of affection. Love moves others to love, and a mother's love is as powerful as any. 'And you!' the woman continued. 'You're a good boy, too. Go see your mother! Your mother is waiting outside to talk with you.'

Heads turned towards the door, where Mary stood. How many recognized her? She covered her face in her hands and wished that no one were looking. It was only Jesus' attentions she wanted.

Then Jesus was speaking again. Not coming to the door, not leading her out alone –

Jesus asked in a loud voice, 'Who is my mother?' He fell silent.

Mary gasped. Why would he ask such a thing? She peeped up. He was not looking at her. He had raised his right arm and was pointing solemnly... at Simon. At James. At Philip. At Andrew. At Joanna. At *Joanna*!

Yeshi? Here?

'These are my mother!' Jesus declared. How harsh his tone. 'The one who does the will of my Father in heaven, *that* is my mother, my brother, my sister.'

Mary scarcely heard the latter. She was out of the courtyard now. She was out of the village. Even before she'd made the decision, the decision was made for her: Mary was on her way to Nazareth.

The widow was going home again.

Alone.

PART FOUR

THE BELOVED

MAGDALA, MATTHEW, ELEAZAR, MARYAM

===

Magdala stinks. The odour is rotting, nearly intolerable. In the summer the wind scarcely moves through the town, which lies in a basin. The heat cooks everything, thickening the air. You want to get out on the lake just to breathe!

The fish that the sons of Zebedee and of John caught was transported south to the town of Magdala, where it was salted and sent westwards to ports on the Great Sea, to Asia and Macedonia, Achaia, Rome.

Fish was dried and pickled in Magdala, the brine saved to be mixed with wine. Fish was turned into an eye-watering sauce, *garum*, with which the rich and the delicate cooked their magnificent meals.

And since all this – the fishing, the processing, transportation both by land and by sea, buying and selling in quantity, satisfying wealthy palates in wealthy houses whose floors were mosaics, whose walls were painted, whose uneaten food was thrown to the dogs: since all of this, and every exchange within it, offered opportunities for taxation, some grew very rich on the shores of Galilee, and some were pressured almost to death, and some were driven mad.

O fisherman! Where do you get the capital to buy the linen to make your sails? And whence the capital to buy the flax that makes your nets, the lumber from woodsmen, anchors and weights from stonemasons? Why, from the broker who bought the right to lease you fishing rights from the chief tax collectors of the industry, who bought *their* right to leases from the machinery of the court of Herod Who himself owes tribute to the emperor in Rome.

Crushed almost to death. How much of the fish you catch is left to you? How much is owed the broker? How much is consumed by taxes?

In Magdala, how do you obtain the clay vats in which to salt the fish? And how do you get the fish? And how do you get the salt? And how do you get the wines for the brine and pickling? Once again, between the chief tax collectors of the region and your work stands another collector, a publican who sells you the license, who may loan you the capital to pay and to pay and to pay...

Fisherman: what do you think of that broker? How do you feel about the tax collectors who measure every move you make – even in the private places of your houses? Do you desire a house in the western hills where the breezes blow and the fish don't stink? A house near the estates of your brokers and your tax collectors?

Fishermen aren't free. Not even those who own a boat or two.

But the fisherman who rose up and followed the Lord – he experienced a freedom he could not have imagined before. It came of a strange equality. For the tax collector who likewise rose up to follow the Lord walked beside that fisherman in the same freedom precisely.

When Jesus said, 'This is my mother, my brother, my sister,' indicating several of us who had left our lives to follow him, Simon broke down and wept. This man drew attention when he wept. Simon wept unprettily. His eyes grew puffy, his forehead red; snot streamed from his nose into the bushes of his lip-whiskers; his lips bubbled and puttered – and, as little Reuben once remarked, he drooled.

But I understood the big man's tears. There passed through me too a thrill of gratitude, and I stood the straighter, gazing at him whom Simon called 'Lord', taking the word as my word now: *Jesus, now and forever, you are my Lord.*

And even as the pledge flew forth on the beams of my eyes, Jesus was looking back at me. I swear, he answered, *And I love you.*

Not in something uttered. But in the twist of his body, ankle to chin; in the tension while he held my gaze; in the vast landscapes of his knowing; and in this, that he parted his lips and showed the rims of his white teeth, smiling. Jesus loved me. I shall hereafter – both in this account and in the assizes of eternity – be known as nothing save his 'Beloved'. *The Beloved*: seek no name for me, nor any other character else. Or read your own name into my person. I have none of my own.

Jesus smiled. The moment has lasted my lifetime.

Then Simon was in front of Jesus, booming moistly, 'All right. Enough. Gotta make an ending here.'

In fact, he was opening a gangway for the young fellow whom Jesus had healed (whose sins the Lamb of God had forgiven) that he might join his mother again. Simon was using his own body to divide the bodies before them. But he meant as well for Jesus to follow. He kept turning and winking. I do believe this blunt, marvellously bellied fisherman feared that Jesus was as crushable as bird-bones in the wolf's jaw.

'Out of the way, good friends. Isn't this a wonderful day? Yessir! A day to remember. Out of the way.'

We became thread, drawn through the thickish cloth of the assembled crowd: Simon, the young man healed, Jesus, Joanna, disciples, disciples, and then me, last of all.

When we stepped out into sunlight, Simon full of confidence walked off in one direction while Jesus turned and walked in another.

Jesus took the road that led outside the town and finally to the east-west highway by which fish in large clay jars was carried to the ports and the ships of the Great Sea.

At the crossroads a small building had been constructed with a linen awning broad enough to shade both to the doorway and a table set up before the door. Behind the table sat a dour man, clean-shaven, soft white hair, long-necked and lean. Lounging against the walls of the building were four soldiers, armed. This was a tollhouse. This man collected the fees of those who travelled past him, something per person, something per cargo by weight and commodity and quantity. He was known as well to be a broker controlling several substantial leases. It was to him that Zebedee and John owed half their livelihoods.

Jesus entered the shaded area. He knelt down on the ground across the table from Matthew. They were eye-level one with the other. Jesus said, 'Do you know who I am? Do you know my name?'

It was then that Simon came huffing and puffing down the road from the north.

'James! Andrew! I lost you!'

The disciples in sunlight were wondering whether the Master intended to pay the toll-tax.

Andrew said, 'Simon, be quiet.'

Simon squinted. He ducked his head to see the figures beneath the awning: the dour publican and his Lord Jesus, the two of them facing each other as if discussing some intimate thing.

'Lord, *no!*'

Simon's disgust was immediate.

'His name's *Matthew!* He's treachery! This guy's almost ruined my father and James's father and half the fishermen on the western shores. You don't *know* this blood-loving son of a vulture!'

Jesus, nodding to the tax collector as if to say, *Wait a minute,* turned. 'If you knew me, Simon,' he said, 'you'd know I know the man before me. Know him and love him, too.'

Both Simon and the tax collector coloured, Matthew slightly, Simon in a sweating flush of crimson: 'But – '

But Jesus had already returned to Matthew. He reached forth his right hand, palm up. By stages Matthew recognized the invitation, put out his own hand, permitted Jesus to take it, and watched as it was raised to the Master's lips and kissed. Without releasing the hand, Jesus said, 'Matthew, follow me.'

There was a moment when everything in the green countryside was still. Then Jesus – like thistledown on an ascending wind – stood up. He kept hold of Matthew's hand, drawing the broker to his feet as well.

He led Matthew around the table towards the disciples, then paused with a bouncing bow, formal and funny at once. Matthew blinked. The face of the Lord reflected the sun as brightly as does the silver tray that catches the blood of the Passover lamb.

I think we bowed in return, feeling a little foolish. And Jesus, beaming, said – not just to Simon, but to all of us said, 'Forgive him, even as he will forgive you and your fathers and your families.'

Oh, what a feast the blessed publican gave us then! Two nights later. Under lamps of the purest olive oil, wave after wave of servants bearing dishes straight from the fires.

There was salted fish, if we wanted it. Fish pickled, but also baked and broiled and minced. Fish boiled in milk. Or taken with an egg. We ate various muttons that had *not* been sacrificed, but had rather been made savoury with mint and rue – and saffron, which is more expensive than gold. Cheeses, onions, leeks, watermelons, pomegranates, almonds, breads sweet as honey. Ah: breads from the wheat of Egypt! Quail, rock doves, sparrows – meat in slivers so tender, sweet and melting, one bit it between the front teeth, lightly.

'It is all and my all, forever,' Matthew said in an embarrassed speech at the beginning of the banquet – and I believed him. If he didn't know how to read, he knew figures. He, who had never initiated a family, was releasing his house to his sister and her husband. Moreover, he had invited a host of tax collectors to share with us this last, outrageous meal. And the soldiers that had endured the heat of the day with him, they were at the tables too. And Zebedee and his wife, and John and his wife, and those they hired, and those who wove the baskets the fishermen used. To find women at the banquet table among the men is in itself unusual; but there were several here of soiled reputations who were as welcome as anyone else – and there was one who crouched in a corner, her back to the wall, peering at Jesus from behind a mass of tangled hair, by turns giggling and sobbing. When I'd passed her earlier in the evening, I couldn't help but smell her. Her clothing, her hair, her person: she stank of rotting fish.

Jesus reclined to the right of Matthew, our Lord the guest of honour.

After the courses, drinking wine, we began to sing songs with the unhappy consequence that Simon closed his eyes and raised a roaring he himself considered melodic. It deafened the rest of us.

As is the custom, Jesus offered the guests a riddle: 'What's sweeter than honey?' he said. 'What's stronger than lions?'

It was Joanna, Chuza's wife, who answered, yet with something that wasn't an answer. 'No, but isn't that the meaning of Samson's riddle,' she asked, 'given at his wedding feast?'

'Right!' This was James, excited that he actually remembered the story: 'Samson killed a lion. Later he found that bees had built a hive in its carcass. The sweet in the strong, right?'

Jesus smiled, but without assent. His eyes twinkled under the lamplight. He looked up at the beams in the ceiling and repeated himself: 'What's sweeter than honey? What's stronger than lions?'

A sudden, convulsive sob drew everyone's attention to the corner of the room: the unkempt woman. In that moment no one could ignore her presence, nor could she pretend we weren't looking. She covered her face completely in her hair; but from behind that wretched veil, in woeful tones, there came a single syllable sung on a frail note, as though she were crooning, *Uhhhh* –

Jesus said, 'Yes, Maryam, wise Maryam, you have the answer. But say it more clearly: What is sweeter than honey? What is stronger than lions?'

The tangled woman sang her single note again, and the word we heard was: 'Love.'

'Undermining righteousness, this Jesus!' someone growled outside the balustrade. 'He scorns Moses! He treats sinners as if they were favoured. Lord God, forestall the pollution of your people!'

At such spectacular banquets as this, it was common for people to come and ogle the food, the dress, the politesse, the guests, the entire flame-enlightened event. The excesses of the rich were entertainment for the many. Nor were they, slipping through Matthew's courtyard to stand behind the low wall that gave into the dining room, turned away.

Among these on this particular night were students and teachers of the law of Moses, several of whom had heard Jesus' teachings during the past months. One or two had travelled from as far away as Jerusalem, and then had suffered a personal assault when he, Jesus, without apology, forgave the sins of those who came to him, and then blamed *them* for their natural and lawful questionings. *Who does he think he is?*

The man who was ashamed of Jesus' praise for Maryam (*He treats sinners as if they were favoured*) noticed that I had noticed him. He beckoned me to come to him. I did. He was, I supposed, a Pharisee, his fringes and tassels long enough to knock at his ankles.

'Why does he eat with sinners?' he asked with genuine appeal. 'Did he explain it? Did he teach you this thing?' The Pharisee's accent came from Jerusalem. He was gap-toothed, a gummy space separating his two front teeth. Those behind him, whose heads bobbed in agreement, I took for students and scribes.

'I met him, Jesus of Nazareth, when he was a youth,' the Pharisee said, gripping my elbow, speaking intently into my ear as if imparting a confidence. 'I delighted in his clarity, his intelligence, his precious questioning. Yes, and I have spoken often of that meeting, telling the teachers to watch that boy, for he would become a rabbi for all of Israel! Only last week I came here, to Galilee, to watch in wonder the things they tell of him in Jerusalem – and to praise him.'

The gap-toothed Pharisee shook his head. With longing, watery eyes he looked over the balustrade at Jesus. 'But this... but I,' he stammered. He let go my arm and struck his breast. 'Ach, but the things I've seen today! I am sick at heart. I will seek this good man's return to goodness. Or why does he eat and drink with tax collectors, and sinners? Can you explain this? Why does your Master accept gifts from those who have accepted goyish Rome?'

His face was contorted nearly to tears. He was much more sad than angry, and his sorrow seemed to derive from an honest devotion to the law – as well as from a tremendous disappointment in my Lord. It was the evident strength of his emotions that disabled me. His meaning was greater than his question. I couldn't answer him.

But Jesus could.

'Eleazar!' he said, the word a whip-crack: 'Do you affirm that I heal?'

I turned. Jesus had not arisen. He was leaning on his bolster still, but staring straight into the eyes of my interlocutor. He must have heard everything.

I think the Pharisee – Eleazar? – nodded. 'I have seen it,' he murmured unhappily. 'I saw as much this morning.'

Jesus continued: 'Those who are healthy have no need of a doctor. Those who are sick have every need. Go and learn what Hosea means when he gives us the words of the glorious God by saying, 'I desire not sacrifice, but mercy!'

'For I, my friend,' Jesus persisted, 'have come not to call the righteous, but to call sinners to myself.'

'Gap-toothed', I've called the poor Pharisee. Well, he was *gat-toothed*, too: his teeth splayed outward like a goat's. It vitiated somewhat the sad man's sadness in my eyes. I tended to see a teacher diminished by the shape of his teeth.

After the banquet Jesus walked alone to Magdala. There was a full moon, bright enough to cast shadows and to make human faces plain, though it rendered them bloodless as marble. Moonlight sculpted the fleshly expression and seemed to fix it like an image in rock on the mountain.

Maryam told me this story: that something roused her from sleep.

She had buried herself under rough linen – the stuff of torn sails – against a tower in which fires cured the fish. Although she never thought she slept in those days, her mind spinning with lights and accusations, with whole companies of hateful spirits, she must have fallen asleep in spite of it all. Because something roused her. Something, or perhaps a nothing: it was the perfect silence that brought her fully alert. And then she heard a steady breathing outside her covering; and it seemed to her that the greater heat was there, not in the tower behind her.

She pulled the linen back.

There, above her, was a face pure white, its planes and angles shining, the eyes pools of shadow beneath an overhanging brow, the cheekbones starkly beautiful.

Maryam felt paralysed. Nor could she open her mouth. And this caused her an increasing anguish, because at the sight of this man, stone-still, a screaming began in her. One voice, five voices screaming. Seven. And the sound was increasing. It caused her organs and all her bones to vibrate. If she could open her mouth, she'd scream with the screaming. But she herself, she could not move. It was not that Maryam was in hell. It was that hell was in her.

And all around them the night was black. Magdala had receded.

The man spoke. Despite his bloodless, alabaster brow, his was the voice she'd heard at the banquet.

Jesus.

Softly he said, 'Begone.' Maryam exhaled, and one of the screamers ceased screaming within her.

'Begone,' he said again. Though it seemed to her that she couldn't draw breath, she exhaled again, an extended sigh, and a second screamer ceased.

'Demon, begone,' he said. Seven times he said *begone*, quietly, neither force nor fierceness in the command, until Maryam felt depleted and pliable. The breathing was her own again. So were her bones and her motion. She sat up. She looked at Jesus and whispered, 'Blessed is the womb that bore you. Blessed the breasts that suckled you.'

'No,' Jesus said, kneeling now before her so that their eyes were on a level. 'Blessed rather are those who hear the word of God and keep it.'

Then he said, 'Maryam, you are not yet altogether safe. Sweep the place where the demons dwelt. Set everything in order – and let the word of God come into you and make a habitation there.'

Then rising, he said, 'Come with me. There is a woman I know who will love you like a daughter. She will wash you and anoint you and make you an ornament in the world.'

Maryam told me that no woman had touched her at any time during the last ten years. Therefore, though she had not cried under Jesus' transforming ministrations, when Joanna began to scrub and to brush her hair, Maryam burst into tears of humility and gratitude.

'Do you know who I am?' she had asked.

'It doesn't matter,' Joanna had answered, her massages causing the scalp to tingle. 'Jesus knows you. And whomever the Master knows, he makes her good for everyone else to know.'

AT NIGHT, AT SEA

—

'The kingdom of heaven,' said Jesus, 'is like the farmer who sows good seed in his field. But while everyone is sleeping, an enemy comes and sows darnel among the wheat, the weed that mimics goodness. In time the wheat sprouts and forms green heads — but so do the weed seeds sprout, revealing themselves. The servants say to the farmer, "Sir, where do the weeds come from?" And the farmer says, "An enemy did this." "Do you want us to tear them up?" "No," says the farmer, "because you'll root up the wheat as well. Let them grow together until the harvest; then I'll command the reapers to collect the weeds, to bind, to bundle and to burn them. But the wheat I will gather into my barn."'

Great crowds were pressing upon us. We were in Capernaum, by the Sea of Galilee. The day had been long, and the Lord continually mobbed. Fishermen left their nets to hear him. Fish processors came, lumbermen in their leathers, beggars in rags. The lame. The blind. As many women as there were men, babies on knees, babies at breasts, babies naked. And sunburnt farmers from villages north and west and south of here, farmers convinced that the teacher knew the soil, knew their troubles, knew *them*, because his stories were so personal and familiar.

It was becoming evident that Jesus liked to speak in parables. For some of those who came to listen, a parable was as easy to enter as entering their own homes. They took the meaning right away. For some the door was harder to find; they remembered the story, of course; we all did; they only lacked maturity. But for others the stories of Jesus remained mysteries, mute, for which these people blamed the teacher, as if he were taunting them somehow. Too bad, since by his parables Jesus was uttering things that had been hidden even from the foundation of the world.

'The kingdom of heaven,' he said, 'is like the mustard seed. When the farmer plants it, it is so lowly and small as to go unnoticed. Nevertheless, when it grows, the mustard becomes the greatest shrub in the garden. And who's to say it won't thereafter match the tree at the end of the world, whose leaves are for the healing of the nations? Unto its branches the birds of the air may come and find a perpetual perch.'

Evening was coming. We hadn't eaten.

I shook my head in order to clear it. I was suffering such a wooziness of thought and such weightiness in all my motion that I wondered at myself. I had not been overly worked. What could be causing this weariness in me?

And then with a start I realized the quality of the love that lived between my Lord and me: that I read his physical signs unconsciously, unconsciously transferring his condition to myself. *Jesus* was the one exhausted, not me; *his* limbs were laden, not mine. In me was merely the lover's mirror – though it felt real, and it was, in fact, true, but true to the Lord, and true to my love for my Lord.

'The kingdom of heaven is like the yeasty dough a woman folds into three measures of flour – until the whole is leavened by a little.

'The kingdom of heaven is like the treasure hidden in a field which, when a man finds it, he hides again – then, filled with joy, he rushes off, sells all he has, and buys that field for himself.

'The kingdom of heaven is like the merchant in search of fine pearls. When he finds a single pearl of the greatest value, he goes and sells all that he has – and buys that one alone.

'Those who have ears,' Jesus cried, 'let them hear!'

Immediately, privately, he said to us, 'Please, take me to the other side of the lake.'

Grant this to my brother Simon: as soon as he saw a need in the Master, he threw himself headlong at solutions.

'Thanks to our pretty publican,' he said with a blustery affection (meaning Matthew, of course), 'our boats are ours again. James, John, let's go get them. Set the sails. We'll take the wind tonight.'

But while the fishermen went to prepare the boats, a scribe forced himself close to the Lord. 'Teacher,' he declared, 'I'd like to study with you. I'll follow you wherever you go.'

Jesus, so tired his voice was cracking, said, 'Foxes have holes. The birds of the air have nests. But the Son of man has nowhere to lay his head.'

One of the disciples, seeing the sails ascending their masts, whispered quickly, 'Lord, I want to come. I will come. But, please, let me go to bury my father first.'

Jesus answered, 'Let the dead bury their own dead. You: follow me.'

Indeed: the disciples followed Jesus into the long boat, positioning themselves evenly upon the thwarts, while he himself took a seat in the stern.

Late in the evening, when the last light was dying in the west, we set sail eastwards into darkness, towards the country of Gentiles.

Within minutes Jesus had curled up on the backmost plank, his arms crossed, his knees drawn up to his chest.

I found a little cushion in my bag and carried it to him. His eyes were already closed.

'Jesus?'

No answer.

I took the liberty of lifting his head in order to slip the cushion beneath it. The flesh of his temple was warm, his hair a rough kink on the pads of my fingers. When I laid his head back down again, he didn't so much as stir.

Crack! Ka-BOOM!

As if by the knives of dragons, lightning shreds the heavens. Thunder follows. Wind is a fist, cracking the boat, tearing the sail, nearly swamping us.

Again: that lightning, fast as thought. A white, stuttering light illumines waves twice the height of our boat, frozen in fury above us, foam ripped by the wind. I see Simon likewise frozen, at the mast, a blade in his hand, his arm upraised to cut cord, his mouth open, roaring. I cannot hear his roaring. Darkness. The boat whirls. The tremendous waves come down with weight and an astonishing cold.

Lightning: every passenger fixed in white terror. Some lie under the thwarts. Maryam sits wide-eyed, prim, erect. Simon is hauling sail. Darkness.

The ancients told stories of primordial monsters whom God was forced to fight, *Yam* and *Nahar* and *Tannin* and *Bashan*, powers whose evils created such rage in the waters, such horror in heaven, that creation would lose to chaos.

Even so, now, this storm: the sailors aboard, hardened by years on Galilee, do nonetheless fear that this is the end of things.

Lightning! Lightning: Simon has tossed the sail. He is almost at my ear, gripping the gunnel in both hands, his lips retracted, his beard ripped backward, his eye glaring wildly at the stern – where Jesus…

Where Jesus lies curled exactly as before, his head on my cushion, sleeping!

The boat heaves hugely up. It rolls. It slants down the wave, sending Simon somewhere above me, scooping the seawater in. Darkness isolates us. Yet, as from a kingdom's distance, I hear Simon's pewling cry: 'Lord, save us! We are perishing!'

Marvellously, though neither the wind nor the waves have abated, Jesus speaks above it all! I hear him – we hear him – say, *Why are you afraid? Have you no faith?*

Lightning flashes, revealing Jesus on his feet! Standing on that backmost plank!

Darkness swallows the sight.

But if thunder follows this last flash of light, why, it is the voice of Jesus himself, rebuking the chaos: *Peace!* he bellows. *Be still!*

And immediately there is a dead calm.

All around me I hear people gasping, trying to catch their breath, coughing water out of their lungs.

Someone is moaning.

And someone murmurs, 'What kind of man is this, that even the wind and the sea obey him?'

LIGHT

‘What kind of man’, indeed!

He who wrestled the seas to obedience would confront as well an army of demons. And if the first challenge had been chaos erupting in nature, then the next was the destruction of civilizations; it was the reduction of humans into a bloody bestiality by the Uncreator, by the Despiser of God and his image and his handiwork. By the Devil.

Forgive me. Forgive the cosmic breadth of my observations. But I remember those several days with an elemental dread. It was as if the horn that Daniel saw might break forth again to sweep the stars from heaven and trample them on the ground.

Yet… yet at the same time I began to glimpse a glory in my Lord which was, yes, equal to such evils. How can I explain the conviction that began to grow in me then? If bolts of lightning could shatter the heavens, then blacken them completely, well, this one, Jesus, was *pure* light, unvarying light, the light at the first of the world. In Jesus was a life which enlightened us, every one. He shined in the darkness, and the darkness could not overcome him.

SWINE

—

As soon as our boat touched shore on the far side of the sea, there went up a wailing in the hills beyond, inarticulate – human, wounded, brutal.

We looked and saw that the basalt hills were riddled with holes, the stones which closed them whitewashed, signifying tombs. Narrow paths had been cut in the hillsides. And a man was leaping leopard-like down the sheer face of the nearest hill – and it was he who produced the catamount wailing: *Youuuuu* –

His was the only motion in the dead-scene before us; yet his vehemence, his ferocity were was so electric, they gave tongue to every tomb: the graves themselves were echoing his lament.

Simon and James were in the water behind the boat, preparing to drive its bow up onto the beach. Andrew and John had taken lines with anchors landwards –

But the spectacle of that madman dropping like the falcon from a high bluff to the ground had stopped the fishermen in their labours. They gaped. Then Andrew began to draw back to the boat.

Youuuuuuu –

The man had hit the strip of flatland between the hills and the sea. He was sprinting straight for them. For Andrew and John. He was naked. His legs and chest had been scored with slashings, some still glistening red, some gone to scars. Blood had spattered his flesh, dried black and cracked. Unclean! Most horribly unclean was this man, this animal swallowing ground, preparing to attack. His wail broke into an animal gargling.

No, but he wasn't after Andrew. He saw none but Jesus, who

had already jumped down from the boat and was walking evenly in his direction.

What do you want with me, youuuuu... Jesus! Youuu... Son of the most high God?

'Demon,' said Jesus, 'be still.'

As if tripped, the man flew forward, grounding himself at the Master's feet.

It was wonderful how alert Jesus was, how fresh in the morning after the night that had threatened to kill us. His rest during the storm must have been sleep indeed, reviving him. He stood lightly now, on the balls of his feet, like a spearman watching the feints of his enemy.

Jesus said, 'Come out of this man.'

And the demon's guttural thrust: *Swear to God, you will not torture me!*

'What is your name?' Know the name to control the enemy: 'WHAT IS YOUR NAME?'

My name is Legion! For we are many.

On a hillside some distance south a huge herd of swine was snuffling the soil, feeding. They numbered about two thousand, with twenty-five herdsmen to control them.

Not into the abyss – so the demons struggle to save themselves: *Send us not into the abyss, but there, over there, into the swine.*

Jesus turned his eyes from the man who lay hacked and naked before him to that grunting carpet of pigs in the distance.

Now, I can't be altogether sure of the following detail, nor did I question the Lord about it; but I believe his cheeks rose up beneath his eyes. I think that Jesus smiled. And then he said, 'Go.'

Go, he said, and suddenly the air felt crowded, though nothing more was seen than a wrinkling of the wind, and nothing was heard at all: an absolutely silent clamouring. And all at once every head of the two thousand pigs snapped up with woofing sounds. The herdsmen went erect. The pigs began to snort like wild hogs, their tails stiff, a stripe of standing hair all down their backs – and the herdsmen, reading the signs, took to their feet.

Down the hill the pigs were running. Down the hill in masses and out onto the strip of flatland, stampeding. And while the herdsmen watched, stupefied, the pigs drove into the sea, raising foam and a great wave seawards.

For perhaps the quarter part of an hour, pigs rushed into the water, the last ones pushing the first ones farther and farther from the shores; pigs grunted and thrashed and rolled and drowned, and none, not one, even considered returning to dry land – until all were dead and a marvellous calm came down upon the morning.

Twenty-five herdsmen lingered, staring at a sea full of swine, like barrels bumping against each other, like a great piggy island – the livelihoods of many people – floating away.

Lo, how the demons have gone to the sea, and both bound up by the word of my Lord!

Then the swineherds, too, were running away; and soon enough we discovered where they went. For within the hour villagers and townsfolk began to show up. At first they stood back, but then they crept towards our boat and the fire we'd used for warmth and for breakfast. Gentiles, every one of them. They gawked at the man that had been naked, the habitation of 'Legion' until this very morning.

He was sitting by Jesus on a flat black stone, washed and fed and dressed, his hair brushed, his face astonishingly young and innocent. Maryam from Magdala had washed and brushed the man's hair, murmuring, 'Hush, hush, little brother. Hush.'

'But,' the Gentiles protested, 'no one could hold him. None of us could bind him before. The Devil inside of him snapped our chains! He broke even the irons on his feet!'

Several of the swineherds pointed at Jesus: 'That man!' They were shaking with anger, but too fearful to come anywhere close to *that man*. 'He did it! He commands the devils. And he destroys as if he were a devil himself! Look!'

The villagers looked out to sea, where pigs were heaving on the slow-rolling waves. They looked with a growing horror at the clean young man – his very sanity seeming to bewilder and to scare them. They looked at Jesus, mild beside the man. And they began to shrink backward.

'Get out of here,' they said, a certain madness increasing the pitch of their voices. 'Get away from us. Go back where you came from!'

Jesus nodded, agreeable but unsmiling. He rose to go. The disciples followed his example and got up as well. We kicked dirt on the fire, gathered our baskets, began to drag the stone anchors back from the beach.

But the man whom Jesus had healed suffered a sort of panic as he watched our preparations.

'Sir,' he said to Jesus, who had just vaulted into the boat. The young man stood knee-deep in the water, gripping the gunnel. 'Sir, please, let me go with you.'

Jesus raised a hand to keep the fisherman from pushing off, then he gazed at the man a moment.

Finally, 'No,' he said. 'I have something of immediate importance for you to do right here, among your people. Talk. Tell your story. In all the cities round about, proclaim how much the Lord has done for you, and the mercy he has had upon you.'

'Legion' no longer, that single soul stood on the beach for as long as it took us to reach the horizon. He was smiling. For Jesus' 'something to do' can become a reason for living, the very purpose of a young man's life.

NEIGHBOURS

—

'Teacher?'

Jesus was standing. The rest of us – two hundred, maybe three hundred persons – were sitting in a spreading semicircle around him. We had gathered in a rucked, rocky field above the seashore outside the walls of Capernaum. The breeze blew cooler here than in the town.

'Teacher?'

Wherever Jesus went, people came with need. Whenever people came, he responded, healing, holding, stroking, teaching –

'Teacher! I have a question!'

The man who rose, demanding attention, was well-known to most of us. He was skilled in the laws of God. People went to *him* with questions they considered of the greatest importance, and he was proud to ground his advice always on a detailed knowledge of the Scripture. Not once, not thrice: he made pilgrimages to the Temple in Jerusalem five times a year.

'If, as you say, no one knows the Father, the Lord of heaven and earth, except... the Son, then why don't you *tell* us: what must someone like me do to inherit eternal life?'

I think the question was a challenge. I think this lawyer, under a show of seeking answers, really sought to humiliate the Lord. I think he, the legal expert, had felt insulted by the words Jesus had just uttered, and especially by the fact that Jesus uttered them not in a teaching but in the form of a prayer:

I praise you, Father, Lord of heaven and earth, Jesus had said, raising his hands to heaven, *that you have hidden these things from the wise and the learned, and revealed them to little children! Yes, Father, such is your gracious will.* Jesus lowered his hands next and spoke directly to the people, saying: *All things have been handed over to me by my Father. And no one knows who the Son is except the Father; and no one knows who the Father is except the Son – and anyone to whom the Son chooses to reveal him.*

Both the sentiment and the divine intimacy must have offended the lawyer: What about a common (wise!) human like myself? What must I do to inherit eternal life?

But Jesus, his eyes dancing, questioned the questioner; or in other words, challenged the challenger:

'What is written in the law? What do you read there?'

Smiling, feeling equal in the contest, the expert quoted the Torah: 'You shall love the Lord your God with all your heart and with all your soul and with all your strength and with all your mind. And love your neighbour as yourself.'

'You've answered correctly. Do what you say,' said Jesus, 'and you will live.'

'Yes, but – '

The lawyer wasn't finished. The contest wasn't over. Perhaps he had added the Levitical passage about 'your neighbour' in order to set a snare with which to trap his rival.

'Yes, of course, but – ' and now the lawyer's second challenge: 'Who *is* my neighbour?'

Jesus ran his hand up and down his walking staff. He nodded, as if acknowledging the difficult nature of the question put to him. He fingered the whiskers beneath his nose. And then he announced: 'A story!'

The lawyer was at liberty to sit or else to continue standing. Folding his arms, he chose the latter. Jesus, therefore, walked close to him, as if they were friends gossiping in the marketplace.

He said, 'A man was travelling the winding, downhill road from Jerusalem to Jericho when, at a narrow pass, he was jumped by robbers. They stripped him, they beat him, and they left him for dead by the side of the road. Now, it happened that a priest was going down the same road. But when he saw our victim, the priest passed by on the other side. Then came a Levite who, when he too saw the victim, passed by on the other side. Finally there came a Samaritan leading a pack animal. When he saw the victim he was moved with pity. Immediately he poured wine into the poor man's wounds and sealed them with oil and bandaged them, then lifted the fellow bodily to his own donkey and carried him to the first village where there was an inn. He stayed with the wounded man that night, and on the following day gave the innkeeper silver coins equal to two days' wages. "Take care of my friend," he said, "and when I return I'll pay you any extra expenses."'

Jesus put a hand on the lawyer's shoulder and looked up into his eyes.

'So,' he said, concluding once again with a question of his own: 'Which of these three do you think proved neighbour to the fellow who had fallen into the hands of the robbers?'

The lawyer's response was soft, but whether because of shame for himself or because of honour for the Master's wisdom, I couldn't tell. Moreover, there was a commotion at the Capernaum gate; several people were rushing out, chattering, making for our field.

I heard the lawyer say, 'The one who showed mercy, he proved to be his neighbour.'

Jesus pressed the taller man's shoulder. 'Go,' he said as softly, repeating the appeal he'd made before: 'Go and do likewise.'

'Hallo! Hallo, Jesus! Jesus of Nazareth!'

We all began to stand.

Leading an anxious group, his tunic hiked to his waist, his fat legs pumping, his head bare, someone I recognized as Jairus, ruler of the synagogue, came running among the rocks. He dropped to his knees at Jesus' feet.

'My daughter,' he puffed, 'my little girl, twelve years old. She's dying. She's *dying*, Master, right this very minute!'

Without a word Jesus began to jog towards town. Simon took off, then the rest of us followed. I passed Simon, whose step was muscled and lumbering, but was hard pressed to keep up with Jesus, even though his pace was rather more even than fast. He was light, his muscles smooth, perfect for the snap and pull of running. He cornered with swift dexterity. By sweaty effort three of the disciples entered the city gates just behind the Lord.

But soon the crowds thickened around us.

Simon, ploughing through people by swipes of his big arms, shouted, 'You know where you're going?'

Immediately Jesus stopped and started to look around behind him.

Simon lifted one of his paws. 'Here,' he shouted. 'I'm over here.'

But Jesus said, 'Who touched me?'

'What? Who *touched* you?' Simon boomed with laughter. 'Must be a dozen folks pressing against you right now.'

'No!' Jesus responded, his eyes flashing from face to face in the crowd. 'Somebody touched me.' He fixed on a woman who was bowed down, trying to scuttle backwards. Directly to this woman, though not unkindly, Jesus said, 'I felt the power go out of me.'

'Yes, yes, yes, yes,' she repeated, trembling with fear. She too fell at his feet. The crowd pushed backwards, expecting judgment.

As quickly as a sparrow chirping, the woman poured forth words: 'Twelve years I've been bleeding. I'm poor from paying doctors who only made me worse. I thought, I thought, *If maybe I touch the fringe of his cloak,* and I did. And I am well. As soon as I touched you, my bleeding stopped.'

Jesus made an island of quiet with his eyes. It embraced the woman who looked up at him steadily, without fear. He said, 'Daughter, your faith has made you well. Go on, now. You're free, and you may go in peace.'

While Jesus lingered here in the street, Jairus caught up with us. At the same time one of his servants came running from the ruler's house. She seized his hand and kissed it.

'Come,' she said. 'No need to worry the teacher any more. I'm sorry, sir. Your daughter has died.'

Jairus drew breath and snatched back his hand. His eyes widened, his mouth began to open. But before he could give voice to his sorrow, Jesus stepped towards him and spoke a word of sharp precision: 'Do not be afraid,' he said. 'Only believe. And come.'

With his right arm he encircled Jairus's back, with his left hand gripped the poor man's elbow; then, holding for stability, touching for the comfort, Jesus led the ruler of the synagogue back to his own home.

Three disciples went before them, making a way through the crowd.

When they entered the house, they found a host of townsfolk in full mourning cry, weeping and wailing, pulling their hair.

'What's the matter with you?' Jesus called above the teary uproar. 'Why the commotion? Why the tears? The child is not dead. She's sleeping.'

Immediately the weepers turned to jokers. They laughed at him. They hooted until he, still supporting Jairus and speaking with an unassailable dignity, said: 'Get out. Every last one of you false bawlers – get *out* of here!'

It was a mob most wondrously offended that huffed dry-eyed, then, out of Jairus's house. And it was peace that took their place.

Into the room where the girl was lying, a large room devoted to her illness, Jesus led her father, her mother and the disciples who were with him. Candles were burning at her head and her feet: respect for the dead, signs that someone was already beginning to arrange for her burial.

As always, Jesus made the time and space his own by gazing closely at the one in need of mercy: the white-faced slip of a girl, eyebrows high, eyelids closed, her small jaw open as if upon a cry of surprise, the child's whole aspect as still as stars.

He reached down and took her hand. '*Talitha koum!*' Jesus said: 'Come, little girl. Stand up.'

And she did. She closed her mouth and cleared her throat. She stood up and began to walk around. Her parents were overcome with amazement.

Jesus said, 'I don't want you to tell anyone about this, do you hear me?'

They nodded. They couldn't speak. Even the little girl nodded, though who knew what she understood and did not understand about her circumstances.

'Mother, a porridge?' Jesus said to the woman. 'Boil a little barley in milk. Get your sweet daughter something to eat.'

DEPARTURES

═══

Thereafter we were travelling Galilee again, Jesus walking among us with his staff, and talking, talking, gathering crowds, but touching the individuals one by one, healing them. First we followed the shores of the sea, Bethsaida, Chorazin, Magdala, as far south on the sea as Sennabris. Next we turned inland village to village.

News regarding this Jesus of Nazareth preceded us wherever we went, healer, teacher, prophet, storyteller, wonder-worker: *He raises the dead! I swear, the man's like Elijah. He raises the dead!*

People knew him on sight, whether or not they'd seen him before. His physical description must have attended the descriptions of his deeds, and great long quotes of his teachings spread throughout the land.

Yet, despite his goodness (even now at my old age, I know nothing but the highest good of him), opinions regarding Jesus were fiercely divided. He was adored. He was sought after. His very presence caused kindly people to stutter.

He was despised.

Jesus of Nazareth: friend of the poor no less than of the publican! Jesus of Nazareth: eats with whores, treats with lepers, touches the clean and the unclean alike, walks with those who are in – and those who are out – of favour, criminals, bandits, officers of the royal court. Jesus of Nazareth: a glutton on account of all that he consumes, both of food and of drink, ready always to accept *anyone's* hospitality. No refuser of gifts is he – and like a rounder stays up late at night, talking!

So they said.

And this say I: in Jesus of Nazareth was the coming of the kingdom of God! For it seemed to me that the very authority of God was made visible through him, to *my* eyes. Ah, me! You must know that I could not live those days as commonplace. I lived in a constant fever of wonder as the stature and the glory of my Lord kept increasing, yea, though his bones were small and his pretty person neat. In him was the authority of the Creator over all creation. I thought that, and I, by my attachment to him, felt elevated. In him was the power of God against every manifestation of the Enemy. In him was the mercy the almighty Redeemer had showed to Israel, but mercy in Jesus was for every human enslavement, by cruel dominions, by sickness. By death. Even death.

I couldn't help it. How could I help it? I loved him. I loved *him* with such swelling in my breast it sometimes felt like suffocation. But the knowledge and the measure of my love were never so clear as when my Lord was hated. Strange. I yearned for every soul who met him to love him as much as I did. Yet it was the soul who refused to love him, the soul who despised him, that caused my love like fire to stream from my eyes upon my Jesus.

Like Nazareth – but for reasons grander and less provincial, because the city saw itself as grand and unprovincial – Bethsaida rejected him. So did the town of Chorazin. What? Did they fear that a powerful good might turn into a powerful evil, especially if it could not be controlled? That *power* was the reality here, while good and evil were merely attributes? Or what? Did the manifest freedom of this power, its independence of all things earthly, terrify them? Did the leaders fear for their leadership? Did the priests fear for the subversion of the world which the Lord God and Moses had ordered? Did power and goodness in a single individual threaten chaos?

Or what? Had God in Jesus come too close? And the heat and the light had started to scorch the souls that loved the darkness?

But I've got ahead of myself. Let me tell you what caused us to leave Simon's house in the first place – what sent us from this pleasant base for Jesus' ministry – to wander Galilee again.

After he'd warmed the cheeks of Jairus's chalk-white daughter, I expected Capernaum to gather in the synagogue and to praise the God of heaven that life had proven greater than death. As ruler of the synagogue, Jairus had merely to mention the possibility, and it would have taken place. But one of his sons was soon to succeed him in that position and possessed already a certain authority among the people; and all of Jairus's sons (years older than their sister) saw neither God nor goodness in the mercy Jesus rendered her. This to me is a breathtaking mystery: when the child walked flushed and healthy out of her father's house into a public sunlight, her brothers and several loitering mourners reacted with confusion. But then, when Jesus stepped out behind her and took her shoulders in his hands and bent and kissed the crown of her head, their confusion turned to rage. They began to scold their sister. They cursed Jesus.

Capernaum, the town on which he had lavished so much time and so much kindness, became one of the first self-consciously to reject him.

Wherever Jesus walked that next week, the brothers pursued him. When he paused to teach they raised their voices louder than his, taunting him, demanding he answer them.

'You're destroying us! Lacerating us!' they shouted. 'You tear our families apart!' they yelled, gathering the curious, persuading the sceptical to agree. Crowds came as much for these verbal assaults as for the Lord: 'Wherever you go, *wherever* you go,' cried the brother soon to rule the synagogue, 'friendly people fall to fighting! Our father will not speak to us! Our little sister hates us.'

And when Jesus began to respond to their assaults, the crowds grew larger, seeking excitement, and opposing opinions solidified.

'Show us a sign!' – this from a scribe who had joined the party hardened against the Lord. 'Let it be a sign from heaven! We know that miracles can come from anywhere. You: give us proof you have authority from God!'

Jesus answered the scribe in an even, unimpassioned voice. But his words drove Capernaum crazy: 'It is an evil and adulterous generation that asks for a sign. You get no sign from me except the sign of Jonah. Just as he lay in the belly of the sea monster for three days and three nights, so shall the Son of man lie three days and three nights in the heart of the earth.'

Our last day in Capernaum was a sabbath.

At about noon a tanner and his wife approached Jesus with

their son, himself a grown man, but possessed by a demon. Except that his business with Jesus was so important, the tanner would have stayed outside the town and cried at a distance: he knew that the stench of his trade was upon him. Few people could abide the odour. But the demon had taken both sight and speech away from his son: 'Please,' he said, almost witless with embarrassment. 'Jesus?'

And with no show save the command, 'Come out,' Jesus cast the demon out of the tanner's son. The young man covered his eyes against the sudden sunlight and said, 'Bright! Mama! It's so bright!'

And immediately Jairus's oldest son, surrounded by scribes and by the Pharisees who now were making lists of the sins of this blasphemer, shouted, 'You are mad, Jesus of Nazareth! And we know the source of an evil miracle. You do what you do by the power of the Prince of Demons.'

Jesus whirled towards his accuser, his eyes flashing.

'I refute you with the words of your own mouth!' he snapped. 'A family torn apart, a house divided against itself – no! It cannot stand. You are right! Sons against their father, father against his sons, no matter who refused the other first: the house of Jairus is indeed in danger of destruction.

'But if, then, by the Prince of Demons I cast out demons, how shall the kingdom of Satan stand?'

For a moment his accusers were silent.

Then Jesus leaped to a stone bench and cried out so loudly, much of Capernaum heard it: 'But if it is by the Spirit of God I cast out demons, then the kingdom of God has come upon you! Can you know? Can you take the benefit? Or will you become a desolation, since you refused to know the time of your visitation?'

Jesus knelt right where he was, on the stone bench in the sight of the people, and untied his sandals. He took them off, stood up, and held them high. Then he slapped the soles so smartly together ('Madman, madman,' mumbled his accusers) that puffs of dust smudged the air. Finally he tied the sandals to his feet again, stepped down, embraced the family of the stinking tanner, and left Capernaum forever.

We all did, the men and the women whose hearts were bound

to his, none of us fully aware of what had just happened or what was yet to come. Tremendous Simon plodded in silence; quiet Maryam (Maryam who seemed to me woven of gossamer) went in his wake, Joanna (who had chosen to dress no more sumptuously than the rest of us) walking beside her. Dour Matthew and Andrew and Susanna, James and his brother John, Philip and Nathanael and Thomas the twin, and James the son of Alphaeus, Thaddaeus, Simon the Cananaean – and one new fellow who was more familiar with Jerusalem than any of the rest of us. He was born and bred in that region, and his attachment to Jesus had only begun on the sabbath of our departure. He had been thunderstruck, he told us, by Jesus' last speech ('the Spirit of God' and 'the kingdom of God') and then was absolutely captured by the sandal-slapping. 'What do you think he meant by that? Oh, God! – it was a thrilling thing to see!' This fellow stood tall as a bullrush, his bones as slender, his hair like the floss of its flower. 'Every whack,' he cried, waving his arms, dancing like an osprey, 'was a whiplash! Did you see their faces? Did you see how Capernaum turned purple?' The new disciple's name was Judas Iscariot.

And so, as I've said, we travelled the seashore north to south. Then we turned westwards and visited villages in Galilee where we'd never stopped before. And we were received. And we were rejected. And both opinions were intensifying. And Jesus repeated his conviction over and over: 'The kingdom of God is near, so near.'

At last, he gathered us all together near the slopes of Mount Tabor and requested that we share an evening meal together, that we plan to spend the night here, outside, rather than in anyone's house. He said he had something to ask of us.

For the most part, we washed and ate in silence. Jesus himself spoke blessings over the food, and then he held his peace until all had finished, and the place had been cleaned, and a good fire sent crests of light across our faces. We sat in a circle, Jesus by the fire in the midst of us.

'There is an urgency,' he said. 'I have taken you as disciples to myself... in order to send you out again. Now is the time. We can't wait any longer.'

When he spoke with his back to the fire, he was in silhouette.

I couldn't see his face, but only the shape of him. When he moved to speak on the other side of the fire from me, it was his back I saw, his slender neck, and the waves of heat distorted his voice. Yet I heard him in my heart. I have not forgotten the words. They became an instruction even after his days on earth had come to their conclusion, and I went out alone.

'Tomorrow you will begin to journey, two by two,' he said, 'through all the villages in Galilee. Go to the lost sheep of the house of Israel, and preach as you go, saying, "The kingdom of God is at hand."'

A log slipped; a column of sparks rose high into the night. Jesus turned to see it, and I saw his face: solemn.

'Heal the sick,' he said.

Simon barked, 'Us? You mean us? We get to do what you do?'

'Cleanse the lepers,' Jesus continued, and Simon ducked his head down. 'Cast out demons. You have already received goodness without paying; now give without pay. Take no money, carry no bag for your journey, nor two tunics, nor sandals – for labourers deserve their food.

'Whenever you enter a town, find out whose house is worthy and stay there until you depart. If a house or if a town will not receive you, will not listen to your words, well, then shake the dust from off your feet as you leave – '

'See?' breathed Judas, grinning and wiggling his eyebrows. 'What did I tell you?'

'Listen, children,' Jesus said, and his tenderness broke my heart: 'I send you out as sheep in the midst of wolves. Be wise as serpents and innocent as doves. Don't, don't be afraid. Aren't two sparrows sold for a penny? And not one of them falls to the ground without your Father's knowledge. But even the hairs of your heads are all numbered. No, do not be afraid: you are of so much more value than a heaven of sparrows.'

Oh, my Lord, how likely and how whole I felt beneath the blessing of your farewell. Where could I go and be severed from your Spirit? Nowhere in Galilee. Nowhere in all the world. If I could climb the sky, you would be there. If I dropped through a crack in the earth, you'd be down there too. If I took the wings of the morning and dwelt in the uttermost parts of the sea, even there your hand would lead me, and your right hand hold me.

With confidence we departed in the morning. Two by two. Some on the international road that went north and south from here, some on the road that went east and west.

My partner and I selected a narrow footpath running east-north-east towards a fertile ridge whose spine was dotted with farming villages. Before we entered a stand of trees, I paused to look back.

I saw Jesus, the Lamb of God whom once I had watched descending a mountain, now ascending Mount Tabor even towards the top of it. Alone.

I did not say in my soul, *He is tireless.* By now I knew better than that, though he could make such a climb with relative ease, Jesus, light as the fox afoot.

What, however, I did say in my soul was this: *He has gone to the mountain to pray. Hear him, heavenly Father.* And I wondered whether he ever wept when he prayed. Could weariness cause my Lord to weep?

PART FIVE

$\mathcal{M}$ARY

A STORY AND A STORY

═══

The widow Mary wants to run. She wants to hike her robes to her waist and dash free-legged over the ridge of Nazareth eastwards to Mount Tabor. But she restrains herself. She can't let eagerness control her, not when she does not know how she will be received; not when she cannot be sure whether her son is still on the mountain; and not when the news she bears is so miserable. And she is herself aggrieved by the news, truly. But Mary has ever been capable of colliding feelings, to be joyful and fearful at once, to love her darling and to blame him.

Moreover, she is not as young as when she and Joseph ran the long night back to Jerusalem in search of their headstrong boy. Nor as limber. Nor as light: her thighs and her hips are melons and lentils, a good thing at home, a hard thing on the road.

And she has a mountain to climb.

Shortly before noon today two of her son's disciples passed through Nazareth and paused to see her. So she discovered that he was on the mountain alone. Alone. And, as she construes it, in need.

Mary has suffered the burden of loneliness. She hadn't done too badly when her son went south to study and to arrive at his Father's purposes for him. Nazareth supported her. And she never doubted that her son's pursuit of his Father was good and right. But this last period, after having seen him again, having travelled with him and helped him and experienced the sweet potency of his presence and observed the world's response to him – this last half year has been horrible. She doesn't complain that most of Nazareth has avoided her. Some neighbours remain furious at her son's insult to their village; some, she feels, are ashamed of *their* actions towards him. But, though neither group will talk to her or even look at her, Mary can endure their silly, cruel treatment.

On the other hand, if her son has dismissed her indeed from his mission and his life, then why does she eat? Why does she breathe? There is no reason for her existence.

The angel Gabriel called her 'favoured' on account of Jesus. *The child to be born of you will be called holy, the Son of God.*

But Mary has ever been more than a womb! She has been a mother. It was *given* her to be a mother, and a teacher, a provider, a source of nourishment and of wisdom, both. It was given her by God! And she accepted the role with complete obedience. And what's more, she delighted in it. So who is to take that from her now? *Take that, and you have taken my life.* Reject her, and God, even God, has rejected a portion of his promises. Reject her and God the Father – it seems to Mary – will have rejected a portion of himself.

This latter loneliness has been more than crushing; it has been frightening.

So she will go and see her son. He may well maintain his formal indifference towards her. Whether she is prepared for that, she doesn't know. She just does not know.

But this she knows: there is a piece of news which she must speak to him. *She* must, and none other, for there is no one else in all the world who understands the depth and the weight her story will have for Jesus. She is herself aggrieved by it. She is in mourning. But he: he will behold himself therein, and the horror of his future.

It is six miles' walk from Nazareth to Mount Tabor. A traveller can lighten her load if she takes no bag, no second tunic, no belt with money. Or else a traveller can take a little barley bread and a few fish in a pouch just because the mother in her can't help it and she's sure her boy hasn't eaten in days and must be hungry. She can take chicory leaves and mandrake root for the sleep they can afford a tired man, and hyssop for a tonic. And wine.

The path near the bottom of the mountain is steep, switching back and forth at sharp angles; but then it rises more gently near the summit. If Mary chose not to run before, now she cannot. She climbs not patiently but slowly, often stopping to catch her breath – and then to look around.

The sun, a perfect furnace of red, stands westwards over the Great Sea at a height not higher than her own; and even as she gains the summit, the woman can see three other mountain peaks set aflame by the sun: Mount Carmel, near the sea; Mount Gilboa, south in Samaria; and Mount Hermon, that snowcapped majesty, mostly north of her. The valleys below are in darkness. And it seems to Mary that these four mountains are the pillars upon which the vaults of heaven are founded. So much glory. *Too* much glory for a shortish widow woman! Ah, what did she think she was doing here? Wilfully, wilfully come to reprove the almighty Lord and God for (possibly) rejecting her? Oh, my.

'Over here.'

'What?' Mary wakes to more immediate surroundings. She frowns – 'What?' – and squints towards the sun.

'I'm over here.' It's Jesus, sitting on a slab of dressed and broken stone, the same flaming light on his face as strikes the mountains abroad. He gazes at her without surprise, without judgment, but with mild inquiry, tilting his head.

'Oh. Yes, it is you, isn't it?'

'You came looking for me.'

Mary takes a moment before answering. At this instant, and under his gaze, she feels exquisitely isolated – as if his looking were a bright light, allowing her to be seen but not to see in return. Isolated, yes: and at the same time brave. This is Jesus, after all, whom she suckled, whom she held, in whose features she recognizes herself alone; and no one else is near to distract his attentions. It's *her* turn now!

'Yes. I came from Nazareth to this mountain and to the top of it to find you.'

'Why?'

'Yeshi, I will not be abashed by you.'

Jesus nods and says again, 'Why did you come?'

That he should ask the question a second time sends a swift heat into Mary's cheeks. 'I came because I am your mother,' she declares, lifting her chin, daring him to interrupt. 'Whatever you say, however you behave, it was the Lord God who appointed me to be your mother, and I shall *be* your mother so long as we both shall live.'

More gently, somewhat defensively, digging in her pouch: 'I came because even the Son of the Most High has to eat some bread and some fish once in a while.'

And this next, as she quits the digging and lets her hands drop, with a terrible tenderness: 'I came because I have news from Perea and Machaerus, Herod's stronghold east of the Salt Sea. My news, Yeshi. I'm afraid it's bad news. But I refused to send anyone else to tell this thing to you. I am your mother: I've come as much to comfort as to wound you.'

Cousin John, the son of Zechariah, is dead.

The sun has gone down into the sea. All the flames are out. Mount Carmel remained a dark hump against the westering sky awhile, but now has been swallowed by the night. Heaven is sandy with stars, the myriad marks of God's promises, the heavenly hosts all holding their breath – so Mary imagines – preparing to weep with Jesus.

They both sit now, her son on the same smooth stone, she on the ground, growing chilly in the night.

She tells the story.

I first heard this news from John's disciples, who came in search of friends. They wanted to speak with Andrew and one other. They wanted to know where you were staying. I couldn't tell them, could I? But I promised to carry the news to those that needed most to hear it.

Yeshi, and I have details of the same story from Chuza, Joanna's husband, who was actually there, since he couldn't refuse an invitation from his overlord. The details are... detestable.

I heard the story twice. It must be spreading across the countryside. You understand, don't you, why I had to hurry to you as soon as I knew where you were?

But Mary couldn't see her son in the moonless night. He was the shadow that blotted out ten thousand stars. He was a dark figure bereft of light. He didn't answer. She plucked up her courage and continued, now giving her story a certain formality, as if she were bearing witness:

Herod Antipas, who calls himself king of Perea and of all Galilee, both

159

the upper and the lower parts — though he is king in nothing but name;
Herod Antipas, still striving for the power and the glory of his father —
though the impossibility taunts and belittles him; Herod Antipas, who stole
his present wife from his brother (well, but I'm a woman, and I say it was
she, Herodias, who caused that mess, jumping from the bed of a ruler-
husband altogether too dull into the bed of a ruler-husband of massive
ambitions, therefore…); Herod Antipas, who is weak before his wife but,
like the peacock, must display his strength in colour and feathers and
spectacle, gave himself a birthday party.

He made it a grand banquet, inviting his stewards, his topmost officials
from everywhere in Galilee and Perea, inviting his military commanders as
well, and granting them all quarters in the apartments of high Machaerus,
which, Chuza says, affords its guests a sweeping view of the Dead Sea and
the hills beyond. Such magnificence governed by such meanness.

There is a fine hall in that palace, the painted ceiling supported by a forest
of stone columns, tables enough to accommodate half a hundred diners, and
space for their entertainment both during and after the banquet.

And lamps! So many lamps of brass and silver and alabaster, that there
were no shadows in that room. They hung by chains from the roof beams;
they flickered in niches every three feet along the walls; they stood on stands
and sat on the tables and warmed the room. And as the banquet passed from
eating to drinking, they lit the faces of Herod's friends with a moist and rosy
glow. Wine, to gladden the hearts of flush-faced men.

Musicians played, and singers sang.

How old was Herod on this recent birthday? Forty-seven? Forty-nine?
Not yet feeble. But foolish. And who knows? — maybe the ageing had begun
to trouble him. His father died at sixty-nine; but his father was already king
at the age of twenty-seven!

Musicians played; a pretty little girl walked a leopard through the room.
They were chained together, neck to neck. Herod laughed loudly, praising the
show; then all the guests expressed their delight by slapping the tables; and
Chuza saw the hair rise up all down the leopard's back. He feared for the
girl. Who binds a child to a cat three times her size?

Musicians played, and dancers danced.

And then came the dancer that silenced the room. This was no servant.
Nor was she the sort of woman who danced to make a living. She was
royalty. She was born to her grace. Her limbs were both long and strong, her
feet so able to grip the floor that she could bend her body backward and not
fall down. At a certain point, she pulled the pins from her hair and whirled

it like a lace on the wind, like a winnowing. At that gesture, Herod Antipas gasped.

Ever since the girl had initiated the dance, high and light on her bare toes, she'd been looking at none but him. And he, nodding and smiling and nodding, had kept fastened his attentions altogether on her, the motion, the tawny flesh, the smoky brows. But this last, the loosing of her hair and its wild whipping around, seemed to sting him. It brought tears to his eyes. His nostrils flared. He lifted himself halfway from the cushions, and everyone else in the room – whether to mimic their king, or else to show their own fascination – did the same. And then it was the room went silent. Even the musicians paused to watch. One piper played. He produced a slender note, repeating it in husky admiration – and she danced. She made his one note the string she walked upon.

Chuza admits his own – even his physical – entrancement. But then he noticed that Herodias was watching from behind a screen at the far end of the hall. With but a slight dipping of her head, Herod's wife was marking time to the dancer's dancing. She was not smiling. The rigid calculation in Herodias's eyes suddenly snapped Chuza free from his dizzy trance, and in a flash he knew who the dancer was, this damsel who held the room, the powers of Galilee and Perea, the armies of Herod, in her power. It was the daughter whom Herodias had brought to her second marriage. Salome. Fourteen years old. Unmarried.

Finally even the pipe fell silent.

And Salome bent forward in a low, thrilling bow.

Herod Antipas jumped up. 'Confusion!' he cried. 'You have struck my senses – my heart, O beautiful child – into the confusions of youth. I am young again. Oh, how sweet and how young I feel! Stand up.'

Until his command, she had kept her face but inches from the floor. Now she stood and presented Herod with an expression of untarnished innocence.

'What do you want?' he said. He passed his hand underneath his nose. He did it again. 'Ask for anything you want and I'll give it to you. I swear it. Even up to half my kingdom is yours. Just ask.' Herod rubbed his nose hard. Perhaps it itched.

'Father,' she said, and he almost collapsed. Had she never called him her father before? 'Father, grant me a moment. I'll be right back.'

Herod threw up his right hand grandly, shouting, 'A moment, my child!' The girl skipped to the screen where her mother was waiting. They whispered.

Straightway, she came skipping back and, smiling, blushing and bowing again, she said, 'Nothing of your kingdom, Father. Not even a foot of your land. I ask for a just punishment. The head of one of the prisoners in your dungeons. The rabble-rouser. Give me the head of John the Baptizer' — and then as an afterthought — 'on a platter.'

Salome stood up and beamed with sweet affection upon her stepfather. 'I'll wait here. John the Baptizer isn't far away. And see? There reclines your captain of the guard.'

Yeshi, Chuza is quitting Herod's service. Even now he is closing the books. And then he'll return secretly to Nabatea; or else he will come to you. You ask me, I'd say he'll come to you. Not just because of Joanna. She has never pressed him. But her goodness, her kindness towards all people, has made his obedience to Herod Antipas a shameful, a burning thing. When he must pressure the tenants, he tells me, he hates himself. And he thinks that it is your spirit which has filled the spirit of his wife. He will find you. He will follow you.

Herod Antipas dropped to the floor. He affected to recline, but his body was stiff, intransigent. He stared first at Salome and then at all the guests who awaited his response. He had promised. He had sworn. The weakness that made his wife an unrighteous force in his life (so say I!) would have become a public scorn if now he reneged on his sworn promises.

Herod glanced towards the captain. 'Go,' he said. 'Do what she asks.'

After the captain left, no one moved. The joy of the banquet had been ruined — but not by Salome's request or Herod's command! Rather his distress over having to make the command. He put his face into his hands. And officials wondered what was the matter with their overlord. John the Baptizer had held him up to a public ridicule. Ridicule would destroy the trust of the people. Why would he regret a necessary beheading? Intestinal delicacy? Weakness?

Salome maintained her birdy perch.

Herodias actually stepped out from behind her screen and took up a position in the room, her arms folded beneath her breasts.

And in less than a quarter hour, the captain of the guard returned. Carrying in two hands a broad silver platter, fluted at the sides. Which he gave to the smiling Salome. Upon which was the head of cousin John. Rolled over on one ear. Yeshi, his mouth was open, his tongue thrust out, as if he'd never ceased to speak.

Mary stops. Surely she could tell him how John's disciples then buried their master, the prophet who had never been a reed that was shaken by the wind. They laid his body in a tomb, John, whose life had been cut down in its prime, but whose word would echo forever hereafter.

But she's given her son enough, Mary has. And she's in the dark. Can she go to him? Would he accept her comfort now?

'Yeshi?'

'It was from this very mountain that Barak and the prophet Deborah fought Sisera, the commander of the armies of the kings of the Canaanites.'

Jesus speaks, as always, quietly. But there is an intensity to his voice which heartens Mary. He *has* received her story. It has affected him.

'This mountain,' Jesus says. 'Mount Tabor, once covered with forests – '

No one else is here. He says these words for himself, surely. But he must be talking to Mary too. It must be that she is included: a story for her story.

'In the days of the Judges,' Jesus says, 'when no one travelled the roads in Israel; when the Canaanites had crushed the villages to powder, the prophet Deborah rose up as a mother in among the people of God. She gathered the captains of Zebulun, the princes of Issachar, the warriors of Naphtali, and placed them under the leadership of her general, Barak. Barak brought them to this mountain. They waited in the forests here.

'Then Sisera and all his armies attacked. They drove their chariots into the valley below us.

'*Up, Barak!* Deborah cried. *The Lord has given Sisera into your hand,* this mother in Israel prophesied: *Doesn't the Lord go out before you?* The heavens broke open, the rains came down, the wheels of the chariots mired in mud, Barak and the Israelites rushed down this very mountain. Afoot they fought the Canaanites. By the swords of the Lord they defeated them.'

Mary watches the black form of her son. He throws back his head and lifts dark arms towards the sky, a gesture so dramatic it takes her breath away.

Holding his arms aloft, Jesus sings the snatch of a song in tones of anguish, in a howling supplication, in Hebrew: *From the heavens the stars came down to fight. From their courses they fought against Sisera.* And then, no song at all, but a wail: *O Adonai Sebaoth! O Lord of hosts!*

But no prayer follows the invocation. And in a moment Jesus begins to speak again.

'This is a story of the courage of women,' he says. 'Sisera escaped. He sought safety in the tent of Jael: most blessed of women is Jael! For Sisera wanted water, and she gave him milk. Sisera wanted to sleep, and she covered him with a rug. Sisera slept, and Jael crept up to him and hammered a sharp peg through his temple. Jael did this thing. She destroyed the leader of the enemies of God.'

Jesus stops speaking. His black figure, the mere darkening of stars, bows forward, placing his face upon his hands. He whispers, 'Oh, Mother, Mother – how I loved my cousin.' Jesus is crying.

Mary shivers. The mountain has grown cold; but it is the depth of her son's emotion that most unsettles her.

'Yeshi?' she says. 'Can I hold you?'

He doesn't move. He makes no answer.

'I told you truly,' she says. 'I've come to comfort you.'

Again, time passes without a response. But she who always tends to talk too much, now schools herself in silence. It is late, so late. The night has surely passed the midnight watch.

'Mother?'

'What, baby?'

Jesus says, 'You are my Deborah.'

And this is permission enough. Mary moves towards her Yeshi. She kneels before him, draws him down from the cooling stone and into her arms. He curls on his side before her. She takes his head upon her knees. She has something for him to drink. It will ease him. It will close his eyes. Wine in which a root has been soaked. Crushed leaves for the taste and for the effect.

In time and in the silence between them, Mary whispers, 'Father, into your hands I commend my spirit.'

And Jesus whispers the same: 'Father, into your hands I commend my spirit.'

Tears moisten the cloth at Mary's thighs. And then her baby sinks into a very deep sleep.

SAVE MY SON

Here is something Mary thinks about while her son sleeps on her knees, while she keeps watch through that night:

That there are three women in the story Jesus had recounted. Deborah and Jael, to be sure – courageous, victorious, and happy thereafter to be home again. But that Canaanite captain, Sisera: he also had a mother. In the Scriptures and in its fullest telling (for it was a woman told it in the first place, Deborah, with a woman's and a mother's sensibilities) the story ends with Sisera's mother, staring out her window, waiting for her gallant son to come back home again.

'Why is his chariot so long a-coming? Why don't I hear the hoofbeats pounding?'

She stares through her lattice at the empty road and answers her anxieties: 'Of course: they're finding and dividing the spoils! Colourful clothing for my son! Colourful clothing embroidered! Embroidered cloth for my neck, too – '

Jesus called Mary his 'Deborah'. The name and the invitation fill her with such warm gratitude that even the midnight mountain air can't chill her any more.

But Mary considers the nameless woman who waits in vain for the child whom she bore, the baby she named Sisera. Mary considers how the womb stirs and yearns for its children, even after they have grown and gone off to other lives. The womb remembers. The womb knows how to weep.

Jesus draws a quick breath. He holds it. He releases it with a slow groaning. Mary puts her hand to his forehead and finds it moist. He's dreaming. He must be dreaming.

Father, make his sleep his comfort. Don't scare him with dreams. Don't trouble him with visions.

Here's another thing that Mary considers during this long night, a someone-thing: Herod Antipas, murderer, putative king, the lackey of his putative queen.

Surely, she thinks, *Jesus knows how far his name has travelled.* Herod has heard of Jesus, his words, his deeds, his effect upon the people. Grand, powerful, comely: they follow as sheep do a shepherd. And perhaps Herod is eaten with the fears the unrighteous feel when wounding the righteous, fears that God knows *only* righteousness. For it was scarcely a week after he had beheaded John the Baptizer when the king began to wonder aloud whether this Jesus might be that John come back to life again. Didn't they preach the very same thing? 'The kingdom of God is at hand!' And couldn't that word be a warning? – the promise of terrible judgments upon those people who were constrained to use force for the good of all?

Come the morning, and Mary must find some effective (but not over-motherly) way to persuade her son to get out of Galilee. Herod spends as much time in Tiberias – a bare twelve miles from Mount Tabor! – as he does in Perea. Soon enough he and his wife and his soldiers and their swords will come dangerously close to the places where Jesus has been teaching and healing. Herod hates preachers of broad popularity, preachers bold enough or foolish enough to utter judgment against their rulers. Herod is afraid of crowds. Crowds become mobs. Mobs are an irrational monster. Herod kills prophets of John's calibre. And worse than that is Herod's suspicion that this prophet *is* John.

The eastern horizon is beginning to define itself against the grey light of the dawning. The stars across the Jordan are being swept away. Even still her baby sleeps unmoving, his knees drawn up to his chest, hands tucked between his thighs, cheek on his mother's leg as though it were his pillow – and Mary considers his sorrow. And this is the last thing she thinks before the night and her watch must come to an end:

Cousin John, rawboned, whose hands and fingers were large enough even in his youth to pick up melons, one in each, grinning: John had attended Jesus' first Passover. John had obeyed the call of God first, making a way for Jesus. John the Baptizer had baptized him. John the prophet had been her son's Elijah, declaring the dignity and the sovereignty, the messianic greatness that lay in the hands of Jesus: *I baptize with water; but there comes one after me who will baptize you with the Holy Spirit and with fire.* John had lived an austere life, denying himself the foods of the fat, the clothing of the comfortable. Jesus had loved him. Jesus, sleeping on her lap – he loves John still. And now that dear man has once more preceded Jesus, this time down the road of no return.

Ah, my God, my God: how hard you are on those you call.

Mary begins to rock, slowly, back and forth.

In a moment she opens her nose and hums a narrow melody.

Morning makes a crimson rim at the eastern edge of the earth.

And finally Mary turns her humming into singing:

But you are the bulwark round my son;
You are his glory, you his crown.
To you, so grand with promises,
   This mother cries:

He lies beside me, sweet and sleeping:
Let him awake within your keeping.
Keep him from fear before the foes
   Assailing his soul!

Arise, O God! God, save my son!
Break the teeth of the wicked one!
Crack his enemies on the jaw!
   Save! Save us all!

PART SIX

THE BELOVED

SHEEP

===

'Ho, ho!'

Simon appeared in the doorway. He threw out his arms and burst into laughter.

'Ha, ha, ha! Whooo-wee, Jesus! – but didn't we have a good time!'

His arms wide open, he stomped into the room where Jesus was sitting on a stone bench. He bent. He clasped the Lord around his chest and heaved him into the air and kissed him on the cheek, just above the close, curly beard. 'It was wonderful!' he roared.

'Simon, Simon!' This was Andrew, entering at the same door: 'Put him down!'

But Jesus was in no hurry to hit the floor again. His eyes flashed merriment. He grabbed Simon's neck and kissed him back.

'Why,' cried Simon, 'you're lighter than my grandma!' He held Jesus out and gave him a shake. And in that moment Simon discovered – we all discovered – a secret Jesus had been keeping from us as long as we'd known him. He was ticklish!

This is how Jesus laughed: by a turning *down* of the corners of his lips. By opening his mouth just a crack. By arching his eyebrows, by shedding tears, and by coughing! He cough-laughed. He choke-laughed. He laughed weeping.

And when Jesus, held in the huge paws of the fisherman, started to snort his laughter, then Simon had to put him down indeed, and quickly – because the big man was himself collapsing under his own astonished, helpless laughter.

'He's ticklish! Jesus is ticklish! Ha ha ha ha! Oh, ho ho ho!' Simon was a sight, lying on the floor, kicking his feet.

Mary went over and slapped him on the top of his head. 'Stop that! Stop mocking my boy!' But she was grinning, and her hair was exploding.

And everyone was laughing now.

Maryam from Magdala – oh, the woman warmed my soul. I'd never seen her completely happy before. She had covered her mouth with her hands, but her eyes gazed on Jesus with such a dancing, sweet affection that she was a feast for mine.

Andrew had given up trying to contain his brother. Judas, all arms and legs on the floor, giggled and giggled high in his nose. Matthew, that lugubrious chalk-man, was actually smiling.

We were home again.

Well, not *home* home. We had no house, no village to call our own. But where the Master was, that would always be the place of our habitation; and the separation which we had all just experienced – and now the peculiar joy of our reunion – these made that wonderfully clear.

Ah, how good, Lord! How good it is to be here.

Joanna and Mary calmed our hilarities by bringing water that had been cooling in goatskins. 'Take the dust out of your throats,' they said, adding the caution: 'All this racket has drawn a crowd outside.'

And then we began to tell Jesus all that had happened to us during our travels, our preaching, even our healing.

'Lord, in your name even the demons submit to us!'

Jesus, sober again and as always not a whit dishevelled (I think it was the precision of his hairline and the perfect shape of his skull in every profile which gave him the appearance of perpetual neatness), Jesus replied, 'I saw Satan fall like black lightning from the heavens.'

Simon gasped. 'Satan?' he whispered.

'Nevertheless,' Jesus said, 'do not rejoice in this, that the spirits submit to you. Rejoice rather that your names are written in heaven. And blessed are the eyes that see what you see. For I tell you that many prophets and kings desired to see what you see, but didn't, and to hear what you hear, but couldn't.'

Mary and Joanna were sitting among us again. Jesus' last words had put us all to silence. We could hear the increasing clamour outside. It made my chest hurt.

'Lord,' I said, 'would you teach us to pray, just as John taught his disciples?'

An innocent question. But Jesus looked at me and repeated my words softly: 'Just as John... taught.' He drew a deep breath and held it a moment, lifting his chin in a gesture that looked like bravery but felt like sadness. He glanced briefly towards his mother. It occurred to me that something had happened in our absence. When I got the chance, I would have to ask her what.

But Jesus was speaking. 'When you pray,' he said, 'pray like this. Say, *Our Father who art in heaven, hallowed be thy name. Thy kingdom come. Thy will be done on earth as it is in heaven. Give us this day our daily bread. Forgive us our debts even as we also forgive our debtors. Lead us not into temptation. Deliver us from evil.*'

There came now such a round thumping on the outside door that Maryam jumped, frightened.

Jesus sighed.

'Simon, my bully boy,' he said, 'we'll need your tough arms and all your bluster in a moment. James? John? My dauntless sons of thunder, can you find us boats?'

And to the rest of us he said, 'You've had a difficult trip. Come away with me, just yourselves. We'll row to a quiet place apart and get some rest.'

To be sure, Simon did a fine job of wedging through the noisy multitude, smaller disciples on either side and Jesus just behind him. And to be sure, James and Andrew had found boats by the time we arrived at the shores of the lake. But we did not succeed at leaving the crowds behind.

God help them all, they came along.

Not in the boats, of course. They ran along the shoreline! Even as we pulled for deeper water, even after we'd rowed for several hours, they kept pacing us. They wouldn't quit! In fact, it looked as if the farther they went, the greater their numbers grew.

Nor could Jesus stop watching them. His lips closed on a thoughtful line, that muscle pulsing in his jaw, he, scarcely blinking, seemed to be embracing them by his eyes alone.

They were peasants, that moving mass now fixed in the

vision of my Lord. It was out of the tiniest villages that they came, where entire families lived in a single room, and five such rooms gave onto a shared single courtyard – and in the courtyard dung was dried to heat small stoves, and goats fed from low stone mangers. Landless peasants, Herod's off-scouring, thin legs, dishevelled hair: they ran with their tunics tucked up. They ran in rags. Some wore the cloth caps of labourers. They ran with an astonishing stamina. They ran with nothing in their hands. None carried money. They could scarcely hold a coin longer than a day. They hated what money stood for, since this was the only thing their ravenous masters, religious or wealthy or royal, would accept in payment for their taxes.

Jesus had risen up in the boat, the better to see the multitudes, his nostrils flaring.

Finally he said, 'Put back to shore.'

'Back to the place we left?' Simon was at the tiller. 'What about your rest – '

'No. Straight to the place where those people are. Look at them. Ah, my soul, just look at them,' he said as if to himself. 'They are like sheep without a shepherd.'

By the time we reached them, there must have been a full five thousand men gathered, standing, waiting for us – and the place where they were, though grassy, was desolate, not a town or a village anywhere nearby.

Nevertheless, when Jesus stepped out of the boat he began immediately to tell them stories. And they listened! All the noise they made while running, all the noise was gone. There was wind; there was the plashing of the water; and there was Jesus:

'Suppose you have a friend who lives close by you, even shares the courtyard with you,' he called in that clear, articulate voice. 'Now, suppose another friend knocks on your door, having walked from a faraway village. It is midnight, yet you open your door and invite the traveller in; and then you discover your cupboard is bare. So you go to your neighbour and knock on his door. "Friend," you call out, "lend me three loaves of bread. A friend of mine has just arrived, and I have nothing to set before him."

'Here's my question: what would you do if that neighbour

refuses you? What if he calls through the door, "Go away. The door's already locked, and my children are in bed with me. I can't get up. I can't give you a thing."

'I tell you, if friendship won't get your neighbour up, boldness will. Persistence will. Knock and knock and keep on asking, and the neighbour will surely rise and give you all you need.

'Ask, and it will be given to you. Seek, and you will find. Knock, and the door will be opened unto you. For everyone who asks receives; everyone who searches finds; and to everyone who knocks the door will surely open. Which of you parents, if your children ask for a fish, would give them a snake instead? Or if they ask for bread, would you give them a stone? If you, then, who are evil, know how to give good gifts to your children, how much more won't your heavenly Father give the Holy Spirit to those who ask him?'

Who was it interrupted Jesus then? His mother? Maybe. There was a time when it would have been Mary, but something was changing. I doubt it was Mary. Simon? No, he was as lost as I was in Jesus' words. Philip? Could have been.

Someone stepped over to him and whispered, 'Lord, it's late in the day. This place is deserted. Send the people away so they can buy food for themselves.'

Well, if it was Philip who spoke, he kept his voice low. Jesus, on the other hand, responded as loudly as if he were still preaching.

He called out, 'You give them something to eat!'

Yes, it *was* Philip! I remember the look on his face, a sort of ghastly horror. Embarrassment. 'Shhhh,' he hissed. 'It would take eight months' wages to feed this lot. You want us to go and spend that much on bread just so they can eat here and not somewhere else?'

And Jesus, very loud: 'How many loaves do you have?'

'Shhhh! I don't know.'

'Go and see.'

Philip ducked his head, as if he could sneak away unseen after that exchange, and giving off a strong odour of sweat he passed among us, 'going and seeing'.

Jesus waited, smiling.

All the people waited too, nodding and smiling. Sheep.

When Philip had finished his search, he went to Jesus carrying a small pouch.

'I'm sorry, I'm sorry,' he whispered. 'We have only five loaves of barley bread and two dried fish.'

'Good,' said Jesus, thoroughly delighted by the news. He turned and spoke to us, to his disciples: 'Move among the people. Seat them orderly on the grass, in groups of hundreds and fifties.'

A test? Was this some sort of test? To send us as stewards into a multitude which, after obeying our commands and then discovering there's nothing to eat, must become an angry horde?

They *looked* hungry. Surely, they had often known hunger.

I confess that I went about Jesus' command with no little fear. Many of the men were tough-skinned and dirty. Sleeveless tunics revealed arms made hard by working. Hands were hugely callused. Both men and women were barefooted. Children crawled naked on the grass. These people farmed, but for the sake of other people. They knew hammers and anvils. They stood in the water to fish. They wove a rough wool. Here a job and there a job, they barely survived. Well, but Jesus was no different. They knew him also as a carpenter, here a job, there a job, and no room at all.

Indeed, then: like sheep content in pastureland, they obeyed us, dividing into perfect flocks with passageways between them. I returned to the Lord, quaking. When I looked, whole hills were covered by humanity, all seated on the ground.

Again, a fine quiet came to the evening.

Jesus took the loaves and the fish and looked up to heaven. He gave thanks. Then he broke the loaves. And broke them, and kept breaking them, giving the pieces to us, as well as the fish, which we carried to the people. And the people ate. All of them! Oh, my God! Oh, great God of Israel! – as if it were manna the multitudes ate their fill and everyone of them, men, women, children, were satisfied!

I fell to such grinning my face began to crack. Of *course* my Lord would make it right!

And after the crowds had eaten, Jesus asked whether we were hungry. It's true; we hadn't eaten at all that day – nothing since the cups of water Mary and Joanna had brought us.

'Well,' he said. 'There's exactly enough for each of you. Gather up what the people haven't eaten.'

We did. We gathered the equivalent of twelve baskets of bread and fish.

'Put out to sea,' Jesus said. 'Eat in the boats. Return them to those from whom we borrowed them. In good time I will be with you. But I'll dismiss this people first, and then I want to be alone awhile.'

To pray. I knew as much by now. He always went on high ground for praying. And he did this not on the easier days, but on days most difficult. When any other mortal would eat and sleep in order to recover, Jesus climbed high in the night and prayed.

It occurred to me as we rowed away that perhaps we hadn't passed the test – if indeed there'd been a test. For earlier he had invited us to go with him to a quiet place apart. In the end, he was going there alone, and I wondered whether we had been dismissed.

What I am constrained to tell you next embarrasses me fully as much as my anticipations of an angry crowd – and my ignorance, therefore, of my Lord – embarrassed me before.

I loved him. But him whom I loved, I did not know. And it may even be that my loving diminished Jesus in my sight. Love wants to be loved in return. And human love seeks – assumes! – the human in the beloved. When the beloved, then, reveals qualities of a wholly *different* nature, it is downright frightening.

That Jesus is ticklish, well, that is a comfort.

But that he can multiply five loaves into food for five thousand men, plus women and children! That is the beginning of fear.

And that he can walk on water –

Long after midnight, close on to the dawning, we found ourselves rowing against a rising wind. We were going west. This wind blew hard straight out of the west. Four men rowed in each boat, each man with a single oar. The harder we pulled, the harder the wind pushed back. And then one by one, those of us facing the way we had come seemed to see a pale light upon the water.

'Look.'

'Yes, I see. Simon! What is that?'

'Marsh gas.'

'No! Not over the open lake. Not in a wind like this.'

'What *is* that thing?'

In the earliest moments of the dawning we began to see that a mist lay on the lake; in that mist the pale light seemed a shade, indistinct.

'It's coming closer. It looks like it's catching up with us.'

'Is that possible?'

'Row! Row, boys! Row as hard as you can!'

'What can move across the water like that?'

'It rises and falls with the waves.'

'It's taking shape.'

'Legs! Striding legs, and a head.'

'O God! It's a haunt!'

'A what? What did you call it?'

'A ghost!'

We all set up a howling then. And by the time the ghost had caught up with us, walking, seeming prepared to pass us by, no one was rowing. Our boats rocked and tossed with the waves.

The ghost put a hand on the stern-board right by Simon, and spoke.

'Cheer up,' it said. 'I am – '

Simon cried, 'You are – '

And spontaneously I said, 'Jesus. It's Jesus.'

'It is I,' Jesus said. 'Don't be afraid.'

But Simon couldn't stop at well enough. 'Lord,' he bellowed, 'if it is you, command me to come to you on the water.'

Jesus, smiling, said, 'Come.'

Simon didn't say, *Really?* But the sudden delight in his eyes and the clapping of his hands gave the appearance of a child invited to play with adults.

Jesus stepped back, away from the boat.

Simon grabbed the stern-board and vaulted onto the water. He grinned magnificently upon Jesus and took a step. At that same instant a wave rolled high behind the Lord. It broke around him as if he were a monument. But when the same wave gathered and crested over Simon's head, he bleated and began to sink.

'Help!' he bellowed now a different tune: 'Lord, save me!'

Immediately Jesus reached out his hand and caught Simon by the back of his tunic and hauled him up out of the water as easily as Simon had picked *him* up yesterday.

'Big man, little faith,' said Jesus, dumping him into the boat. 'Hot and cold, you are,' he continued, stepping into the boat himself. 'Shilly-shallying Simon! Why do you vacillate?'

He sat and the wind ceased. The sea grew perfectly calm.

Ahhh!

And hadn't the same thing happened before? And hadn't I been filled with wonder then? What had happened in the meantime?

Severely, I began to examine my love for Jesus, how it was not – how it had proven not to be – large enough. I myself, *I* vacillated more than Simon, but all quietly. For I had delighted to find the divine in Jesus! I took *pride* in his power over demons, over creation. Yet on this day, in the midst of ten thousand, I mistrusted him. I expected his failure. I feared for my skin. I, who had scorned my brother Philip – I was even now under the judgment of my own most bitter scorn, for my beloved was so much greater than my love. And so much more steadfast than my heart. Once I exulted that there was nowhere I could go, but that he would be there with me. *If I took the wings of the morning and dwelt in the uttermost parts of the sea* – But here, upon the sea, I thought I saw a ghost.

My Lord, my Lord: as if I needed to know it all over again, my Lord was the Lord of the sea!

Save me, I said in my soul, dropping my eyes, unable to look upon the man who had got into the boat with us. *Lift me higher. Lift me, Lord, unto yourself.*

BEFORE HIS FOES

We left Galilee. Once Jesus had made up his mind, we walked west without stopping in towns or villages any more, west on the road that passes north of Sepphoris and thence to Acco-Ptolemais, a port city, mostly Gentile, on the Great Sea. Once at Acco-Ptolemais we turned north and continued on the coastal road towards the regions of Tyre and Sidon.

When, a while back, he had sent us out on our own, two by two, Jesus had instructed us to 'go to the lost sheep of Israel'. Now he was leading us altogether *out* of the lands of Israel, into the lands of the nations and pagans.

If he were going alone, I suppose that Jesus would have covered twenty miles in a day. The energy in him was that taut. He shivered like a swift steed yearning to break forward and to run; but he was restraining himself, I believe, for the sake of the rest of us. No one could have flown as fast as he.

I don't think he was angry, though none could blame him if he were. Rather, something was on his mind, some driving conviction which he seemed, by the fierce bunching of his jaw muscles, the muscles in his temple, to be chewing, chewing, never swallowing.

When we were near Sepphoris, his mother had approached him on poor, pumping legs and asked whether we might detour several miles to Cana, so she could let Chuza know where we were. Jesus didn't even answer: he chewed, he trembled, he walked, and we followed. His eyes were like hard beams, peering dead ahead into some black tomorrow. And after this blind oblivion towards his mother, even Simon didn't try to interrupt these ruminations.

To anyone who would listen, however, Judas winked and chattered away: 'I bet he's got a plan! I've figured the Master out, how he thinks — and he's working up a scheme, you mark my words!'

Judas, ever the enthusiast, Judas, giddy for the future, absolutely idolized 'the Master'. However dark the Lord's mood might become, however complex his mind and his meditations, for Judas Iscariot all was bright simplicity; he followed Jesus in the expectation of one thing: adventure! *You bet! The world will know his name — and ours!*

'Just look at that face!' Judas babbled, waving his arms like a long-legged stork attempting to take off. 'Look at that forehead! It's the prow of a boat! It cuts through the waters! And you just *know* he's devising a way to cut through the mess around us. Stupid rulers! Folks grown rich on Roman loot! And priests and the legal eagles who would eat the hearts right out of us!'

Judas's 'legal eagles' may, in fact, have had something to do with our leaving Galilee. It is on their account that one might be forgiven for thinking that Jesus walked in anger.

Eleazar the Pharisee and the lawyers and the scribes whom he had gathered as a sort of delegation around him had made us a full-time occupation. Wherever we preached in Galilee, that pack showed up, observing Jesus, disputing him, attacking him with greater and greater fervour.

'Why do your disciples break the tradition of the elders?'

Though they framed their comments as questions, they weren't seeking answers. They sought mistakes by which to humiliate this teacher before the crowds and so to prove him false. Or evil.

'Why don't your disciples wash their hands before they eat?'

And Jesus, fearless before his foes, never ducked the challenge. In fact, he seemed to thrive in the fight. His complexion darkened; his brow grew so ruddy that copper colours flashed in his hair; and the conflict was always intensified by his answers.

'This people honours me with their lips.' Jesus answered their charges of breaking tradition by quoting Isaiah: 'But their hearts are far from me!' And raising his voice to the multitudes, Jesus called his interrogators 'Blind guides of the blind. If a blind man leads a blind man, they'll both fall into the pit.'

'Even you.' Eleazar, the gap-toothed Pharisee spoke with a slow, acrimonious judgment, his sorrow turning into censure – as if he must now save the greater family from a disobedient, dangerous son. 'Jesus, Jesus, even you refuse to wash your hands before you eat.'

Both he and our Lord had accepted the invitation of another Pharisee. Eleazar had just pronounced a blessing over the food, and Jesus, unwashed, had reached into a common bowl of honied gruel with his fingers. Then, at Eleazar's parental *Jesus, Jesus*, he returned the gruel back to the bowl, causing Pharisees physically to draw back.

Jesus said, 'You Pharisees clean the outside of the cup, but inside you are full of greed and wickedness. You fools. Didn't the one who made the outside make the inside too?'

'Woe to you,' he pronounced in a terrible calm: 'For you tithe every little thing, mint and dill and cumin! But you neglect the weightier matters of the law, justice and mercy and the love of God!'

Such was the tenor of these contentions in Galilee. We continued to cook our meals on the sabbath, ignoring the laws requiring rest: 'The sabbath was made for the people of God,' Jesus said, 'not people for the sabbath.'

And he would heal on the sabbath. Not quietly or privately. Publicly, in the synagogue, calling attention to the deed.

'Here,' he announced to everyone present, 'is a man with a withered hand.'

Or, at another synagogue on another sabbath: 'Here is a man who suffers from dropsy.'

Or, 'Here is a woman, crippled eighteen years by a spirit that has bent her in half. What do you say? Is it lawful to heal on the sabbath day?'

And Eleazar, no longer looking at Jesus (he covered his forehead in Jesus' presence), spoke to everyone assembled, spoke as the grandfather of fixed authority: 'There are six days for work. Come on those days to be healed, but not on the sabbath day.'

And Jesus shot back: 'Hypocrites! Doesn't every Pharisee under the sun untie his donkey on the sabbath? – and lead it out to drink water on the sabbath? Why, then,' he demanded, his complexion grown very dark, 'shouldn't this woman, a daughter of Abraham whom Satan has bound these eighteen years, also be unbound and set free? On the *sabbath*?'

In their faces, as it were, he restored the withered hand, he healed the dropsy, he straightened the woman, and he said, 'If you had heard and learned the word of God which I gave you before, *I desire mercy and not sacrifice*, you would not now be condemning the innocent! For the Son of man is Lord also of the sabbath!'

The common folk, the displaced farmers now bound by the royal and the rich, shepherds who sheared a stranger's sheep, women who crushed a stranger's grapes and wove a foreigner's clothes, fishermen in everlasting debt for their boats – for the very right to fish! – artisans indentured to Herod in Sepphoris and Tiberias, widows, orphans, beggars, even the bandits who prowled the hills: all of these, the multitudes, heard themselves referred to as 'the innocent', and they grinned. They remembered bread at the hands of Jesus, and compassion, and how his fringes took their diseases. They loved the carpenter who both built and healed in the despite of rulers and authorities, and they rejoiced. Rough their joy. Uncouth their boisterous praise to God. Impolite the rancorous volleys of their laughter –

And unhappy the rulers, Pharisees, scribes, forced to receive the contempt of the mobs of Jesus. Outraged (mutely!) the leaders forced to suffer his stings in public:

'Woe to you, scribes and Pharisees, hypocrites!' Jesus cried in the marketplaces, eyes afire: 'You slam shut the kingdom of heaven in the faces of all these people! For you yourselves do not go in, but when others try, you stop them!

'Woe to you, hypocrites! You devour widows' houses, then turn and make a show of your religion by praying prayers that wander as far as the Jordan.'

The conflict had long gone past debate. It had ruptured into warfare.

Late one night, near the end of the second watch, a bandit stole into our camp from the darkness surrounding us. Like a raven he swept over the sleepers. But Joanna felt his passage. She woke and looked and cried out: 'Robbers!'

Simon was awake immediately, reaching for his short sword;

but the bandit had already grabbed Jesus and yanked him up against his chest. A man like an oak, and firelight showed his hair to be magnificent, long and black and banded at his brow.

'No need for your sword,' he said. 'I only have something to say to this one.'

This one, this Jesus, was offering no resistance. He'd found his footing in front of the captor and was standing lightly upright and complacent.

Simon growled, 'Who are you?'

'Does it matter?'

'No! Not if you hurt him. You'll have no breath to *breathe* a name!'

'Calculate before you promise, partner. The night is filled with my men. You have how many fighters here? Four?'

'Look out, fool!' Simon was choking on a helpless frenzy. 'That's Jesus of Nazareth you *think* you got! A prophet, mighty in words and deeds!'

'I know his name.'

'And,' said Mary, stepping around the low fire, 'I know yours.'

To our amazement, the woman walked up to the black-haired brigand, and bent, and kissed the back of the hand that held her son.

Firelight caused Mary's wrinkles to wreathe, smiling, smiling, and her night-hair looked like hay.

She said, 'You're another Jesus, aren't you?' and reached up and laid the flat of her hand upon his cheek. 'You are the son of my friend, the widow Anna, who was the wife of Abbas.' Now Mary patted Jesus' shoulder. 'It's OK, Yeshi. He's from Nazareth too.'

Jesus – the son of Anna and Abbas – actually bowed his head and shuffled his feet, verily abashed.

Jesus – the other one, *our* Jesus – stepped easily out of the bandit's embrace. 'Why don't we sit,' he said. 'Mother? Some water? Simon? Some kindness?'

They sat. We all strove to relax but eyed the darkness which was vast around our solitary fire.

The Lord said, 'You wanted to throw me over the brow of a hill.'

'I hated you,' the brigand responded. 'Arrogant, ignorant of how hard our lives, sitting in our synagogue, accusing us.'

'Is that confession?'

'It's the truth. Why should I be sorry? But I've heard of you since then. Wasn't arrogance, I'm thinking now, but boldness and conviction. You're the same with one as with the other. And I've learned about your thinking and your teaching, and I've looked from a distance and seen the things you've done for my people. My poor, beat-up people. I don't hate you. And I'm thinking, we're not different, you and me. So: I'm here to make you a proposition: join us. Fight with us.'

Someone gasped. Someone else giggled. Mary appeared with cups and water.

'Your word, your wit, my strength and strategy,' said the Nazarene bandit, taking a cup. 'Fight with us.'

A nervous rustling passed through our company. *Fight?* When bandits were caught their punishment was always, always the same: they were crucified.

But the one who had giggled whispered, 'Do it, do it!' Ah, of course: it was Judas Iscariot.

Jesus took a slow drink, then repeated a thing he had said to us long ago: 'Blessed are the peacemakers, for in the end they shall – by God himself – be called the children of God.'

'So you say,' said the bandit-Jesus. They made a notable contrast, the small one nimble as a child and ever trim, the large one bull-like for muscle and crowned with such a wild mane of black hair he could have been the rebellious Absalom. 'So you say,' he said, 'but it isn't peace that follows you where you go. My friend, it's division.'

'But not by iron,' Jesus responded. 'By my word. Those who take the sword, partner, will also die by the sword.'

'There are good reasons for dying, by the sword or arrows or hanging or torture. There are good people for dying *for*.'

'Agreed.' The Lord looked away. He closed his mouth a moment. Then: 'With all my heart, I agree. But those who take the sword do also kill by the sword. And I cannot find reasons good enough – nor people evil enough – for that. Listen: when I have gone my way, when I have finished all that I have come to do, then I will give you peace. All of you,' the Lord said, including everyone around the fire. 'All of you!' he repeated in a loud voice for anyone listening in the darkness: 'But it is my peace I'll give to you, not the sort the world gives.' He sighed. He set the cup of water aside. 'Little children,' Jesus said, 'let not your heart be troubled. Please, don't be afraid – '

Suddenly he clutched at his breast as if kicked. He groaned, and Simon cried, 'What? What, Lord?' The big disciple started to rise, pointing at the bandit: 'Did you – '

'Kindness, Simon!' Jesus barked. Small beads of sweat glistened in his lashes.

Silence followed.

Finally, Jesus the brigand, the son of Anna and Abbas, said, 'We, neither of us, will change the other. I'll go now. Let me go... in peace. But I have one other thing to tell you.'

The Lord raised his eyes to look at his townsman. There was no other gesture, except a thinning of his lips and a pulsing of the muscles in his jaw and in his temples.

The other said, 'You must know how deadly things have become.' He stood up and looked down on Jesus. He was like a pillar above us, his marvellous hair a part of the darkness. 'The maidens who bring us food, who travel the cities as ears and eyes – lately they've brought a bitter report. The Pharisees are conspiring together, my friend. Right now they are preparing plans for your destruction.'

And so the bandit vanished.

And so we left Galilee.

BREAKING STRIDE

Here's a perplexing event. I will tell it as it happened and let you make of it what you will.

We skirted Tyre on its eastern side (where they made a purple dye from mollusks, sending out an awful stink on the western winds) then travelled north for half a day. We stopped and prepared to spend the night near the mouth of the Litani River. Jesus walked inland alone, towards the tremendous cliffs on the north side of the Litani. By morning he was sitting on the shore-rock, his staff across his knees, staring over the Great Sea, as grim, internal and tense as ever he had been since leaving Galilee.

We rose and ate and repacked our possessions. Just as we were shifting things to our shoulders, Jesus approached us, walking briskly. 'Peace be with you,' he said by way of greeting, but didn't pause for our response. He led us immediately onto a rising, jagged path by which we would soon ascend to the high ridges east of here. Clearly, our journey had taken its second broad turning.

'Son of David?'

As we climbed, a woman began to follow us, a Syrophoenician of dark complexion and shining cheekbones, no more than twenty years old. Perhaps she'd been bought in Tyre as a slave.

'Son of David!' the woman sang out. 'Son of David!'

She came bareheaded, in the thinnest of shifts. She looked as if she'd bolted suddenly from some house, unprepared. She wore no sandals. This road was stone on stones, ruinous to the flesh. Nevertheless, she ran carelessly and hard until she came abreast of Jesus, then went ahead of him, then turned and pleaded, 'Lord, have mercy on me!'

But Jesus kept his jaw thrust forward and his lips pinched, his eye unturning – his manner no different than it had been for three days now; this was the morning of the fourth. He didn't look at the woman. He didn't answer her. His staff kept chunking at the rock. She quickly fell behind him and many of us.

'Lord,' she cried, running again, stumbling, determined to catch up. 'My daughter is wracked with a demon!'

Simon gave her no quarter. She had to go off the path to pass him by, scrambling over loose scree, climbing higher to patches of vegetation. Nor did Nathanael move aside – swinging the toolbag, it seemed to me, wider than was necessary. Nor did the gangling Judas.

'It cripples her!' the woman cried, above us now, running parallel. 'The demon throws her against walls and pitches her into the dirt. It makes her scratch her own face. Not on me, then. Have mercy on *her*!'

Judas scolded in his high voice, 'Go away.'

Just as she started to angle down towards Jesus again, Simon called, 'Master! Send the yelling foreigner away. She's bothering us. She's bothering *you*.'

This is the part which you must explain for yourselves. I won't even try to make sense of it.

Suddenly Jesus broke his stride. He raised an arm to stop us all, then drove his staff between the stones and faced the woman. His narrow expression, however, did not change. It was as brittle and sharp as the rock beneath our feet.

'I have been sent,' he said, '*only* to the lost sheep of Israel.'

Immediately the young Syrophoenician jumped down from her little height. She dropped to bare knees on the path and said, 'Lord, help my child' – slender fingers woven together, her black eyes open and fixed on Jesus.

He glared down on her. His jaw muscle pulsed. 'It is not right,' he declared, 'to take the children's bread and throw it to the dogs.'

'Yes,' she said. 'True,' she said, with scarcely a pause to breathe. 'But even the dogs eat the crumbs that fall from their masters' tables.'

Jesus stood absolutely still, as if his stance had turned to marble. The muscle in his jaw ceased bunching. His lips parted slowly. He gazed so long at the woman that Simon began to squirm and mumble in front of me. The dark supplicant on her knees, however, waited without a motion, her hands folded against her throat. She spoke no more. Maybe she'd seen a change in the face of the Lord.

'Ah, woman,' he finally said. Jesus sank down on a single knee and took her hand. 'Woman, you have great faith.' Each looked easily into the other's eyes. I smelled chamomile. She must have crushed leaves of chamomile, running off the path. 'And what you ask?' Jesus said to her. 'Go on home. It has already been granted to you.'

They stood up together.

The Syrophoenician woman now passed back down the path, her chin tucked down in sweet humility – every one of us stepping aside to let her by.

There can be no doubt. When she returned to her room, her daughter was whole and healthy.

PETER

═══

Among the gods of the pagans, among the gods of the image-makers, is one they make half man, half goat. He's an ugly sort, loutish face, goat-horns sprouting from his forehead, goatish his ears and his beard, goat the lower regions, legs and tail and the rutting part. Shepherds and goatherds delight in this god. They play the pipes they say he first constructed, cut from the reeds that once had been the girl-nymph Syrinx. They pray to him for the potency of their rams and the fruitfulness of their ewes. But then, this god is believed to increase fertility everywhere the livestock goes, wherever forests flourish and the wild beasts run. In the pagan stories, he is forever chasing pretty nymphs, blood-hot and charged for sexuality, 'playful', they say; lascivious, more likely, unpredictable. Lecherous.

He can drive whole armies of men mad with panic.

Pan. His name is Pan.

At the south-west foot of Mount Hermon is a beautiful city built on a high terrace above the northern reaches of the Jordan Valley. These days that city is called Caesarea Philippi. In centuries past, however, until Philip the son of Herod the Great expanded and improved it, the city was called Panias.

Within the city, on the lower slopes of Hermon, is an ancient, famous grotto – one of a number of natural caves – and within that grotto a shrine. From time out of mind, people have worshipped some deity here: the Baals, millennia back; and before that still, the crawling chthonian gods. Hundreds of years ago the Greeks came and devoted the grotto 'to Pan and the Nymphs'. Hence the city's older name, 'Panias'.

From this grotto springs forth a stream which, having watered the city and its terrace, flows down into the valley as one of the major sources of the Jordan River. From this grotto, then, springs the Jordan – *our* river – which feeds the Sea of Galilee, then measures the length of Israel even down to the Great Salt Sea, where the Jordan goes to die.

There is no God but the Lord!

Yet peoples and nations define themselves by the gods they worship. I have shown you the crossing of two great peoples in Caesarea Philippi, the Greeks and the Jews. Let me elaborate a third.

Less than fifty years before our own arrival at that city, Herod the Great transported blocks of a pure white marble to an area close by the grotto of pagan gods. With money the king had taxed from his people, he brought in architects and diggers and stone masons and engineers and sculptors and carpenters and legions of labourers. Herod raised a dust, and out of that dust he raised a pure white temple dedicated to his personal patron, Caesar Augustus – who had, while yet living, been proclaimed divine, a 'son of gods' – and to Roma, goddess of the city whence the empire controls the visible world. After the temple had been completed, the great Augustus himself crossed the seas to visit Herod. The two kings stood side by side on the porch of this gleaming monument to his divinity.

At an ancient site, therefore, by the grotto which had been regarded as sacred far longer than peoples can count their years, the Greeks and the Jews and the Romans converged, their sources, their stories, and – though there is but one Creator, one Lord of heaven and earth – their gods.

It was to this place that Jesus had been leading us.

It was in Caesarea Philippi that he gathered us privately together. No one recognized him here. No crowds beset us.

And finally, it was on a rocky expanse higher on Hermon than the grotto, the temple, and the headwater of the Jordan, that Jesus unlocked his mind to us, and we heard what thing had been consuming him since Galilee.

We were sitting in a sort of jumble, Jesus facing south, overlooking both the city below and the rich Jordan Valley yet lower than that. The sight was in sunlight, rinsed and completely clear.

I sat by the Lord. Throughout this last, forced journey it had increasingly become my custom to place myself beside him when we sat, when we ate, when we lay down to sleep. My love for him both strong and confused, I was grateful he did not deny me the nearness. But it was his grim, solitary manner which most drew me towards him. Whatever the mystery my Lord repressed, it was not easy on the man. I offered my presence, bones and flesh and a heart of love. No questions, though, no silly speeches of comfort. No words at all. I offered, simply, my being beside him, for – well, for companionship, I suppose. Not knowing his thought or the wrestling within him, I knew no other thing to do. I let him choose the good of it, and hoped he would discard the rest, the whole of me, if he wished.

Directly before the Lord and me, Maryam from Magdala leaned on one arm, her legs tucked under her: pale child, her thin hair lifting stiffly in these breezes up so high. Mother Mary, at the outer edges of the group, squatted as peasants do, on her heels, her knees against her breasts. Simon sat thump on the ground with his legs straight out in front of him. The rest: a jumble, as I said. We neither talked nor twiddled. We waited.

No one doubted that the Lord had something to say. He'd often chosen places 'apart' for private teachings and pronouncements, and the climb this morning – especially since all of us had received explicit signals to follow – was clearly the prelude to some important word.

He began with a question.

Looking at us from under the dark rust of his eyelashes, he asked, 'Who do people say that I am?'

Well, then: reflections upon himself? This was new. Had he been considering the weight and the extent of his name these days? His influence?

After a moment when none of us spoke, several disciples answered at once:

'Herod says, and others say too, that you're John the Baptizer come back again.'

'Some think you're the Elijah who went to heaven on a whirlwind, never dead, ever prepared to return to the earth.'

'Jeremiah!'

'Any one of the prophets of old. Take your pick.'

Jesus nodded and nodded his trim head until the answers exhausted themselves, and people fell silent again. Then he said, 'But what about you?' And, looking directly into Simon's eyes: 'Who do you say I am?'

And Simon answered immediately: 'You are the Messiah, the Son of the living God.'

'Yes,' said Jesus with such resolution that we all released a sigh. Simon's mouth split in grinning. Jesus picked up his staff. 'Blessed are you, Simon son of John,' he continued, granting Simon the full radiance of his favour: 'for flesh and blood has not revealed this truth to you. My Father in heaven revealed it to you!'

Then, reaching the end of his staff far enough to touch it to Simon's shoulder, speaking with a quiet formality: 'And I tell you, you are Peter, my rock-man. On this rock' (*tap, tap, tap*) 'I will build my church – and the gates of hell will not prevail against it.'

Rock-man.

Peter.

A new name. As God gave Jacob his new name? O my Lord, something grand is happening here!

Jesus withdrew the staff, placed it across his knees, and kept on speaking. 'Listen closely,' he said, 'I will give you the keys of the kingdom of heaven. Whatever you bind on earth – while yet you walk on the earth – will be bound in heaven, and whatever you loose on earth, it will be loosed in heaven.'

'Ho ho ho.' This was Simon laughing softly, but laughing. He didn't get up. In fact, he'd flopped flat on the ground, seeming struck with wonder. There was merriment in his eyes. If there was also understanding in his mind, he was a quicker student than I. I recognized with joy that Jesus had uttered a particular and personal blessing on Simon, for his confession, for his receiving the Father's revelation. But what he said thereafter – 'church', 'the gates of hell', 'the keys of the kingdom of heaven' – I could not understand. Not then. Not till a long time later. And I'm guessing that Simon, so jovial in the moment, paid no attention to Jesus' words; or else, without any real examination, he simply assumed he understood. I base my guess on what he did not ten minutes later.

But the big disciple was not given to brooding! And he had

every right to laugh, to enjoy the sweet stroke of Jesus' staff, and to bathe in his fresh blessing. We joined him. We grinned and giggled at the sight of our brother, his vast belly rolling and holding his laughter like swells on the sea.

'Simon Peter!' we chorused. 'Simon *Peter!*' testing the name, teasing our 'bully' brother. 'What's your wife going to call you now? Stone-head? Rocky?'

Soon enough Jesus rose up and knocked the butt of his staff on bare stone. Apparently he was not finished. Moreover, the thin expression had returned to his face. Not that he was not pleased with our behaviour. I don't think it mattered. Rather, he was gazing dead ahead again, into that black tomorrow.

Laughter died. We turned to him. He did not sit. He remained standing, staring south. His staff leaned against Mount Hermon. And I, from my position below, saw an eagle sailing above, swooping, circling on the mountain thermals.

'Listen to me, every one of you,' Jesus said. 'This is what must happen to me. This is what *will* happen. The next long journey which we must make will be, slowly, slowly, up to Jerusalem. We will arrive there in time for the Passover. Then, in that city, I will be tormented by the leaders, the chief priests, the scribes – '

Simon Peter sat up, his nostrils flaring.

If Jesus noticed, he gave no sign. 'I will be tormented,' he said, 'and I will be killed – '

Simon was on his feet, aghast.

' – but on the third day – ' Jesus still was speaking. I don't think Simon heard him. He was moving forward through the group, working his mouth against some sour word.

' – but on the third day I will be raised to life – '

At that point Simon Peter swept by Jesus, grabbing his elbow and pulling him aside.

'God forbid this, Lord!' The disciple's breath rushed out in a hoarse whisper. He couldn't know how loud he was speaking. 'Master, what you're talking about – no. No! This must never happen to you!'

By a quick twist and remarkable strength, Jesus snapped free of the bigger man. He whirled to face him. 'Whom do you worship?' His voice was a knife, his lips curled inward. His eyes shot fire. 'Whom do you serve? God? And only him?' Jesus slapped his hands together right in front of Simon's face, then whirled away again. 'Satan, begone!' Jesus cried, slapping his hands twice more. 'Get *behind* me, you stone for stumbling! You've set your mind on matters of humanity, not on matters divine!'

It could not have been worse if Jesus had cracked the disciple with blows across his face. Simon Peter staggered backward till he hit the moss-covered stone and slid down into a crooked heap, his mouth open, his eyes wide and horrified, he himself gone speechless.

Hardly modulating the tone, the Lord continued to speak, now to the whole group:

'If any one of you plans to come after me, you'd better take up your cross to follow me! If you strive to save your life, you're going to lose it. But if you're willing to lose your life for my sake, you will find it.

'What good would it be if you gained the whole world only to lose your life? Or what could you give in *return* for your life?

'Those who are ashamed of me and of my words... of them will the Son of man be ashamed when he comes in his glory, in the glory of the Father, with the holy angels. Listen to me: there are some standing here who will not taste death before they see the coming of the kingdom of heaven.'

Jesus turned one more time, took up his staff, and walked off down the mountain, leaving us behind to make up our minds, whether to follow.

Let me set it down for the record:

The first to spring up and go loping after Jesus was Judas Iscariot, bubbling with excitement. 'Jerusalem, says he? Yessir! Yessir, the man has a plan, and I knew it! That city's the very centre of things! And I *know* the place like the back of my hand!'

The widow Mary left slowly, heavily, leaning on the arm of her younger friend, Joanna.

Nathanael wondered aloud whether Jesus had need of his tools any more. No one offered an insight. He picked them up and slung them over his shoulder and took his way downwards alone.

Maryam from Magdala would likewise have slipped off the

mountain alone, like a wraith, like the pale vapour of sorrowful sighing. But Matthew saw the child's distress – as if it had been her objection, not Simon's, which Jesus had lashed with his tongue. Therefore, the tall publican rose wordlessly and followed some little distance after Maryam so that she need not know she had a protector. By silent, long-legged striding and an expression that signified nothing but numbers behind it, Matthew made the child his charge and saw her safely down.

The last to leave was Simon. Peter. When there were but two of us, I went to him and knelt and laid my hand on the back of his neck. For a long time he neither spoke nor moved. Finally he said, 'Leave me alone.'

I did.

I shouldn't wonder if he stayed on that mountain shelf the entire night and half the following day. Fasting, surely. Praying?

Though I didn't dare say anything to Jesus, I prayed to the Father on Simon's account.

SHEPHERD

Did shepherds among the Greeks make supplications to that goat-man, that rutting, ugly idol, Pan? Did they play his pipes and sing his songs and, by their pagan rites, beseech him for the new life of their billys and their nannys, their rams and their ewes?

Well, then I have songs to match their songs. And I have truth to put their tales to shame.

Perhaps the shepherds and goatherds exaggerate his appetites. Perhaps their tales were born of the dreams of perfervid minds, giving shape to shadows within themselves, not to shadows without.

Or – what's likeliest in a world aswarm with spirits – this is the case: that the goat-god lives; but what they offer Pan is offered in fact to a demon; and nothing but demons are the nymphs, the naiads of their springs, their fountains, their pools, the dryads of their woods.

If so, then I have the word that must shut the mouths of the hosts of that liar, the Devil.

On the first and the second days, Jesus said:

In truth, in perfect truth I tell you that those who do not enter the sheepfold through the gate are thieves and robbers. But the one who enters plainly by the gate: he is the shepherd of the sheep. The sheep hear his voice. He calls each one of his sheep by name, then leads them out of the fold. When he has brought out all that are his own, he goes on ahead of them, and they follow him, because they know his voice.

They will not follow a stranger! They'll run scared from the voices of strangers, alien voices, unfamiliar.

Ever since I was a child I've known the songs of the great King David. Neither Simon nor I could sing, though between the two of us I knew the lack and he did not. But I have a head for memory. I could recite much of the Psalter. And I could pray.

During the third and the fourth days, I prayed the words that David sang, often, out loud, alone, in the privacy of the night, and in particular for Simon Peter, who was not there to hear the Lord with tenderness say, *I AM.*

I stood upright under the stars and prayed:

Into the valley of shadows, sheep
  Tumble towards death;
A staff to catch (and a rod to keep
  Us) hauls us back.

Into the valleys of dappled pools
  And spring grass, green,
The shepherd leads us, flocks and fools,
  To live; drink; feed.

'Come! Feed on the sweetmeats of your foes,'
  The Lord God cries;
'And down your brows I'll pour the oils
  Of majesty!'

I do. I come. And mercy grooms
  Me, O my Saviour —
That I within your holy rooms
  May dwell forever.

During the third, the fourth and fifth days while we lingered in the villages near Caesarea Philippi, waiting for Simon Peter to return and to join us again (I simply could not believe he would separate himself from us, for what life did he have apart from his 'Messiah'?), Jesus continued to speak to the company in figures, in riddles of a hundred meanings.

He said:

I AM the good shepherd. The good shepherd lays down his life for the sheep!

The hired hand can't be the shepherd. He will not be: he doesn't own the sheep. When he sees the yellow-eyed wolf approach, that rabbit will leap, run squealing away, allowing the wolf to ravage and scatter the flock. He runs because he's hired. He does not love the sheep.

I AM the good shepherd. I know my own, and my own know me – just as the Father knows me and I know the Father.

And I lay down my life for the sheep.

I have other sheep that do not yet belong to this fold. I will surely bring them in as well. They will learn my voice as I call them each by name, and in the end there will be one flock and one shepherd.

This, then, little children: this is why the Father loves me, because I am his love below. For I lay down my life… and will take it up again.

Listen! No one takes it from me! I lay it down of my own free will; I have the power to lay it down. And I have the power to take it up again, which powers I receive by obeying the command of my Father – which is to love you.

And I give my sheep eternal life. They will not perish. No one can snatch them out of my hand.

My Father, who gives them to me, is greater than all. No one can snatch them out of the Father's hand.

The Father and I are one.

On the morning of the sixth day, Simon appeared. Whether he had known our location for some time already, and had worked that long to gain the courage for facing the Lord; or whether he really didn't know where we were, and had to spend his days in searching us out, I never asked him. Nor did he offer to tell me. He just walked up to the group and took a place as far from Jesus as he could.

Maryam from Magdala saw him. She frowned and seemed to consider him carefully awhile: he was a man aggrieved. He couldn't raise his face to look at anyone. There were pouches under his eyes, burrs in his clothing and his hair; his fingernails were bitten and filthy.

Finally, quietly, Maryam went over and sat down beside him. She tucked her legs beneath her robe. She didn't talk. She didn't touch. She didn't even look at Simon. She just sat and gazed away.

Jesus said:

Have no fear, little flock. It is your Father's good pleasure to give you the kingdom. Have no fear.

Shortly before noon on the sixth day, before the sun had reached its zenith somewhat south of us, I watched as Jesus walked over and crouched on his heels before the crushed disciple. He regarded Simon Peter with his eyebrows arched, his hands relaxed between his knees.

'Simon? My rock?' he said. 'Would you look at me?'

The big man slowly shook his head. 'I can't.'

'Why not?'

After a moment, Simon said, 'I think it would burn my eyes in their sockets.'

Jesus kept his position and closed his mouth a moment, eyebeams playing like dapples across the face of the other.

'Simon?'

'What.'

'My rock, my stone? My rock again?'

'What?'

'Look at me.'

Again, Simon shook his head.

Jesus shifted his weight, reached forward, and took hold of Simon's chin whiskers. He pulled the great head up. But the eyes were squeezed shut, the cheeks bunched and straining beneath them.

'Look at me. I have something to show you.'

A flicker of eyelid, and Simon caught himself already looking. He blushed.

Jesus was smiling.

Simon allowed his eyes to dart around, though his head was trapped by the chin whiskers.

'Show me what?' he said.

'Oh, not here,' said Jesus. 'Up there.' He pointed. 'Please, my bully boy: climb the mountain with me.'

Next he asked John to bring his staff.

And he asked James to come forward with John.

Then the four of them climbed Mount Hermon for several hours together.

HIS FACE RADIANT

There are many temples on Hermon, high and low, and chapels carved into the rock of the mountain itself. (But the voice of the Lord, the God of Israel can make the mighty, grey-haired Hermon *skip like a wild young ox*. So sings David.) There are great terraces on its western slopes, where the rain and the dewfall nourish plum trees, cherry trees, pears, almonds. The southern slopes are steeper and rougher. Here the face of the mountain has cracked and grizzled in places, creating fissures and narrow valleys. A path ascends to remarkable heights; villagers from the foothills climb it even to the snows at the top of the mountain, some to worship, some to bring back boats of snow to chill their foods and their drinks below.

Jesus, Simon, John, and James went up by way of this path. Not so far as the snow, but – having departed the path and angled a distance eastwards – to fastnesses of low bush and bare stone.

Jesus didn't speak while they climbed. Neither did he breathe more heavily than had they been hiking on flat land. The three disciples, likewise, did not talk; but that may be due to their puffings and blowings. Simon especially laboured to heave his bulk upwards, stripping down first to his tunic and then to his loincloth despite the cold and the winds at these elevations.

These elevations: through the clear, cloudless air we could see as far south as the Gilead mountains and the Sea of Galilee. How many nations were visible from the summit? All the nations of the world, could it be, from so sacred a place?

Jesus stopped.

'Stay here,' he said to the three.

He went a little farther on his own, down a grade, up a grade, until he stood on a singular rocky prominence. There, again, he stopped. He began to turn around –

And by the time he'd completed the turn towards the three men watching, the Lord Jesus had been transfigured.

His face became radiant, as bright as the sun, burning dark spots into the sight of the astonished disciples. His clothing dazzled them, flashing like sunlight on the sea. They blinked. They rubbed their eyes and looked and saw suddenly that two others were standing with Jesus. One was Moses! – holding the staff that once had split the Red Sea into two walls of water. The other was Elijah, who had not died, but had been lifted on a fiery whirlwind into heaven. They and the Lord were talking together.

'Lord!' Simon Peter shouted, sweating, panting at the glorious sight. 'It's so good to *be* here! If you want, I'll make three tabernacles, for you, for Moses, for Elijah – '

But even while he was speaking, there came boiling down from heaven a cloud of pure white fire, a pillar of sparkling fire which fixed itself between the earth and the vaults above. The disciples fell to the ground in terror. The brilliance felt like flame against their faces. They covered their eyes in the crooks of their arms.

And out of the pillar upon the mountain a voice like thunder uttered words which they could – which these poor mortals *could* – understand:

THIS IS MY BELOVED SON, WITH WHOM I AM WELL PLEASED. HEAR HIM! OBEY HIM!

Simon shook uncontrollably. His teeth clacked like sticks against a fencing.

But then he felt hands on the sides of his head, and the shivering stilled, and warmth overwhelmed him, and he opened his eyes and saw no one but Jesus only, kneeling, gazing steadfastly down on him, two freckles on his eyelid – the common man.

Jesus arched his eyebrows as if in inquiry.

But he said, 'Don't be afraid, my magnificent, immovable Rock.' He tugged at Peter's ear. 'Get up. Put your clothes back on.'

No, but he was speaking to all three of them. He was touching them each on their temples.

'What need of tabernacles,' Jesus smiled, 'when you've got me to cover you?'

As they descended the mountain into the darkness that had begun to pool below, Jesus ordered them to say nothing of what they had seen until the Son of man had risen from the dead.

And in all the days to come, they kept the secret to themselves.

Except that Simon Peter whispered once in John's ear: 'What do you think Jesus means, "Risen from the dead"?'

$\mathcal{M}$ARY

CHILDREN

===

As long as Jesus moved among the villages in Galilee, Mary was able to accomplish certain domestic tasks. When they stayed for several days in one place, she would borrow some woman's loom and weave clothing for the group; if Jesus walked on to another village before she was done, Joanna and one of the men would remain with her until she finished. She was teaching her younger friend how to weave (wasn't it this very skill that had brought them together in the first place?), and seldom did Jesus go farther than a few miles at a time.

Mary supposed they might have carried a horizontal loom from place to place, pegging the beams to the ground when she used it. But, lacking beasts, they had to travel light. And the work could get tangled if it wasn't finished before they had to unpeg it and pack it for a later opportunity.

Likewise, she borrowed clay pots for cooking and ovens for baking and small stone mills for grinding their grain.

While they still moved at an easy pace, Mary could wander the hillsides and the ravines, gathering herbs, leaves, roots, blossoms, fruit, bark – medicines and remedies for the health and the comfort of the group. She had the time to dry them, to crush or boil or make a paste of them.

From the hills near Cana she took squill. It calmed vomiting. And scales from its bulb – dried and sliced – eased the stomach gripes of travelling folk, who often were poisoned by food too old or poorly cooked. In the spring Mary found anemones to cool the fevers of the disciples. Wild mint carpeting the lowlands, wild mint from the fields near Magdala, fought infection in bloody cuts and open injuries. And she knew how to draw resin from the bark of a gum tree, which, as a lotion, healed those cuts and injuries. More than that, the resin helped relieve the brutal coughings Simon Peter sometimes suffered.

Mary had left her home. She hadn't left her craft and her wisdom behind. She loved to do, and she loved the effects of her doing.

But then her son closed his mouth and turned their comfortable wanderings into a steady journey with a destination and a goal. They were going to Jerusalem. Not even entering villages on the way. Jesus was keeping the group close to himself and apart from crowds (as much as was possible) and was teaching them – teaching his followers particularly – of the life of the kingdom coming.

No longer could she spend time finding the right medicinals. No longer could she grind. No longer weave: Mary had to patch the rips and the holes in their clothing. Chuza had joined them when they passed south from Mount Hermon through Galilee. Good thing. He brought monies with which to buy the bread she hadn't time or place to bake any more. He had given his house and his possessions away, a gift to his daughter and son-in-law, and severed all ties with his past life.

(Chuza came with them. Bad thing. When Herod Antipas heard that the influence which this peasant prophet wielded had grown strong enough to draw his own stewards out of his own household, the ruler sought to kill the Lord. Jesus said, *Go, tell that fox, 'Behold, I cast out demons and perform cures today and tomorrow; and on the third day I must, I will complete my course. For it cannot be that a prophet should perish away from Jerusalem!'*)

Moreover, even if she could have continued her sweet, rewarding chores, Mary would scarcely have noticed. All domesticity had gone out of the widow. Her heart had been wrenched. She'd lost the love of it.

Judas Iscariot had begun to annoy her. He fairly skipped through Galilee, flapping his featherless arms, jabbering with a giddy joy: 'Going to Jerusalem! Belly button of the universe! Got a plan, you bet, my Master the king of the hill, and who knows the city better than me!'

Why, that whippersnapper could scarcely sprout ten whiskers on his lip! Thin straggles at his jawline, his fingernails bitten to the quick, deaf to the wisdom or the example of his elders, oblivious to the deep streams in her son and the austere nobility of their progress: self-important juvenile! What was he by now? Seventeen? Nineteen?

'They think they're so wonderful! Wait'll a *real* wonder-worker shows up! Think they're so powerful? Can beat the people down for profit? Ha! Here comes *their* beating, wait and see!'

'Jerusalem?' Chuza asked, fingering his beard with apprehension. He was dark-skinned, his face indistinct in the darkness. 'No. Not Jerusalem.'

Mary said, 'His mind's made up.'

'OK, Jerusalem,' the stocky land-manager relented. 'But not now. People need Jesus all over Israel. Israel? All over the world! Why, my own homeland, my troubled Nabatea, needs mercy and healing. Oh, Mary: persuade him that Jerusalem can wait – at least till after the Passover.'

Joanna's husband was having a tough time adjusting to this nomadic life. The poor, portly initiate: Chuza had to learn to walk and to eat all over again. His weight, his tender feet and uncallused hands, the scrabble ground, lack of a mattress, lack of a bath, plain food, vegetable food, the embarrassment of eating always as a guest, never as the wealthy host, discomposed him more than he had anticipated.

Chuza was game and uncomplaining; but he was also slow and sore and bleeding. Presently Mary was binding his feet with strips of linen soaked in a boiled mint and olive oil. It was late evening. Light came from a dying fire.

'We can handle the multitudes,' she said while working. 'I think this is a passing thing, Chuza, his wanting to be alone.'

'No, no, not the multitudes. The multitudes might be the spark, but they're not the fire that will consume him.'

Mary paused. She pulled a brand from the fire, blew it bright and held it by Chuza's face: the man was deadly earnest, little eyes unwavering. His caution did not come from pampered wealth but from a pragmatism of long experience.

'What do you know, Chuza?' Mary asked. 'What danger awaits us?'

He removed the brand from Mary's hand and laid it back on the fire. In shadow, then, he answered. 'The governor always attends the Passover.'

'Yes.'

'He brings a large and well-armed regiment. Force to fight a riot, if he has to. They'll stand on the roofs of the Temple porticoes. They will stare down into the courts of the Temple, watching the flow of pilgrims – '

'Yes. I know that. I've seen it myself.'

'This governor, this Pontius Pilate – in office what? four, five years now? – has shown himself both shrewd and ruthless. His purposes are purely Roman. He'll keep order by killing a few if he can, by killing the lot if he must. There is no negotiation.'

'Chuza,' Mary spoke softly. 'Why do you raise the matter now? Twenty years ago my husband went up to Jerusalem alone, then surprised me by coming back *before* the end of the festival. He said he'd been run off, barely escaping with his life. The ruler, trying to contain an insurrection, sent mounted cavalry against the tents of the pilgrims. The man was himself a Jew. But on that day Archelaus, the son of King Herod, slaughtered more than three thousand Jews.'

'Mary, please. Pilate will never be so rash. If he were, I'd say we were safer.'

Chuza leaned forward a degree or so and reached hard for his bandaged feet. In Cana a servant must surely have strapped his sandals on; the new disciple's stomach was an impediment to his own operations. Mary would have helped him, if she weren't so absorbed in the conversation. And it was dark now, the fire having fallen altogether into coals.

'This governor picks the leaders,' Chuza grunted. 'Last year he noticed a flow of pilgrims both closer and larger than usual, noticed them as they were leaving the Temple gates on account of the racket they made. His soldiers identified five figures as central to that flow. The men were carrying the lambs they'd only just sacrificed, no weapon, no threat except for the size of the group and a kind of fanatical singing. Shouting, stomping, dancing. I'd have called it the transport of joy.'

Chuza stood up. So did Mary. He winced. She was fixed on his words, not his person, and did nothing.

'Pilate's men came quietly behind and pierced the five through and through with spears: through their lambs and through their bellies, so that the blood of the men and the blood of their sacrifices mingled on the steps of the Temple. They were Galileans. It's the only reason I know the story. No one noticed. There was no outcry.'

Now he took Mary by the shoulders and shook her resistless body. 'Mother, talk to your son. I've seen the crowds that Jesus draws. It is no secret; he *is* the draw; nor does he know how to blend. Please. Politic Pontius Pilate would be content to silence even the hint of a riot by the death of one.'

Where are your angels? Your holy angels? Where is Gabriel, whom you sent to tell me of Yeshi's coming? Why don't I see angels, O God, ascending and descending on my son, even as he said I would see them?

The widow Mary is praying.

On this particular night she has stolen away from the rest of the disciples and found the place where Jesus himself is praying, his arms lifted up, himself on top of a knoll, alone. She will not disturb him. She will not because she cannot. It is the thing she renounced in order to be with him at all. Chuza knew not what he was asking. He had filled her with torment in order that her son might take that torment and change. But what had Chuza accomplished? Only to fill Mary with a torment which she could not release, which she couldn't give away, which she must bear within herself as once she bore her baby.

These latter days were getting harder and harder.

O you angels! O you mighty ones who do his bidding, who obey the voice of the Lord! O you, all his hosts! O you ministers that do his will, come! Come! Come down and counsel his beloved Son that life is better than death, and healing better than affliction!

On the other hand, there were certain consolations along the way.

Oh, my soul: what sort of paradox is this? Exactly when he had set his face towards Jerusalem and seemed consumed by his 'destiny' there, Yeshi had begun to reveal a tenderness altogether new in him and heartwarming in his mother: for children.

He grew restless when other people, strangers, seekers, challengers, intruded on the privacy of the group – call it the 'family' – that surrounded him. But the approach of a curious kid would immediately seize his fond attentions, and he smiled and softened and caused some small mending of his mother's heart.

When they had sneaked by night into Capernaum, one last time to sleep and to eat in Simon Peter's house, under the kind ministrations of his wife and her mother, Jesus asked the disciples what they had been arguing about.

It was bright morning. Most of them were sitting in the courtyard, having finished breakfast. They would leave again that evening after dark.

'Arguing?' said James, John's brother. 'What do you mean?'

'I heard voices last night.'

They all went silent and hung their heads. They knew what the Master meant. In fact, the boys had fallen to fussing over which of them was the greatest.

Jesus glanced out the doorway of the courtyard. 'Leah,' he whispered. 'Pretty Leah?'

A child no more than four years old, a little bubble-tummy girl with fly-away hair, looked inside and smiled.

Jesus sat on the ground and crossed his legs. 'Come here,' he whispered. 'Here, pretty Leah. Sit by me.'

She did. She dashed into the courtyard and threw herself against his chest. He hugged her. (Mary's hand flew to her mouth.) Then he turned the child around and sat her between the wings of his knees.

'This, friends, is greatness,' Jesus announced while Leah stuffed his sleeve into her mouth and sucked happily. 'Great in her lowliness. Listen carefully,' he said: 'Unless you turn, each one of you, and become like a child, you will never enter the kingdom of heaven. Those who humble themselves exactly like my Leah, *they* are the greatest in the kingdom of heaven.'

The child was looking here and there around the hovering group of adults, all looking back at her with mild astonishment. Jesus had his arms around her. She was unafraid, merely curious.

'Kiss me, Leah,' he said.

She twisted around and made a smacking sound in the folds of his robe, then rubbed her face there as if it were itchy. Jesus snorted. He hiccupped and quickly turned her back around, ducking to cover his grin. Of course. Ticklish.

Mary watched her son, a half smile playing at her lips, water in her eyes. Was it ordained that the gentle Yeshi must never be a father?

Oh, her beautiful boy!

So many of the men whom Mary knew considered children as nothing more than property, inferior, lacking rights and status. They were fed and kept for what they might become, not for what they were. They were taught holy codes and duties – and maybe a trade, if they were male – through strict obedience and terrible punishments, whacked like donkeys, drubbed like dogs in the doorway. *Do not hold discipline back from a child! If you beat him with a rod, he will not die. If you beat him with a rod, you will save his life from* Sheol! Abraham and Sarah rejoiced to bear a child. Rachel pined for one. Hannah begged for one. Even Mary's cousin Elizabeth, when she found that she was pregnant, wept, saying, 'God has removed the reproach that was upon me!' Nevertheless, in the cities and the villages and the courtyards and the houses, parents had absolute authority over their children; thus it had ever been: *Whoever curses his father or his mother shall be put to death.* And so what? So parents impoverished, and fathers who had been driven into debt, had in the past and did in the present sell their children into slavery, daughters first and then their sons.

Who, then, would ever choose to exalt a child – a little girl! – as the model of piety before our God? Yeshi. Who would praise inferiority? Who would call the *loss* of status and a baby-dependency 'greatest' in the kingdom of heaven? Yeshi. Yeshi would. And did. But then, he had spoken of God as *his* Father ever since he was a child of twelve years. And he had invited the rest of them to do the same. *When you pray, say: 'Our Father who art in heaven –* '

Yeshi wants, thought Mary, *a whole new kind of family.* In which, in fact, she had no status as a parent. At least, not in regard to him any more. She had accepted the changes, though before God, *that* Father, she would remain forever the mother of Jesus!

But once she had collected her nappy-headed four-year-old

against her breast and whispered, 'Kiss me,' and he had whirled around and kissed her as easily and playfully as Leah had kissed Jesus just now. Once. And therefore the water in her eyes.

'Whoever welcomes one such child in my name welcomes me,' Jesus was saying, rocking left and right with the child in his arms. 'But if anyone causes the little ones, my children or else my baby believers, to sin! – why, it would be better for him to have a millstone hung around his neck, and to be thrown into the depths of the sea.

'Be careful never to despise the little ones who believe in me. I tell you, their angels inhabit heaven, where they gaze forever and ever upon the face of my Father.'

Mary remembered meeting Eleazar the Pharisee in the Temple long ago, when Yeshi had been lost and then, for the first time, had stunned her with his knowledge of his 'Father'. There, in Solomon's Portico, Mary had not spoken to the gap-toothed teacher. Joseph had. And these days she was downright grateful that she hadn't granted him the courtesy, whatever the reason.

Why should the self-important Pharisee turn a chance exchange with an intelligent boy into some heavy obligation which Jesus, the *man* now, must owe him his life long? Why take things so personally? And why turn a personal disappointment into such a public war? Arrogant son of a cockroach!

Eleazar's great and wounded sorrow regarding her son was an insult, pure and simple. Covering his eyes in Jesus' presence, indeed! Eleazar, the lover of the laws of God? Ha! What about the six hundred and sixty laws his kind had ravelled out of the good cloth of heaven's commandments? A *fence* to protect those commandments, did they say? *Ha!* Yeshi was not destroying this people by breaking their laws; Yeshi was breaking down the fence and calling people back to the very core of Torah: Love God. Love your neighbour.

Eleazar's sorrow couldn't be anything less than hypocrisy. His seeming interest in her son's career covered wicked designs: *The Pharisees are conspiring together, my friend.* Mary could not shake the bandit's warning from her brains: *Right now they are preparing plans for your destruction.* It's the reason why they were moving through Galilee mostly at night.

Nevertheless, this Eleazar, feeling the heavy-hearted call to save the nation from the excesses and the blasphemies of her son, found him out one more time, and one more time tried to trap him in his own words. His traps, however, had been fixed with iron teeth – for he approached Jesus not only with his regular gang of Pharisees and lawyers but also now with men in Herod's employ, at whose request the soldiers of Herod would draw their swords.

He waylaid Jesus at eventide – in the ancient city of Jarmuth on a hill so high that a woman could see over the Jordan Valley into Gilead. Eleazar stepped out of a walled alley sighing and groaning, giving everyone to believe that, out of some deep paternal and misguided love, he was offering Jesus just one more chance to prove his wisdom.

'Teacher,' Eleazar said, his hand on the little box bound to his forehead, 'we know that you are a man of integrity. You defer to no one. You refuse to treat people according to their status, but you teach the ways of God in accordance with the truth.'

Jesus said, 'Indeed.'

Mary wanted to punch the old man on his nose! She wanted to yank the hairs of his scraggly beard or slap that hand away from his eyes and *make* him look at Jesus!

'Teacher?' Here it was. The question, the trap: 'Is it right to pay taxes to Caesar, or isn't it? Should we pay them, or shouldn't we?'

There, immediately beside her son, stood Simon Peter and James and John, whose fathers had nearly been killed by the taxes of Rome. And there stood Matthew, who once was despised because he gathered Roman taxes. How could Jesus agree to taxation without risking the wrath of his own kind, the people whom he loved?

But there, beside Eleazar, stood Herod's dumb functionaries who taxed the people as much as Rome did and who flourished on the goodwill of the emperor. How could Jesus reject taxation without risking *their* wrath and his own arrest, in consequence, for subverting the government?

Mary wanted to walk over and kick the man in his pusillanimous ankles. Liar! Hypocrite!

Jesus remained calm. His eyes were steadfast upon the

Pharisee. His complexion had darkened somewhat, but his elegant head neither shook nor nodded. He held his peace so long that Eleazar actually spread his fingers and peeped up to be sure that his adversary hadn't simply walked away. He hadn't. The fingers closed again.

'Pharisee,' Jesus asked, 'why are you trying to trap me?'

Eleazar cleared his throat. 'No such thing,' he said. 'Didn't I just heap praise upon you?'

Jesus said, 'OK. I'll take your question in the spirit with which it was asked. I'll answer. Bring me a coin. A denarius. Let's have a look at it.'

No one moved. By now Judas Iscariot was carrying the money that served the whole group. Most of what Chuza had brought with him went into his money box – perhaps because he, Judas, was the quickest and the happiest to fly into town whenever a purchase was necessary: importance, excitement, adventure, and now and then a thing for himself. He'd bought a sword in Sepphoris: 'For the plan of the Master. You heard what the bandit said.'

But even Judas stayed put just now. His Master hadn't asked the coin of *him*.

Eleazar elbowed the servant next to him. That servant glanced first at the Pharisee and then at Jesus and then back at the Pharisee.

'Do it,' Eleazar said sorrowfully, patient, willing to honour a divergent request in order to get to an answer. 'Show him a coin. This we know: he will not steal it.' A pause; then: 'It's not in his character. To steal.'

The servant fumbled under his robe and brought out the silver coin and reached it to Jesus.

'No. Don't give it to me,' Jesus said. 'Look at it and tell me for yourself: whose image is on the face of the coin? Whose title is written there?'

The servant drew it back and tried to show the coin to Eleazar, who shook his head, likewise choosing to have nothing to do with the coin. Glancing here and there and everywhere, as if someone else should relieve him of the money and the duty, the servant finally blinked at it and mumbled, 'Um. Well. It's Caesar's head. Caesar's image, I mean.'

'Eleazar, my answer,' Jesus said. 'Give to Caesar the things that are Caesar's. Give to God the things that are God's.'

'You can't – ' the Pharisee began to say.

His servant looked at him anxiously. 'Sir?'

Eleazar: 'You can't break coins like breaking bread.'

'Sir?'

'Put your money away! We're going home.'

Herodians, now! And the threat of a royal arrest, even as John had been arrested and imprisoned in Machaerus. But: *It cannot be that a prophet should perish away from Jerusalem.*

That same night Jesus left Galilee and Herod's capital, Tiberias. He crossed the Jordan eastwards into the regions of the Decapolis, where the family camped and slept. In the morning they followed the route that brought them by mid-afternoon to Pella, a city busy rebuilding itself. It had been destroyed a hundred years before. Its people had lingered awhile in their ruins, while others, Jews, moved in. A fine spring of water and good rains and a mild winter made the site rich and productive. And then the Romans brought purpose and money and hope –

After cockcrow, but yet in the cool of the morning, the day after their arrival, Mary and Joanna borrowed clay jars and went down to the spring for water. Ahead of them they heard the chattering, laughing, gossiping of women already gathered there. If men met in the gates of the cities to conduct their business, women met at wells and springs and pools. Mary liked the sense of it.

Their empty jars on their heads, Mary and Joanna joined the women and walked to the stones where the springwater pooled. Some of these women sat nursing their babies, causing in Mary's motherly spirit soft cooings of her own. Others had slung their babies at their backs. And little children dashed hither and thither while their mothers chirped like birds in a bush.

But Mary couldn't help but pay special attention to a small boy who moved painfully in slow circles, a crutch tucked underneath his arm. His right leg was thin, shortened and bent acutely sideways at the knee. He went round and round the stick-crutch, solemn-faced, going nowhere.

'Honey?' Mary set her jar on the stone wall and moved towards him. He paused. 'Where's your mother, darling?' He gazed back at her. 'Did you come with your mother?'

Slowly, he shook his head.

'Did you come to the water alone?' He shook his head. Infirmity had written age into his watchful eyes. What could one so crippled do hereafter but beg for his livelihood? 'Well, can you tell me who brought you here?'

He pointed.

An old woman, herself hunched severely at the shoulders, had just filled a water jug and was dragging it towards a small two-wheeled cart. A goat stood in the traces. Apparently both the jug and the child would be carried home. Someone's grandma would be walking.

All right: when*ever* had Mary resisted her impulse? In an instant she was beside the old woman. Gently she lifted the jug and carried it to the cart and set it inside.

'Mother,' she said to the woman who watched her with almost the same mute expression as did the little boy. 'I know a man who can bless the child.'

All around the pool women broke off their conversations. One by one they turned to consider this wild-haired stranger now come among them, speaking of blessings and of –

'I know a man,' Mary said, 'who can heal the child. Can straighten him. Can make him walk upright and properly.'

One of those who nursed their infants called, 'What man? What's his name?'

Somewhat surprised, Mary swivelled her head and sought the speaker.

'Well, he's my son, you see.' She paused, smiling.

'Not much of a help, sister. We all have sons. And we all have something to say for them.'

Quite clearly, lifting her chin, Mary declared, 'His name is Jesus. He comes from Nazareth. He is a prophet powerful in word and in deed!'

'Really?' A hushed wonder reduced the voice. Women's mouths began to open. Little poppings where infants lost their nipples. '*That* Jesus is your son?'

'Yes. That Jesus.'

215

'Where is he?'

'Here. In Pella.'

'Woman! Blessed are your breasts! Where in Pella?'

Suddenly Mary caught herself. She glanced at Joanna, who looked somewhat worried.

'Well,' said Mary. 'Well, I'm not sure. I – well, I was only inviting this grandmother and that boy.'

Immediately she put her lips near the old woman's ear. 'Do you want to come?' she whispered. 'Do you want to bring the child?'

The grandmother gripped Mary's arm with surprising strength and nodded. Already Joanna was leading the boy towards the cart. Mary took the thin bridle that led the goat and, smiling, greeting and goodbye-ing the rest of the women, started back the way they had come.

It was a climb towards the city. No one talked. The grandmother worked hard to stay abreast of the other women. Mary wanted to run. But she did not want to break the silent woman beside her. Controlling *this* impulse was a mighty act.

As they approached the place where Jesus was – a narrow tableland west of the city – they heard an earnest gaggling behind them. They'd been followed! Women old and young, their children in arms, their children behind them, likewise were bustling up the Pella paths. What could Mary do? Just at the edge of their camp she was overtaken. Several of the disciples, barked and jumped up. Shoulder to shoulder, a kind of militia themselves, they moved forward. 'What do you want here?' the men accosted this great wave of women. 'You have no purpose here!'

'We do!' the women answered. 'We want to see Jesus!'

'Go on! Go on! Get out of here!'

'Jesus?' cried every mother among them. 'Jesus, bless our children! Lay your hands upon our children!'

Simon Peter dropped his shoulders and spread his big arms, preparing to drive the women by force away.

'Simon, stop it!' Mary yelled. 'You're going to hurt someone!'

Ah, when would she learn to shut her mouth? When would she truly trust her son to know and to do the right?

Because, look: Jesus was already behind the brutish disciple, quietly driving *him* aside.

And in the moment when everyone, men on one side, women on the other, saw the Lord in their midst, his arms raised up as if in prayer, the whole congregation fell quiet.

And no one did not hear his words: 'Let the little children come to me.' He was looking at the boy in the cart, walking in that direction. 'You must not block them, Rock-man. Let none of those who love me hinder the children.' Holding the gaze of the wide-eyed boy, Jesus slipped the crutch and all its padding from under his shoulder. 'For it is to such as these,' he murmured, stroking the crooked knee, 'to such as these that the kingdom of heaven belongs.'

Jesus kept the crutch and, standing among the women, turned to face his disciples. 'How can you forget so soon? I've said it before: that those who do not receive the kingdom of heaven as a little child will never enter there.'

And so went the rest of that day, on a high land west of Pella and east of the Jordan Valley. Jesus picked up the littlest ones and sat to receive their bigger, livelier siblings. He laid his hands on the children, and he blessed them.

Mary, his mother, thick in her throat, her vision swimming in warm tears, croaked to herself, one of the songs the women sang on pilgrimage to Jerusalem:

I am not proud within, my Lord,
My mind too high or mighty.
I am not proud without, my Lord;
My eyes are nothing haughty.

Nor do I daze myself with things
Too marvellous for me.
I have composed my restless soul
And set my spirit free:

I am a small girl, newly weaned,
Wrapped at her mother's bosom.
A lamb is my soul inside of me,
Weaned and wrapped and woollen.

She sang the song while returning alone to the pool for the water jar which she had forgotten there.

She sang, she arrived, she sighed, she found her jar, she picked it up – and in a sudden savagery, she hurled it against the stone wall and smashed it to pieces.

AT THE JABBOK

——

As the family left Pella to follow the same route farther south, a young man came running from the city behind them. Altogether out of breath, he fell to his knees in front of Jesus. He smiled and shook his head and slapped his chest and gasped for air.

Jesus stood still, waiting.

The man was... beautiful. His hair, combed in oil, twinkled in the sunlight. He gave forth a charming scent. His complexion was smooth, his cheeks bright pink, his teeth perfectly straight and white, his manner fresh and open and cheerfully self-deprecating. He was clothed in linen that surely came from the finest flax in Egypt; an inconspicuous embroidery defined his sleeves and the selvage around his neck.

When he had caught his breath, he greeted Jesus. 'Good teacher,' he said with an easy reverence. That he was kneeling rendered him neither abject nor fawning. 'What must I do to inherit eternal life?'

'Why do you call me good?' Jesus responded. 'No one is good but God alone.'

The young man grinned at his mistake. But his question had been sincerely put. Here was a man whose education, clearly, was complete; he was turning his attentions to the shape of the rest of his life, and he truly wanted to know how he ought to live it.

Jesus said, 'You know the commandments, don't you? "You shall not murder. You shall not commit adultery. You shall not steal. You shall not bear false witness. You shall not defraud. Honour your father and your mother."'

'Yes! Teacher, yes,' the young man exclaimed earnestly. 'Not only do I know them, but ever since I was a child I've devoted myself to keeping them, to keeping all the commandments. But you,' he said, catching the hem of Jesus' robe and kissing it. He blushed at his own gesture and grinned. 'I know that you have something more to teach me.'

Jesus' countenance softened. He waggled his head in a kind of wonder, then knelt before the young man and took the lovely, tapered fingers into his hands.

'Perhaps you are wiser than you know,' said the Lord. 'Yes, there *is* one other thing required of you. Go back to the city, my son. Go right now. Sell everything you own, house, goods, embroidered robes. Gather the money from your sales and give it to the poor – ' The young man ceased smiling. His eyes slid sideways. Sunshine fled his face.

Seeing this, Jesus turned his words into an appeal: 'For when you, child, are poor, you will have a treasure forever in heaven. Then come and follow me.'

The beautiful young man said nothing. He leaned backwards, took his hands from Jesus' tender grip and stood up, heaving a most heartbroken sigh. How mournfully he walked away. He would not be coming back. He must have inherited tremendous wealth.

Watching the profoundly pious, profoundly dejected fellow depart, Jesus, too, blew out a sigh.

'Ah, children!' he said. 'How hard it is for the rich to enter the kingdom of God. It is easier for a camel to go through the eye of a needle than for a wealthy man to enter the kingdom.'

Judas spoke up, spontaneously, fretfully. 'Well, then! Who *can* be saved?'

Jesus looked directly into that disciple's eyes. 'For you and for every other mortal on earth it is impossible. But not for God,' he said. 'With God all things are possible.'

The farther south and the closer to Jerusalem that they travelled, the faster and the farther Jesus paced ahead of the rest of the family. He spent his nights in solitude, separated. He rose early in the morning and left before breakfast. The disciples were becoming followers indeed, rushing their morning preparations and taking to the road as soon as possible, following at distances behind the Lord.

On the other hand, they never failed to find him in the afternoon, waiting beside the road, lean, erect, his lips compressed, his rusted eyebrows crushing the flesh between them, his soul consumed by thinking.

Once or twice they came upon him while he was talking with other people:

– A young man, a Samaritan, kneeling and repeating thanksgivings. 'Didn't I heal ten lepers,' Jesus was saying. 'Where are the nine?'

– A woman, wearing a thin shift hastily donned, standing abject in front of Jesus, who was himself squatting, writing with his finger in the dust; and a group of men glowering behind him. Jesus was twisting his head towards these men, saying, 'Taken in adultery?' The men, indignant, 'In the very act!' Jesus, agreeable, returning to his dusty scrawl, 'All right, then. Let the sinless one among you hit her with the first stone.' Even as the disciples approached, the older men were walking off one by one, and then the younger ones until they were all gone. Jesus straightened and looked at the women. 'Has no one condemned you?' 'No one, sir.' 'Then neither do I. Go, and sin no more.'

– Pharisees, also on their way to Jerusalem for the Passover. This one was a snarling conversation. It didn't stop when the disciples came near; it didn't even acknowledge their presence. 'Abraham is our father,' the Pharisees were insisting. Jesus overrode them: 'If you were children of Abraham, you'd do what he did. But look at you! You seek to kill me, the one who brings you truth directly from God.' They: 'We, *we* were not born of fornication!' Jesus: 'Your father is the Devil! You do your father's will!' And they, spitting on the road: 'You Samaritan! The demons are flies that drink from your eyes! And demons are worms in your belly!' Jesus: 'You dishonour me. God will glorify me. He will be the judge.' The Pharisees slapped themselves under their arms and snatched up stones to stone him. Peter emitted an astonished, violent roar. For the first time the Pharisees realized that they had an audience. They stalked, seething, away.

The disciples burst into various shouts of victory, Judas slapping Peter on the back.

Jesus whirled and glared at them. Perhaps it was only Mary who heard his whisper and the anguish in his voice: 'Don't you get it? Don't you get it even now?'

Could he, she wondered, watching as he left them right where they were standing; could he be going somewhere alone, to weep the tears she would have wept, in mute frustration?

It seemed to Mary that the hair above her Yeshi's temples was receding. His neck looked strained, the muscles taut and ropy, the hollow below his throat sunken, cavernous. She saw the bones beneath the skin and suffered. When did he eat? When, really, did he sleep? But she had lost the right – no, no: she had renounced the right – to make soups for him, or even to suggest he take more care for himself.

Ah, Lord God! – how she strove for the peace of the weaned child clasped to its mother's bosom. But *she* was the mother of a child who'd long ago refused her bosom. Not peace, then. Anxiety. Her stomach cramped and her stool was liquid and her prayers were growing angry. And why should she castigate her son for carelessness? Worry distracted her as much. Mary saw the filth and the thistles in her clothing; she knew the grit beneath her nails and the furious knots in her hair. Even the pads of her fingers were wrinkled, and the wrinkles streaked. Well – but she didn't care. No, this was the point: she took no care for her own person. She was consumed by the condition of her beloved son.

Late one afternoon about four miles south of Amathus, the family spied Jesus waiting by the blue waters of the Jabbok River. His back was to them, but his head was in profile, looking upstream to the left.

The barley fields beside the river were softly rattling, ready for the harvest. The disciples had already begun to pluck the earliest figs, and high on the hills in the east they'd heard the sheep complaining at their shearing. The latter rains were lightening. Springtime in the lowland. It was spring in the valley of the Jordan. But the spirit of their Lord before them had the effect of a mortal winter.

No one hallooed to signal their approach.

Yet he must have caught motion in the corner of his eye, for he stepped from the water and faced them and then began to stride with purpose towards them.

They hesitated. The company instinctively drew back and spread out, so forceful was his coming – like the eagle that skims the fields for mice.

'Life or death,' he said in clear articulation as he walked, his grey robe billowing. 'It was at the Jabbok that Jacob met the Lord of hosts. Alone on the edge of its upland gorge, Jacob the father of tribes wrestled the angel of the Lord. For life or for death. That he lived was solely by the mercy of God! And his name was changed to Israel.'

Jesus halted ten feet from the family and drove his staff into the soil. It stood upright when he let it go. He moved to Simon Peter, then to Andrew and James and John and Thomas and Maryam and, one by one, to all the disciples.

'Are you so thickheaded? Don't you get it yet?' he said, his lips retracted, his eyes like sickles. 'We are going up to Jerusalem. But not chiefly for the Passover.' Jesus gave each sentence its individual utterance, pausing before he spoke the next. 'The Son of man will be handed over to the chief priests and the scribes.

'They will condemn him to death.

'*They* will hand him over to the Gentiles.

'The Gentiles will mock him and spit on him and flog him and kill him.'

Almost everyone received this punctuated speech in silence.

Everyone except (Mary could scarcely believe the audacity) for the brothers James and John. These had bent their heads together and were whispering. When Jesus paused after 'kill him', their heads popped up, sensing opportunity. And even while he was pronouncing the final sentence – 'Three days later, he will rise' – both brothers stepped forward, stout and frowning with importance.

'Teacher,' they said.

Jesus stared at them.

'We'd like you to do whatever we ask of you.'

Mary stared at them, astonished. Who was their mother? How had she raised them?

Without expression Jesus said, 'What do you want me to do for you?'

They glanced quickly at one another, then proclaimed: 'Let us sit by you when you come into your glory, one at your left hand, one at your right.'

Jesus narrowed his eye. Abruptly he turned on his heel and walked all the way back to the Jabbok, his staff still standing behind.

Maryam from Magdala made a tiny moan, pressing her palms to her breast. Mary saw with what alarm and sympathy the child was regarding James and John, praying for them, she did not doubt.

But the two boys hadn't the sense of a dog when it's been scolded. They stood with their heads high, unruffled, awaiting an answer.

Simon Peter, however, showed every sign of rufflement. And Judas, taller than all, was nevertheless jumping about, trying to get the brothers' attention. 'Hey! You guys. What about me?'

Before the group began to speak or to break apart, Jesus returned and beheld both James and John exactly as Mary might have done, were she their mother: with the sadness and the love and the judgment that knows the future better than her children.

'You don't know what you're asking,' Jesus said. 'Are you able to drink the cup I will drink?'

'Yessir!' they both declared. 'Yes, indeed.'

'Well,' Jesus sighed. 'Whether you're able to or not, you will. You will surely drink of the cup of suffering. But to sit at my right or my left was never mine to grant. These places belong to those for whom they've been prepared – '

'Who do you think you are?' Simon Peter pushed between the brothers and rounded on them. 'The morning stars? Apples in the eyes of the good God Almighty? Which one of us was the first to be called? D'you remember that? And that child over there, *there*!' pointing at Maryam from Magdala, 'shows more trust in the Lord than either of you fish-heads – '

'Sit down!' This was Jesus, exasperated. 'All of you, sit!'

Simon snapped his mouth shut, blinking. Everyone sat.

'You know that the rulers of the pagans lord it over them.' Jesus spoke between clenched teeth. He snatched the staff out of the ground and held it crosswise, on the tips of his fingers. He set his feet apart, an athlete, a boxer light and wary. 'Their high officials, those who sit to the left and the right of kings, tyrannize the people. It must never, never be so with you! Listen to me: whoever wants to become great among you must be your servant. And whoever wants to be *first* must be the slave of all!

'For the Son of man did not come to be served, but to serve!' Jesus levelled the staff with one hand, stretched it out before him, and began to point. 'He came, Simon; James; John; Judas, and every other fool among you: he came to give his life! – as a ransom for many.'

What is this talk? What is this wretched talk of his? And how am I supposed to swallow it? And where are you, O God, the only Father of my child?

Don't you love him? He's your son!

What is the matter with you?

Can't you protect him. Can't you ease his mind? Can't you deliver him from these terrible dreams of dying? Can't you direct his ways towards safety?

Hey, big sir! Hey, God of the word and words! Why do you sit all silent now, on your throne in your splendid heavens, sealed against the world?

When we, your people, go up to Jerusalem this is what we sing:

Who is like our God,
Who sits enthroned on high?
Who stoops to regard
The heavens and the earth?

He raises the poor from the dust;
He lifts the needy from the ash heap –

Sure. But when it's our son who's the needy one, yours and mine, there's no dragging you down to notice! What then? Are we poor pilgrims liars in our mindless repetitions, 'lifts the needy'? Or are you, sir, the liar?

Did I deceive the boy when I repeated your words, your very own words to him – or did you deceive me first? 'The Lord God will give you the throne of David, little Yeshi. Believe it, baby.

You will reign over the house of Jacob forever. Forever, kid, because your kingdom will have no end.' Liar! I see an ending coming –

Ach, I can't talk to you. I start howling, and the next thing, I start crying. I hate to cry. I want the voice of thunderclaps to roar my rage – yes, yes, and even my prayers – to you.

Hear the voice of my crying all the day long:

Fight, almighty God, against the men that fight against our son! Take up your shield! Come down and help him!

Flash your spear against his enemies!

Comfort Yeshi. Say, 'I am your deliverance'!

Shame them, debase them that seek his life!

Let them be like chaff before the blasts from the nostrils of your angels!

Let ruin whack them unawares!

Then! Then, O Lord! Then will my soul rejoice in you, and all my bones cry out, 'Who is like the Lord? – for he rescues the needy from murderers!'

Then will I shout for joy. I'll sing forevermore, 'Great is the Lord! The mighty God delights in the welfare of his servant – yes, and of his maidservant too!'

My tongue will ring in belltones your righteousness and your praise across the countryside both day and night.

If.

You rescue our son from the lions.

OVER THE JORDAN

It was a bare two weeks before the Passover. Some priests had already begun their journeys up to Jerusalem. Jesus and his followers had made camp near Bethabara, across the Jordan from the city of Jericho. Urgency had relaxed a bit. In fact, Jesus the carpenter had purchased wood, nails, iron battens, and had begun to measure the wood for cutting. The family hadn't moved their camp for several days already.

It was precisely here, on what once was called the Plains of Moab, that the people of Israel also encamped while the ageing Moses prepared them to enter the Promised Land. From here, then, Moses left the Israelites forever, walking eastwards to Mount Nebo, from which God showed him the rich earth he would never walk upon. One thousand three hundred years ago. And Joshua – *Yehoshua*, whose mother called him 'Yeshi' – became their leader. He sent spies across to Jericho. And then the whole people crossed the Jordan on dry ground, and marched around that city, marched around it seven days, and seven times on the seventh day, until its walls collapsed, and God took the city for himself, placing everything within it under *herem*, under his holy ban.

This was also the place where John, the prophet, Mary's hard-nosed relative too early dead, had baptized her son.

And crowds began to gather again, perhaps because Jesus had stopped travelling and was lingering rather long in the same small region.

Friends ran and sought their friends, saying, 'John may never have done a sign, but everything he said about this man is coming true.'

And Jesus did not deny them. He seemed indeed to be emerging from his brown contemplations. He was telling stories again:

'When the Son of man shall descend in his glory, when all the angels that sang at his birth shall sing and surround him again, he will take his seat on the splendid throne, and as king over all he will judge the nations.

'People and peoples, the king will divide them the way a shepherd divides the sheep from the goats. The sheep he will gather at his right hand, saying, "Come, O blessed of my Father. Inherit the kingdom which has been prepared for you even from the beginning of the world. For I was hungry and you fed me. I was thirsty and you gave me to drink. I was a stranger and you welcomed me. I was naked and you dressed me. I was sick and you visited me. I was in prison, little flock – and you came to visit me."

'But the righteous will be bewildered, and they will ask him, 'When, Lord, did we see you hungry and feed you? When thirsty or alien or naked or sick or in prison and came to serve you?'

'And the king will answer them, saying, "Listen to me: when you did it to one of the least of these, my sisters, my brothers, the outcasts in the kingdoms of the world, you did it also to me."

'But then the king will say to the unrighteous, "Depart from me into the fires prepared for the Devil and his angels. For I was hungry, and you refused me; thirsty, and you refused me; a stranger, and you refused me; naked, and you refused me; sick, languishing in prison, and you did not so much as visit me."

'Well, and the goats, too, will be absolutely thunderstruck. They will have no memory of behaviours so damnable. "When, Lord?" they will cry. With a frightened, wide-eyed dismay they will plead their innocence. "In God's name, *when* did we see your majesty in such terrible need and did not minister to you?"

'"Listen! For the last time, listen!" the king will decree. "When you chose *not* to do it to the least, the outcast, the despised, the pariah, the abandoned, every one of them a sister and a brother of mine, you chose not to do it to me."'

There were priests in the crowds that heard Jesus' story of resurrections and judgments and glorious endings. Some of these laboured to make their livings. There was a stonecutter among them and several ploughmen from a district north in Perea. They knew the codes of holiness in Torah, regarding love for the neighbour and the foreigner, care for the poor, forgiveness for the debtor. These priests considered the teaching of this rabbi an excellent commentary on Torah.

Other priests, however – those who sat astride their mounts at the back of the crowds – belonged to the House of Kathros in Jerusalem, a powerful and wondrously wealthy family since it alone was permitted to produce spices and incense for the Temple. These priests had made certain purchases in the southeast before bathing in the warm pools of Callirrhoe and then continuing to Jerusalem by way of the river-crossing near the plains of Moab. Curiosity caused them to rein their mules in earshot of this Jesus of Nazareth, that peasant prophet who'd been stirring up the Galileans.

These priests, nothing like their brothers, were scandalized by the story they heard. Nor were they fools. They recognized the force of the prophet's person and the nature of the crowds surrounding him, Jews as much from Judea as from Perea and Galilee. Were they all pilgrims? Were they all coming to the Passover?

In a sudden fury the priests of Kathros whipped up their mules and galloped over the Jordan towards Jerusalem.

'*David* could call himself the shepherd of his people,' they shouted to one another. 'This man is no David. *David* was anointed king. This man is a Galilean! A Nazarene! What audacity to call himself a king! Yes, and what sedition!'

They forded the Jordan as fast as water-mosquitoes, their fine raiment splattered with mud. They ripped through Jericho and nearly killed their beasts by driving them relentlessly up the rough road to Jerusalem.

'And by God!' they cried in horror. '*Only* God will judge the nations at the close of the age. Blasphemies, utters this honey-tongue! Disasters will fall upon Jerusalem – unless we prepare!'

Oh, the chief priests were about to get an earful of the potential insurgency about to cross the Jordan. Oh, what a dramatic Passover this was going to be!

Once long ago – after his baptism, but before he left Judea for Galilee – Jesus made friends with a small family of three unmarried siblings, two sisters and a younger brother. They lived in little Bethany, two miles east of Jerusalem. In the early days, when his name remained unknown and only two or three people went about with him, he'd accepted their invitation to stay with them. One day extended into a generous five while he ate their food, slept on their roof, and taught them lessons of the better part which, he said, 'shall never be taken away from you'.

The oldest of the three was Martha. Actually, she was the householder, sensible, confident, efficient, and as masterly as any man she knew. Mary, both younger and taller than her sister, was by nature reserved. She appreciated Martha's blunt management and her willingness to make decisions. But she it was, Mary it was, who combed and cosseted their little brother in the early days, washed him and dressed him and walked him on cool mornings up the slopes of the Mount of Olives. By the time his voice began to change, she listened to his bright plans – and she watched, alarmed, as he rode a black horse bareback, his face in its mane and the mighty engine stretching its head in a flat-out gallop. He rode like a Syrian, not like a Roman. And he could ride at all because he cleaned the stables, brushed and fed the horses of a wealthy Damascene who lived near Bethphage.

In spite of the loss of his parents, the lad was completely happy. His face illuminated the room, eyes unclouded, filled with laughter, his talk delightful, his prospects excellent. Looking upon him one afternoon, Jesus had said to the sisters, 'I will not leave you forever orphaned. I will come to you.' The rabbi's expression, the languid droop of his long, rust-coloured lashes, showed deep love for their brother. And though they didn't altogether understand his *I will come to you*, neither Martha nor Mary ever forgot the promise. They had placed all their own hopes and dreams upon their brother's future. And shortly after Jesus' departure for Galilee, Martha entered into negotiations with the father of a daughter in Jerusalem, seeking a bride for her sunny brother.

His name was Lazarus.

Now, upon his return to the southern regions of Israel and less than two weeks before the Passover, a frantic message flew from

Mary and Martha to Jesus, east of the Jordan: 'Come. Come right away. Our brother Lazarus is sick unto death. There is no time to lose. Come.'

Jesus' mother heard the messenger, as did a number of other disciples. She knew what love Jesus bore for the little family; it caused her own heart to bump with sympathy, though she'd never met them; and she expected her son to rise up and hurry across to Bethany.

But he answered the messenger with no such urgency. 'It isn't a sickness unto death,' he said. 'It's a sickness unto glory. The Son of God will be glorified through it.'

Mary relaxed. Jesus knew these people. She didn't. Jesus knew the condition of things even from distances away. Mary scarcely knew what was under her nose. She relaxed – and discovered how tight her muscles had become at the thought of crossing the Jordan into the haunts of their enemies.

The family spent another two days near Bethabara, during which time Jesus didn't mention the sickness at all. Rather, he worked as a carpenter and a wheelwright, finishing a pretty little carriage.

'Yeshi,' Mary said, 'I've never seen you make such a thing. Why now? What's it for?'

'For my mother,' he answered, nailing battens to the sides of slats cut into hemispheres for wheels. 'For her ageing, years hereafter. But just now for the mincing Chuza. Poor tenderfoot. Have you noticed the blood-prints he leaves wherever he walks?'

On the morning of the third day everything changed. Jesus rose before the others. He was up and about even before the roosters had begun to crow the dawn light in. Mary heard him stirring. She heard the clank of metal on metal, and saw that he was packing his tools away.

'Up! Up!' Jesus called. 'Get up and get ready. We're going to Judea.'

Judas Iscariot woke immediately. 'Finally,' he muttered to himself.

'Wait a minute!' Simon Peter, rising on an elbow. 'Master, what's the rush? The Pharisees who tried to stone you north of Amathus, remember? They're over there. They don't love you any more than they did then, and Judea is filled with stones!'

Jesus said, 'Isn't half the day in daylight?'

'What?'

'Those who walk during the day don't stumble. They see by the light of the world. Those who walk at night stumble, don't they? Because light is not in them.'

'Well, yes. Even a baby knows that. But – '

'Lazarus has fallen asleep. I'm going to wake him up.'

Roosters in the village nearby began to cut the air with their crowing.

'What? Asleep? Hang it all, I know I'm not clever. And maybe Matthew will explain your riddles later. But, Lord! If the man's asleep, he's fine. There's no need to go.'

'Clever has nothing to do with it, Simon. And the stones of Judea have nothing against your head. I'll say it plainly. Lazarus is dead.'

Mary gasped. Dead? *Is* dead? And Yeshi was building a cart while – ?

Thomas the twin had already begun to roll his stuff away. He stood and looked down on Simon Peter.

'Get up,' he said. Then he spoke to everyone. 'Come on. Let's all go with him, that we might die with him.'

Midway between Jericho and Bethany, Mary approached Andrew, who also had made friends with Mary and Martha in the early days. It was from him she'd heard their names and their stories.

'Run ahead, why don't you?' she said. 'What must Lazarus's sisters be feeling now? Go quickly, Andrew. Tell them their Lord is on his way.'

The Lord and, several hours behind him, the crowds. When the wounded and the hungry had arrived at his camp and found him gone, people told people, and by noon the poor from Bethabara and Abila and Bethennabris and Gadora and villages everywhere in Perea were pouring across the Jordan.

Late in the afternoon Jesus turned left off the road to Jerusalem and took a path to the south, along the lower slopes of the Mount of Olives.

Even before reaching Bethany, they spied Martha running from the village, a dogged, shameless, angry sort of running. Jesus paused. Without removing his eyes from the woman –

whose eyes were clearly fixed on him – he handed his staff back to Matthew. The disciples moved away. Mary alone stayed near her son.

'Not a sickness unto death!' Martha yelled, running. 'What were you thinking? He's dead already! Four days dead!'

The woman was as stout as a *massebah*, the pillar that marked a grave. Her hair was uncovered, knotted behind. Her great neck was so ringed with folds of flesh that they drove the lobes straight out below her ears. Her arms were cedars of Lebanon. She was strong and, on small feet, very fast. And when she came near to Jesus, Mary smiled to find that the woman's height was equal to his. Roundness had reduced her at a distance.

Martha stomped her foot. She was puffing, trying to catch her breath, wanting to scold, all at once. Sweat moistened the folds of her neck. Tears darkened her cheeks with a muddy dust. She stomped the ground again. She drew back a hand as if to slap the man, but then balled a fist and pounded softly on his chest. 'If you had been here,' she gasped, she scolded. 'If you had come when we asked. If you had even believed us. Ah, Lord' – breathing, drawing a very deep breath – 'my bright little brother! Lazarus! He would not have died.'

'Martha, Martha.' Jesus made a dove-like, throaty sound and opened his arms.

Martha's hands fell. She dropped her forehead to his shoulder; he embraced her, and she wept loudly, her arms hanging helpless at her sides.

Finally she spoke into his robe. 'But even now… couldn't you do something? God will give you whatever you ask.'

Jesus said, 'Your brother will rise again.'

'I know,' Martha muttered. Then, pulling back and flushing scarlet, moisture winking in the folds of her neck: 'I know, I *know*! Lazarus will rise. Everyone will rise. The whole *world* will rise' – *how often had the woman heard that phrase from comforters?* – 'at the last day! Which only God knows when *that's* going to be!'

Jesus released her, withdrew by a single step, then gazed at Martha through narrowed eyes. They glittered, his eyes. Two creases cracked the skin between his brows. Under the tight beard, his cheeks depressed and angled towards the corners of his mouth.

Martha's vision was locked by his.

'What?' she muttered. She blinked and began to wring her hands. 'What?'

But there was no blame in him. There was, instead, a fervid concentration and a yearning. And this woman was its object. So said his tone when he started to speak again.

'Martha.'

Hesitantly, childishly, she lifted a shoulder and tipped her head to it.

'Martha.'

'What?'

'I AM the resurrection and the life,' Jesus said, his looking level and endless. 'Those who believe in me, even though they die, yet will they live. And those who live and believe in me will never die.'

Both he and the woman stood unmoving.

Mary, too, was transfixed. Her son had just said *I AM*. He had uttered the name that is never to be uttered, the name by which the God of Isaiah refers to himself! Such daring stunned her. Worse, had Eleazar been here no one could have stopped him from throwing stones. He and all his people would have hurled rocks like thunderbolts.

Jesus hadn't moved. 'Martha?'

She lifted her eyebrows.

'You heard what I said?'

'I did.'

'Do you believe it?'

'Yes, Lord,' she spoke solemnly. 'I believe that you are the Messiah, the Son of God, the one who was to come into the world.'

Martha, thought Mary. *The name means 'Lady.' Even so do we title women of refinement and position.* Mary was filled with admiration for this Martha-Lady, who took the hand of Jesus and kissed it, and then allowed him to lead her, side by side, towards Bethany. She was no less mournful than when she had come running out. But the anger was gone. And when she'd allowed him to take her arm and to lead her, Martha had also allowed him to enter the terrible privacy of grief and to share it.

Just outside the village, Jesus stopped and Martha slipped

ahead. The disciples were not far off, but the space around their Lord and his mother seemed reserved for more intimate communions.

Within five minutes Martha's sister Mary came into sight among the cluttering of houses. She saw him. She began to hurry. Long and dark she was, her hair as long as her waist, dropping in a single braid as thick and rich as a black, combed flax. Behind her came Martha walking, and behind Martha an assortment of comforters: relatives, friends, God-fearers, officious busybodies.

'If you had been here – ' The younger sister's eyes were rubbed red, raw, and her voice very small: 'If you had been here – '

But Martha put a finger to the tall woman's lips. 'Hush, hush, I've already told the Lord our feelings.' And immediately Mary, the sister of Lazarus, dissolved in tears and sank to the ground. Many of the comforters were overcome by her sobbing, and joined her, sorrow for sorrow.

Jesus bowed his head and touched his left hand to his brow, covering his eyes. But his mother saw how his chin bunched and began to tremble. He tried to speak. His voice caught. His hand still hiding his eyes, Jesus said, 'Take me to his tomb.'

Then his shoulders drooped. And he wept.

Someone said, 'See how much he loved the young man?'

Someone else said, 'Yeah, but what's the point? A real healer could've prevented the death in the first place.'

Jesus heard the latter comment. So did his mother: *Perfidious fool! Mocking our intimacies!* She saw that it dried the eyes of her son and set his jaw at an angle she knew as anger.

And when, next, she realized that the mouthy son of a cockroach had followed them to the gravesite, Mary moved through the crowd and pinched him.

'What the – !'

It was evening now, the sky gone green and earth exhaling coolness. Lazarus's tomb was an old one, used through countless generations. Ancient hands had hollowed it in the rock of the hillside. Four days ago its flat stone had been rolled from the doorway, up a gentle incline, that the body of the young man might be laid herein; and then the stone was rolled down, to cover the doorway again.

Jesus took up a position not five feet from the tomb, Martha and Mary on either side of him. People assumed they had come to make a final mourning.

But Jesus said, 'Simon? James? Remove that stone.'

Martha frowned. 'Dead four days, my Lord,' she said. 'That grave's going to stink to high heaven if you open it.'

Jesus took her hand and Mary's hand, and gently turned them both towards the tomb. 'Didn't I tell you that if you believed you'd see the glory of God? Simon, the stone.'

It crunched gravel as the disciples pushed it one revolution upward. The doorway yawned. The fusty smell of old bones erupted, but not the smell of putrefaction.

Then Jesus cried with a loud voice into the darkness: 'Lazarus! Come forth!'

In a moment the young man – the dead man – appeared in the doorway, his hands and his feet wound in white linen, a cloth around his face.

No one uttered a word. The hillside was as still as death. An eagle lay motionless upon a shelf of wind in the twilit sky. Every watcher stood there as if solitary in a yellow wilderness: the watcher and that standing corpse and the wind across dried grasses.

Then Jesus spoke, and everything was as it had been. 'Go on,' he said, gently pushing the sisters towards their brother. 'Unbind him. Let the poor man walk on his own.'

When the crowds from Perea arrived and heard the news, they went mad with delight. *Dead four days, and he raises the dead!* The word spread throughout Judea. And the chief priests in Jerusalem, together with certain Pharisees, called a meeting of their Sanhedrin in order to measure the threat advancing now upon Jerusalem.

'If we let this man persist in his designs,' they said, 'he'll bewitch every rube that comes to the city.'

'He'll seize the crowds and lead them.'

'The whole country will go after him!'

'And you know the consequences of that.'

'Right! Three legions will march here from Syria, under orders from Tiberias Caesar Augustus to take over our nation and to destroy our holy place.'

'God save us!'

'Whoa, whoa! Does none of you understand?' This from Caiaphas the high priest, who wore his hair cropped in the style of the Roman wealth, who worked closely with Pontius Pilate, and who, long in office, received great benefit from the sale of sacrificial animals under the Temple porticoes. 'Don't you see the perfect solution? Right before your eyes?' he said. 'Much, much better it is that one man should die for the people than that the whole nation should perish.'

In earnest, then, the chief priests and the Pharisees set in motion forces which must end in the death of Jesus.

One member of the Sanhedrin, Joseph of Arimathea – who had become a secret follower of Jesus – begged the rest to think rather in terms of a formal, completely legal trial. But what was one voice among so many?

Does anyone know his hiding place? Official questions passed from rank to rank and mouth to mouth. *When is he vulnerable? Where does he go apart from the crowds and lackeys that might defend him?*

BOOK THREE

THE
SACRIFICE
OF
THE
MESSIAH

PART EIGHT

MARY AND THE BELOVED

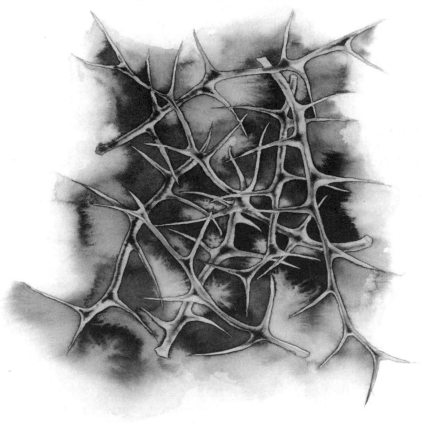

SUNDAY I: THE BELOVED

It rained in the grey-dawn four days before the Passover. Not a heavy rain. Pattering showers and a loamy mist, enough to wash dust from the road-stones and to clean the pinnate leaves of the palms. White and green was the eastern rise of the Mount of Olives; moss green, drab green, and soon a glistening emerald green – for the clouds broke, and the early sun shot through the mist to play on the face of the slopes.

Pilgrims who had spent the night upland of Jericho rose and shook the water from their tents and renewed the journey up to Jerusalem. Parthians, Medes, Elamites, Mesopotamians: the gathering multitudes. It was a difficult climb through the stone gaps and chalky cuts of the Jericho road: fifteen miles between the cities and more than three thousand feet higher into holiness. But by daylight festive Jews were lifting their voices and singing the *Hallel*:

> *Blessed be the name of the Lord*
> *From this time forth, forevermore!*
> *From the rising of the sun to its red descending,*
> *Let the name of the Lord be praised!*

Most were dressed in wool, the unbleached robes of peasants, day-labourers, the poor who punctured the fruit of the sycamore. Peasants wore a cloth cap or went bareheaded and carried hempen bags. But among these were the more fortunate, landowners and lords, whose turbans were pure white, the borders of whose tunics were embroidered, whose linen cloaks

242

were red or yellow, blue, expensive.

The travelling pilgrims chattered in a dozen languages, like geese and ducks and pigeons together. But when they sang, distinctions dissolved and the great host became one:

The Lord is high above all nations!
His glory is higher yet than the heavens!

Who is like our God,
Who sits enthroned on high?
Who stoops to regard
The heavens and the earth?

He raises the poor from the dust...

We heard their long approach from the north-east, their slow ascending over rough hills. They didn't yet know who was in Bethany or what he had done here, but they would. Villagers were already dashing off in their direction to exult in the news.

Jesus was subdued.

'Lazarus,' he spoke softly in a small mulberry grove behind the young man's house. 'You know of stables near Bethphage, right?'

'I know the owner. I used to work there.'

'Good.' Jesus put a hand on Andrew's shoulder. 'Go with him,' he said. 'Tethered outside the stables you'll find a colt. It's unbroken. It's never been ridden. Untie it and bring it back to me.'

'Master, let me go!' Judas, winding his arms into something like a pigtail, pleaded, 'I'm fearless! It might look like stealing – '

Without acknowledging the interruption, Jesus paused so fleetingly it would have gone unnoticed, except that he snapped his teeth together.

'Andrew,' he said pointedly, squeezing the disciple's shoulder, 'if anyone happens to challenge you, say simply, "The Lord has need of it," and all will be well. No one will stop you.' He lowered his hand. He touched Lazarus at the small of his back. 'This colt,' he said. 'I'm going to ride it into Jerusalem. Go.'

His final words were doomful.

I haven't Simon's disposition. I don't fly to extremes. My public manner tends to be equable, neither laughing overmuch nor crying. But by the time Andrew and Lazarus returned with the colt, such heaviness had fallen upon me that I could not keep from sighing: a mood solemn and unutterably sorrowful. *This is the day*, I wept inside. *This is the day*, like picking compulsively at a wound.

Until that morning, until the very moment when Jesus said, 'into Jerusalem', I had allowed something like a veil to hide my Lord's intention. *It isn't now, it's next week. It isn't now, it's tomorrow, and haven't we a whole sleep between?* I wasn't hoping he'd change his mind. I knew him too well for that. But neither did I have to confront the reality. Until – *It's time. This is the hour. Jesus is going into Jerusalem.*

And my mood overcame my mind.

Without thinking I slipped my robe from my shoulders and laid it over the back of the colt. Immediately Simon Peter did the same. And Andrew too. And wordlessly we helped Jesus to sit astride the little beast. He had to bend his legs in order to keep his feet from dragging on the ground; he gave his staff to me; then with his knees alone he directed the unbroken colt towards the pilgrims' way north of Bethany. The colt, amazing me, obeyed. And that Jesus was not avoiding the crowds also amazed – and humbled – me. *Oh, why do I persist in such personal pride? I do not know my Lord so well as I think!*

Whether Jesus had spoken to them, or whether they had instinctively discerned some reason for it, our women stayed in a group behind. Only the men went with Jesus. All of the men including Chuza – and in the forefront, Judas Iscariot.

Seeing the crowds on the Jericho road, and remembering, perhaps, my own compulsive gesture, Judas burst into a frenzied fit of laughter and (so I supposed) did me one better by tearing the robe from his own body and whirling it high in the air and, laughing like a jackal, throwing it down on the mud in front of the Lord. The colt lifted its hooves and walked across the robe – and then I realized how swiftly news about Jesus of Nazareth spread among the multitudes; for all at once there were twenty, fifty, *hundreds* of peasants throwing down their garments as a carpet to cover the way that Jesus was going.

And the Pereans who had arrived in Bethany soon after

Lazarus was raised from the dead – they too now joined the pilgrim throng.

Surrounded by people, surrounded by their deafening song, we ascended the Mount of Olives, and I saw agile young lads scurrying up the trunks of date palms, knives in their teeth; and I saw them whack the long leaves off – even as Jews had done triumphantly in the days of the Maccabees – and pilgrims below snatched up the leaves. Children, women, everyone caught a fever of the hope of such another victory again. And I began to recognize who these people were: the dispossessed! The poor, farmers forced from their lands, artisans, tenants, women whose feet were blue with a rich man's grapes, fishermen crushed under taxes, beggars who still found reason for worship and for Jerusalem. These danced before the Lord. They knew the name of Jesus, he from Nazareth! They waved the branches and they sang:

Hosanna, Hosanna!
Blessed is the kingdom that comes!
Blessed is the son of David!
Blessed is he who comes in the name of the Lord!
Hosanna in the highest!

But then we cleared the top of the mount and saw Jerusalem laid out before us. And there – glorious – on the near side of the city across the Kidron Valley, was Moriah, the Temple Mount, that magnificent, busy esplanade and all its courts and all its gates; and surrounding it, the lofty porticoes and all their marble columns, blinding white; and elevated, its doorway facing us, the Temple itself, sheathed in gold, radiating an aureate fire in the morning sunlight. Glorious, I say; but suddenly the bright glory dimmed. An awe-ful sensation came over me, and it seemed that the shouts of the pilgrims diminished to a distant roaring, and pilgrims dissolved into strengthless phantoms, and Jesus, my Lord alone, was left. For he was weeping.

Tears shined on his cheeks and darkened his beard. He swallowed. The rims of his ears were red, his eyebrows up. His mouth was moving. And in a sacred manner I heard the words as if within my heart:

If even now you knew the things that make for peace!

There was an eagle high above us, sailing in circles over three mountains together, of Olives and of the Temple and of opulent Zion.

O Jerusalem! Jerusalem! Killing the prophets and stoning those who are sent to you! How often I have yearned to gather your children together as a hen gathers her chicks beneath her wings – and you would not! Behold your holy house, therefore. Behold: it is forsaken.

The small colt nodded and was moving, and the mystic moment passed. Faces flushed with triumphant pride were close beside me, smelling of sweat and breaking my ears with yelling.

And as we came close to the gates of Jerusalem, new waves of people poured out to meet us, both pilgrims and the poor and widows and Pharisees, and some of the latter fought through the masses to bellow at Jesus: 'Hang it, man – this could destroy the city! Command the people to shut up!'

And Jesus, no longer weeping, an iron light in his eye, shouted, 'If these people held their peace, why, the very stones would take up the cry!'

On the thunder of the multitudes, then, he rode into Jerusalem and straight towards the Temple. At its gates he turned the colt loose and took his staff from me, then mounted the steps upon his own power, passing into the third round of holiness, arriving – still besieged by the raucous crowds – at the Royal Portico.

When he was a child of twelve, Jesus had seen the beasts and the birds sold here for the pilgrims' sacrifices. When he was a child he smelled their smells; he heard their bawlings, their bleatings, the tramp of hobbled hooves, the sudden flutterings of caged wings; but then his attention was on the lamb in his arms.

As a man, however, observant of the Scriptures, as a prophet, as the Son of God, Jesus' attention was seized by the beasts. And the money. And the trade. He looked around this hawking market with an increasing rage. Slight of stature though he was, he was light on his feet as well. And his muscles were metal bands and his dexterity devastating.

He raised his staff like a hammer and brought it down with such fury that a counting table cracked in half. He raised it and swung it again. He crushed cages and split stools and broke money boxes and spilled their coins in defecations of the beasts. Merchants tried to escape; sheep were released and oxen cut free, and the lowing cows swung their great heads in confusion; with a whip of cords Jesus drove the livestock towards the stairs and out of the Temple; and Judas mimicked his Master, kicking at dried goods, laughing, slapping the cheeks of the passing merchants. 'I knew it!' he shrieked. 'I knew it! Here we go! The plan is just beginning!'

But Jesus had already left that hero to his own sport. Judas, feeling suddenly naked, went up on tiptoe, spun his head to find his Master, then saw the slight, distinctive skull.

Striking his staff on the pavement, Jesus was striding through the Court of the Gentiles, through the gate called 'Beautiful', across the Court of the Women, and through the Nikanor Gate, where he mounted steps to the topmost. There he stopped. He faced the inner courts and the high altar and the open doors through which the interior of the Temple was made visible. Then the Lord cried out in a voice like the *shofar*, like a trumpet in the morning: 'You chief priests, hear me!

'You Levites responsible for this holy place, hear me!

'And Caiaphas! High priest profiteering in the Temple of God, listen to me!

'It is written in the Scriptures, *My house shall be called a house of prayer!* But you have made it a hotbed of racketeers and robbers! You've turned the Temple into a den of thieves!'

Close at the back of my neck I heard a quick sucking of air, then an expulsion as stinging as spit: 'To hell with you, you demon!'

I felt the spray of that curse.

And then with low malice, the sentiment was refined: 'Die in the sight of your despisers. Die, humiliated, the death of your deserving.'

I moved several steps forward, tucking myself into the crowds, then looked back. I should have known; the man was from Jerusalem, after all, the bitterness had been personal: Eleazar the Pharisee, so angry that his eyes were moist, the bridge of his nose bone-white, his lips bright red, his chin whiskers flecked with spit.

It must have been by some wonderful counterfeit that Jesus escaped both the Temple and the city. None of us could find him. None of us had seen him go.

But all of our women had stayed behind in Bethany.

And knowing the love he held for Lazarus and the sisters, I suggested that he might have returned to them. Where else could we have looked?

We crossed the Kidron and hurried back, filled with dread, afraid that Jesus had already been snatched away to prison. My stomach felt like a bowl of hot water, every step spilling the heat into my bowels. If the authorities still needed a reason to arrest him, well, the Lord had surely given them one. Ah! What a doomful day!

But when we ran down the path into Bethany, we saw a dark figure standing on the roof of Martha's house, almost lost in the shadow of the Mount of Olives.

It was the Lord. His time hadn't come. His time had not yet come. I pressed my forehead against the trunk of an almond tree and wept; and the white flowers, now browning, dropped their petals all around me.

MONDAY: MARY

—

When Mary heard what Jesus had done in Jerusalem – actually baiting his enemies, driving them (unnecessarily!) to even wilder furies – every nerve in the woman wanted to whip him with a willow switch.

He was sitting on Martha's rooftop, gazing imperturbably to the east where, below the declining hills and the cliffs that rimmed its shoreline, lay the Great Salt Sea. Wide black masses of bitumen had been vomited to the surface of the sea. In shape and size they looked like decapitated bulls – and at their edges were boats and little men labouring in the heat, little men hauling the sticky substance aboard their boats.

'Like a Moses smashing golden calves! Like a Jeremiah, I tell you what!' It didn't help Mary's disposition that she had to hear the news of her son's worst, maybe even his only, violence again and again from the likes of Judas Iscariot. 'Mad as a Maccabee, he was, kicking, kicking – what? What do you call it? Ha! Kicking the Abomination of Desolation out of the Temple! Whoo-eee! And here's the beauty, here's the genius of the tactic: the whole mob that followed us into the Temple cheered! What a roaring! Who would *dare* to attack him then?'

'Pontius Pilate, you idiot!' Mary spat.

But Judas, cavorting like a hoopoe bird, was oblivious. 'Even the kids piped up. Little *kids*! Squealing, "Hosanna to the son of David," just like their daddies! Driving the chief priests mad! And this is just the start. It's the first skirmish. Because, look: he used none of his wonders, only his arms. Oh, glory! – wait and see what's coming – '

'Nonsense!' Mary: 'What do you know, you… boy?'

' – today, maybe. Tomorrow for sure! Smack his sandals together, and make a darkness everywhere. Blinding folks! Darkness so thick they can touch it! Spank the dust with his staff, and all the dust'll boil up in clouds of gnats. Stick his staff in the water, yessir, yessir, and the waters of Jerusalem'll turn to blood! Tomorrow. But no later, I'll tell you what: no later than Wednesday when *all* the pilgrims are in Jerusalem for the Passover! I know. I know.'

Self-proclaiming bullrush! Undereducated brat!

Mary rushed into the house and begged Martha's sister, that younger Mary of the long, black braid, to use her loom. It was already strung, a piece already begun. Mary shot the shuttle back and forth between the threads of the warp and beat the weft with nearly savage slams. She needed to work. She had to shut away the babblings of that immature fool. He didn't listen. He didn't watch. He didn't learn from his elders. He lived in silly dreams of derring-do and impossible heroics. He knew nothing of Jesus nor of the times nor of consequences nor of the immensities that hung as heavily over human behaviours now as the waters covered the seas. He was himself a madding gnat, whose single gift to the family had been his bright enthusiasm – till now, his status reduced to a gnat.

The fact that the mobs cheered Yeshi was *not* to his benefit. It was precisely what would draw the attentions of the governor. Mary and Chuza had assessed matters earlier this morning. Joanna, Maryam from Magdala, the women in general had put their heads together, and Matthew in particular had lent his balanced intelligence to their analysis: Jesus as a healer, as a rabbi, even as (*pace* Judas) a wonder-worker was of no interest to Pilate. Claims of divinity, however blasphemous in the eyes of the Pharisees, in the eyes of Pilate, whose sky was lousy with deities, were little more than foreign curiosities. But that Jesus might amass a following large enough to destroy good order and Roman authority, *that* Pontius Pilate would crush as the very purpose of his rule in this place. By every account he was a pragmatist. If he had to, he would release foot soldiers, archers, lancers and cavalry in the thousands upon the people. But if he could, he'd take the leader alone, and no skin off his nose.

Moreover, it was Chuza's conviction, and Matthew's agreement, that Pilate would be in conference both with Herod and with the high priest regarding these matters. Through them the Roman might more peacefully contain this odd, obstreperous, one-goddish folk than through direct coercion.

'Mother,' Chuza said, 'matters are much worse than they were several weeks ago. Then the people merely came. Now he inflames their ardours – making a procession of his entering the city! Did you do as I suggested? Did you tell your son about Pilate's methods?'

'I did,' Mary said. 'Well, and I didn't. I mean, I can talk, but I haven't any influence. And we have a covenant, he and I. Without it I wouldn't be here at all: his will is his Father's now, and none of mine, and I must not interfere.'

'He wants the crowds?'

'I don't know that,' Mary said.

'He seeks notoriety? Maybe to emblazon his message?'

'It *is* a message more than prophetic.'

'I think – ' Ah! That pale waif, Maryam from Magdala, was actually speaking in a gathering larger than two. 'I think the crowds are the ones. The choosers. They want to come.' Her talking was a nasal hum, almost bereft of consonants. 'Because he is Jesus. They could, you know. Just. Love him.'

Mary looked sharply at the girl-woman and understood and suffered a spasm of sympathy for her against the days that must be coming. Of course: unassuming Maryam had spoken rather more of herself than of the crowds. Maryam loved Mary's son. Aye, and love it must have been that had brought this delicate spectre out of her madness at Matthew's banquet long ago. What would happen to Maryam hereafter, when love was sundered? Would she slip back into that protective isolation, that madness again?

Chuza was speaking. 'He seems in no hurry to go out into public spaces today.'

'It's a comfort,' Mary sighed, 'but a passing one. He will surely keep the Passover. I know that. And not on the Mount of Olives. In the walls of Jerusalem. O God!' A visible shuddering passed down her body. She hunched her shoulders and wrapped her arms around herself. 'I know it, I know it, and I do not sleep on account of it.'

'Mary,' Joanna said. 'When did you last eat a decent meal, Mary?'

'It doesn't matter. I'm fine.'

'You are my closest friend,' Joanna said. 'I've loved you since you laughed in the marketplace and made my wedding dress.'

Mary looked at Joanna. 'A long time.'

'The only reason your clothes are clean,' Joanna persisted, 'is because I washed them and Martha patched them.'

'Yes. Of course. Thank you.'

Maryam got up and moved towards Mary and sat down beside her, gazing off and saying nothing.

Chuza said, 'You must listen to my wife. Look after yourself. Take some porridge.'

Matthew (of all people, the dust-coloured publican!) said, 'You're thin. You're going grey – '

'My hair has *long* gone grey!'

'I'm referring,' Matthew said in reasonable measures, 'to your complexion – '

And Mary exploded: 'Since when did I become the centre of this conversation?'

'Your turmoil' – Matthew again – 'isn't a secret.'

Mary stood up and stormed out of the house, only to find Jesus speaking with a group of the disciples in a way she quickly found repugnant.

'And you remember,' he was saying, 'when I sent you out two by two without a purse or a bag?'

'Of course,' Simon Peter responded. 'Good days, those were. Good deeds we did, too.'

'Without money or means, my Rock, did you want for anything?'

'Not a thing. We ate well, slept dry, and were welcomed wherever we went. We went, you know, in your name.'

'All right,' Jesus said, 'but things are changing. You'll be going out again. I promise you that.'

Things are changing! Of course they are. Force them and they will surely change.

Yeshi's eyes were level, the rust-brown gaze upon the disciples and through them, both at once. He was, and he was not, with them; and as far as Mary could tell, the men were unaware of that terrible cleft within her son.

Inside the house, misdirected pity. Outside the house, a herd of munching, flyblown cattle.

'When the time comes and you must go out again, know this: Satan is arising. Therefore, those of you who have purses, put money in them and take them along. Those of you who have bags, fill them and take them. And if you have no sword, sell your cloak and buy one – '

Ah, Yeshi! But aren't you the one in control?

' – for it is written, "He poured out his soul to death, and was numbered among the transgressors; yet he bore the sin of many." This, even now, is being fulfilled in me – '

Judas Iscariot thrust his long neck forward and ran from the group to his bundle by the house. He drew out his sword, and clamoured, 'Lookit! Lookit, Master! I knew what was coming! I got me a sword already!'

Jesus frowned. The expression was sudden, and for the instant his looking was altogether here, in this place, focused upon the exuberant, pop-eyed Judas – who took the frown (how *could* the fool?) for commendation.

'And Simon has a sword,' Judas bubbled, 'and that makes two of us!'

By then the Lord's expression had dissolved into a brown imperturbability.

'Enough,' he murmured. He turned towards the stairs at the side of Martha's house and began to climb them to the roof. As he went he said, 'It is enough.'

And Judas launched into that self-important tirade which drove the mother of Jesus back into Martha's house in order to put her hands to work, attacking the loom with a vicious weaving.

O God, you know my son!
Remember him and visit him;
Bring retribution down upon the heads of his enemies!
You are long-suffering, O God:
Do not take my son away.
Consider the reproach he has suffered for your sake,
And say to him what he will hear from none but you:
'Enough! It is enough.'

When your words came unto him, he ate them!
They were his joy, his heart's delight;
For you are his Father. He bears your name!

Why should his pain —
No! No!
Why should my pain be unending?
Why should my wounds be so grievous and incurable?

Truly, truly, truly, O you mighty God,
You have deceived me!
'Go this far into the desert,' you said to me.
'Go without water.
'Go past the point of no return;
'And when you are thirsty even unto death,
'I will be for you streams of a living water.'

Well, I went, O God, trusting in your word!
And now I am thirsty
Even unto death.
And the stream that should have been flowing
Is dry,
You liar!

And God answered Mary, saying, *If you repent, I will restore you, so that you may serve me.*

And Mary answered God: *No, thank you.*

And God said, *If you speak what is precious and not what is worthless, I will make your service glorious. You can be my mouth.*

And Mary answered, *No.*

And then, giving the weft such a whack it seemed she were knocking an ox on the head, she said, *Amen.*

TUESDAY: THE BELOVED

I had seen the Temple long before I met Jesus. Already as a young man I'd gone up for the Passover among brothers and sisters, and had stopped the practice only when I cast my lot with John, whom many people called the Baptizer – and who had introduced us to Jesus, whom *he* called 'the Lamb of God that takes away the sin of the world'.

It wasn't until Tuesday, then, three days before this year's festival, that I realized how many of these more recent brothers had never even seen the Temple before.

Sunday had separated us. Sunday had overwhelmed us with crowds and shoutings and inciting gestures and the furies of certain leaders of the Pharisees and chief priests. I scarcely noticed the others then.

But when we went to the Temple on Tuesday Jesus remained mild – seemed actually to be as slight as he was – when pilgrims began to press us on all sides. He was subdued in all he said and did. No emotions were provoked. And though Pilate's legionnaires, armed and armoured, paced over the roofs of all four porticoes, watching our movements; and though the policing forces of the chief priests, level with us below, followed our movements on foot, trailing us across the esplanade, eyeing us, whispering, waiting – yet this time I had the leisure to observe my brothers. Overawed. Chastened by the glory. Giddy on the Temple platform which, within its temenos, was more spacious than four of their villages.

While Jesus sat in the porches of Solomon and taught those who weren't as bedazzled by miracles as they were hungry for righteousness (*If*, he said, *when you stand to pray, you hold anything against anyone, forgive him first, and your Father in heaven will forgive you*), those disciples newly come into the Temple expressed a variety of wonders.

Matthew sat down in the Court of the Women near the room where oil was stored. He bowed his head and made a cup of his hands in the space between his knees. When he looked up again he didn't move but gazed towards gates of Corinthian bronze in a private, undemonstrable silence. Here he remained during our entire time in the Temple.

Nathanael inclined towards pieties. He went down to the Huldah Gates at the low south side of the Temple where he washed himself in the ritual baths – oh, what quantities of water in Jerusalem! – then reascended the steps with a tingling sense of cleanliness and gratitude.

Thomas the Twin ('Let's go, that we might die with him') had apparently forgotten the proximities of death. He strolled up and down the Portico of Solomon, touching the magnificent, pure white pillars – fifty of them! – which held the roof aloft. Again and again he passed within earshot of Jesus' teaching, sometimes pausing to dwell on the Lord's sonority, if not to interpret the words, so that the carved capitals of the pillars and the sunlight and the wash of the voice of Jesus all created a world of which Thomas could say, 'Good. It is very good.'

In time Jesus concluded his teaching. He rose up and left the portico, and Thomas followed him into the Court of the Women, where they sat near Matthew. Soon Simon Peter came, and Andrew and James and John and Philip.

At their first arriving, Judas Iscariot had flapped his arms and chirped. Truly. He threw himself into a gangling dash, ploughing through the people, approaching every corner of the massive platform, then pursing his lips and nodding. 'I disagree,' he spat, as if in an argument with some blunt fool: 'I disagree, and I know what I'm talking about!' Judas spent a hard half hour staring with wicked cleverness at the Fortress Antonia which overlooked the entire Temple area from its height behind the north-west corner, wherein were garrisoned Pilate's forces, a fastness which (*Look out, you stupid fools!*) could be conquered only by – but surely by – the wonders of God in the hands of his Master.

Judas, satisfied, loped back to the place where Jesus had stood on Sunday, at the Nikanor Gate, its stones overlaid with plates of silver and plates of gold as thick as a tall man's thumb.

On the east side of the gate the rabble crouched and lay about, impoverished and infirm. Beggars stretched out their hands and rattled their bowls and muttered perfunctory benedictions upon the souls of those who dropped a coin therein – and Judas found this somehow musical, an exquisite accompaniment to his dreams and exultations.

On the west side of the gate, across the Court of the Priests and the Israelites, the high Altar of Holocausts sent up billows of savoury smoke to the nostrils of God; and behind the altar blazed the golden Temple in a noonday sun, its doors beset on either side by the great bronze pillars, Boaz and Jachin. Judas turned round and round, his arms extended, his mouth wide open like the kid who catches raindrops, and he laughed.

Suddenly he bounded down the steps and swam through pilgrims to Jesus, who sat near the chamber of oil reserves with the rest of the disciples.

'Now!' Judas cried. 'No need to wait! Let's do it right now!'

What we were to do, or who particularly was to do it with him (all of the disciples? He and Jesus alone?), Judas didn't say. Didn't, perhaps, have the chance to say.

'Shut!' Jesus snapped, clapping his hands as if to drive demons away, 'Up!' Judas blinked and stumbled. Jesus clapped his hands a second time, staring fiercely at the fresh-faced disciple: 'Sit down!'

Judas sat.

Simon Peter glanced at Judas and pursed his lips. He knew the tone of Jesus' voice. He knew its ruinous effect.

Jesus said, 'And listen. Open your clogged ears. Ignore the sounds inside of you. Listen.'

Listen to what? To which? There were multitudinous groanings and sighings of prayers. There were bleatings and baaings of sacrificial animals, flappings of birdwings, commandings from priests, songs of the Levites, conversations, the treadings of the thousand-footed faithful, timbrels and psalms in various tongues arising from knots of pilgrims –

Listen to what?

Jesus pointed. He sent our attentions to the shofar-shaped treasuries which were attached to the columns all around the Court of the Women. With regard to Judas, however, he did more than merely point and suggest. He took hold of the hair at the back of the young man's head and aimed his face to each of the bronze treasuries, one at a time.

'Did you bring the money box?' he asked.

As much as Jesus' grip allowed, Judas shook his head. 'You didn't tell me to.' The poor lad was in pain. Not from his hair. From this demonstration, rather, which he didn't understand, either its meaning or else what it had to do with him.

'Listen,' Jesus repeated, releasing Judas. 'What do you hear?'

The young disciple, his neck splotched red, strained to listen, hearing nothing, apparently, because he was hearing everything.

'Matthew,' Jesus said, 'what do you hear?'

'Money,' Matthew said.

Ah! Yes: men of importance, men of evident wealth, their clothing dyed in purples and blues, were dumping Tyrian currency into the treasuries, the coinage clinking and clanging and rumbling against the thin bronze receptacles.

'Judas,' Jesus said, 'what do you hear?'

Judas said, 'Money.'

'Right. Good.' Jesus patted his shoulder. 'Now, look over there' – Jesus pointed towards the Nikanor Gate – 'and watch.'

A very old woman had just pulled herself up to her feet. She began to shuffle through the Court of the Women in a direction somewhat slant of us. She pressed a begging bowl in both hands against her stomach. Soon, though she took desperately small steps, we knew her direction, if not her mind: she was moving towards the treasury just to the right of us. As she crept by, I saw her in profile: a long translucent nose; eyelids loose, the low rims sagging from their eyeballs, her mouth working like a Pharisee's at prayer. When she reached the treasury she brought forth the begging bowl and turned it slowly over above the bell-like mouth, and two tiny bits of metal fell from the bowl into the bronze.

We could hear nothing of the fall.

'Judas, my brother, my bright disciple,' Jesus said. 'Know the difference. Live by it: those rich men who contributed wonderful sums to the Temple were contributing something of their surplus.

It never touched their need. But this widow who gave two copper mites – she has given more than ten such notables combined. For she gave all she had. It was everything she had to live on.'

My brother. My bright disciple: Judas took the words as an immediate redemption. All was well! He was back in his Master's confidence, enthusiastic and ready! He unfolded himself and jumped up. 'Want me to run for the money box? I can. I will. Is that what you want?'

Jesus sighed. He stood and started to walk away.

'Enough,' said Jesus to the air in front of his face.

It was a brooding Lord who led us to the south-western gate and down its dizzy flight of stairs into the low Tyropeon Valley and thence around to the Kidron.

Judas – his sky cloudless, refulgent with sunshine – kept craning his neck to see to the top of the Temple's magnificent retaining wall, eighty feet above him. Most of its ashlar stones were three feet thick and nine feet long; but some near the bottom courses were four times those in length. They were well-hewn and fitted perfectly and of such density that the largest weighed a hundred tons. How had Herod hauled such behemoths here and up and into place!

'Just look at those stones,' Judas marvelled. 'What a plan! What a triumph! I'll betcha Rome never built buildings like these!'

'Buildings like these,' Jesus said without turning to look at Judas. 'I tell you, the time is coming when not one stone will be left upon another. And marble and cedar and columns and capitals, gates and porches, walls and roofs – it will all be plundered and crushed to the ground.'

Judas paused while the rest kept walking. 'But we've come to take it, right? Not to tear it down. Master? Right?'

On the west side of the Mount of Olives there is a small garden and a pressworks which renders oil from ripened olives. Accordingly, the garden is called 'Gethsemane'. To this place, to Gethsemane, Jesus led us that afternoon. He turned to face Jerusalem, then sat on the low, horizontal branch of an oak tree, as if this garden had been long familiar, a haunt of his, perhaps, in the days before John had baptized him.

We all sat on patches where the ground was dry, on stones, on our robes.

'When, Lord?' Simon Peter, too, was gazing westwards to the Temple, his great brow puckered and troubled. 'When will the beautiful stones fall down?'

Philip said, 'Will there be some sort of sign before it happens?'

Quietly Jesus began to speak of terrible things.

'Watch out that no one deceives you,' he said. 'Many will come in my name, braying, "I am he." Frauds.

'And watch out: when you hear of wars and rumours of wars, don't be alarmed. Such things must happen in the term of this world and aren't yet the end. There *will* be war and earthquakes and famines and plagues and portents in the heavens. But they are only the beginning of the birth pains.

'And you – ' Jesus closed his mouth a moment, breathing through his nose. 'Be on your guard. You will be handed over to councils. They will beat you in the synagogues. You will stand before governors on my account. And kings. And brutal emperors. But first, to every nation, the good news must and will be preached.

'And when they do arrest you, when they bring you to trial, don't worry for what you will say. Say whatever comes to mind, because it won't be you – it will be the Holy Spirit speaking through you.

'You will be hated because of my name. But endure, my little children. Endure to the end and you will be saved.'

Simon Peter whispered, 'The end? Is that what we asked? About the end?'

'When you see Jerusalem surrounded by armies,' Jesus said with a sibilant, articulated clarity, 'you will know that desolation is near. Let Judea flee to the mountains. Let cities rush to the country because of the great distress on earth. For Jerusalem will be trampled by Gentiles.

'And after the suffering, the sun will be blackened by day, and by night the moon will give no light, and the stars will fall like cinders from heaven, and every celestial body will shudder, and they will see the Son of man coming in clouds and in great power, the king in an ineluctable glory. He will send his angels to the ends of heaven and earth to gather the elect, and these things! – when these things start to happen, stand up! Raise your heads! Your redemption is drawing near.'

The silence that followed swarmed with fears and pictures and thoughts unfinished.

'But, still – ' Simon Peter broke the silence. He was dragging all his fingers through his hair. He seemed even now to be clinging to the question which launched this grim vision of the future. Well, it was a simple question, after all. Simon tended to return to the simple when complexities wanted to swamp him. 'But still, I mean: when, O Lord? When will the… end come?'

And the Lord, for the first time in this discourse, shifted his eyes from Jerusalem to us.

'I don't know,' he said. It wasn't a joke; it wasn't a slur; it wasn't a dismissal. It proved to be a primal mystery. 'No one knows that day or that hour,' Jesus said, 'not the angels in heaven, not the Son. It is only the Father who knows. It is only the Father who will ever know – until the end is upon you.

'Simon, John, James, all of you, and all to whom you will preach throughout the world: keep watch. Keep alert. Keep awake. Don't fall asleep. You do not know when the master will come. In the evening, at midnight, at cockcrow, at dawn. Keep wide awake – or what will happen if the king on the clouds of his glorious power should find you sleeping?'

WEDNESDAY: MARY

=

'Martha, did you make the oven yourself? This clay is seamless.'
'It comes from Bethlehem.'

'Really?' Joanna said. 'I know the reputation but I've never seen one before. Smooth sides. Perfect hollows for the dough. So finely porous. I'll bet nothing sticks or burns.'

'The Syrian once thought to marry Mary. He tried to strike up negotiations with me – there being no other family except me, you see. There being no inclination to marry the older sister first, you see.'

'I do.'

They worked in the courtyard. Martha – the fat at her neck and her arms shaking – was shaking wicker baskets over a thatch of dry grass on which had been placed three cakes of dried dung. Bread baskets made of peeled willow branches. Every crumb in every basket had to be burned. Martha blew hard into the weaving, because if but the tiniest crumb could not be dislodged, the whole basket had to be burned.

'He gave me the oven as a sign of good faith. Mary saw no good in a foreigner who wouldn't fear God. He saw no reason why Mary's opinion should count at all. I saw no value in debate. I kept the sister and the oven, both.'

'Let's use the oven.'

'What?'

'Oh, come on, Martha. Let's don't burn the leaven. Let's bake it.'

'Well.' Martha stood erect and placed her hands on her marvellous hips. There, by the doorway, was Maryam from

Magdala, peering up from beneath her eyebrows with a sweet appeal, nodding. And suddenly over the edge of the roof hung the head of Lazarus, upside down and grinning: 'I'm hungry.'

Martha giggled. 'Let's,' she said. 'Let's have a party!'

Up to that point the women had spent Wednesday cleaning Martha's house, her courtyard, her storage rooms and all her holdings. Actually, house-cleaning had been their secondary consideration. Primarily, they sought all *hametz*, to remove it from the premises. They'd burn it or eat it or give it away – perhaps to the Syrian who stabled his horses near Bethphage. Nothing leavened, nor any leavening at all, could be left in Martha's keeping by noon tomorrow, Thursday, the day of preparation for the Passover. Yeast-bread, yeasty dough, beer and every other fermented food, gone: for the Passover celebrated Israel's escape from Egypt, when the Lord God commanded the people to prepare themselves for the flight, eating unleavened bread with their loins girded, their sandals on, and their staffs in their hands.

But then, all in a twinkling, it was decided that *hametz* should not be burned nor given, but eaten away, with other foods that were not forbidden, but were savoury and satisfying and could gladden the heart.

So while some of the women kept searching for *hametz*, others began to chop and to dice and to boil water in copper pots, to bring honey and fruits from the market, and a crushing of nuts for delicate crusts.

It had been a warmish winter. Barley would be ready for harvesting right after Passover and in time for the wave offering. But for now they swept the bottom of the barley bin and ground the last grain on the saddle-quern in the courtyard and kneaded a dough with honey and nuts and stuck pats of the dough to the side of the oven and baked it there. They cooked fresh eggs and brought forth pickled ones. They plucked quail and cleaned them. Maryam from Magdala heated a malodorous fish sauce, then slipped the quail therein to steep through the afternoon. She promised (dipping her head and smiling like a beldame with a secret) to make of the meat an unforgettable dish.

Through most of the year Martha raised a vegetable garden, harvesting in their seasons cabbages, beetroot, leeks, turnips, onions, cucumbers, lettuce, lentils, beans of several sorts, peas.

She grew a sort of muskmelon. And watermelon. She dried what she could, stored root plants in cool caverns underground, and ate what couldn't be preserved. Martha had a little orchard too, a sycamore, fig trees, two almond trees, a grove of mulberries for the black fruit, from which she made a sweet wine. And close by the house she worked a bed of herbs, mustard, cumin, chicory, garlic.

On this Wednesday Martha stinted nothing of her gardens and her stores. Everyone, all the women, abandoned every gloomy thought and turned their hearts to the banquet to come. Tonight there'll be no sorrow, my Lord. Tonight we're throwing a party!

They giggled, chewing myrtle berries to sweeten their breaths.

Joanna kissed Chuza elaborately, then wheedled from him the coin he hadn't given Judas – absolutely the last of his personal currency. She mounted a horse behind young Lazarus and rode into Jerusalem, where she purchased spices most expensive: saffron, cinnamon and ginger for the flavourings; calamus for the scent it would deliver that evening; and, from a garden in the city so well known she'd heard of it in Galilee, roses in profusion.

The women looked at one another and laughed outright. They chattered at high decibels. They gabbed about their husbands and silliness and lovemaking and children both lovely and stupid. They noticed – and at the same time they refused to notice – that a strange extravagance had overcome them. They would not think about tomorrow (in spite of the feast that must follow tomorrow): they'd enjoy it all today! They would feed on life today.

No sorrow tonight, my Lord! And tonight there's no tomorrow!

Mary, the sister of Martha, went to a small niche in the wall of an interior room and lifted the cloth that covered it. She touched an alabaster flask therein, which was filled to the wooden stopper with perfume. For three years she'd been accumulating nard by dribs and drabs until finally her flask was full. The woman had saved twelve ounces of genuine nard. Compulsively, now, she wrapped her hands around the flask and drew it out of the niche and turned, her braid swinging a midnight rope.

Mary, the mother of Jesus, went alone to wander the forests and the fields and the stony hills nearby. Alone, but not in loneliness. She had laughed with the same abandon as did the rest of the women. She, too, allowed herself a flushed and hectic hilarity. She had come out alone, singing wordless hosannas, in order to gather herbs and condiments according to her own particular knowing: sorrel for salads and sauces; mallow, the whole of which – the fruit, the leaf and the seed – was good to eat, and whose properties would both soothe abrasions and keep a swollen stomach from tightening up too much; rue for its pungency, though she knew it best as medicine against the bite of an insect; and lemon grass and hyssop and black cumin for cakes and coriander and chamomile.

And after everyone in the pretty evening had gathered and reclined and washed their hands, then – against custom, against ten laws and twenty religious restrictions – it was Martha, not Jesus nor any other man, who stood up and raised her hands and uttered a blessing before the meal: 'Father, blessed are you for bringing bread forth from the earth.' She broke the fresh barley bread and began to distribute the pieces here and there among the diners.

There were no long tables in the village of Bethany, nor anywhere else east of the Mount of Olives. This banquet was celebrated at square wooden boards which had been set, not on four legs, on tripods in order to manage the uneven ground. Three people reclined around each single board. All now drew their food from central dishes, eating with flat wooden chips and drinking from glass cups. But all the people of Jesus' family were in talking distance of one another, some in the courtyard, some in the rooms, several reclining on the roof beside the parapets over which they leaned to look down and to talk.

Suddenly Joanna started to sing:

Awake, O north wind! South wind, come,
And whirl across my garden!
Take my fragrance far abroad,
A savour for my lover;
Bring hither, winds, my lover!

A wedding song!
Simon Peter, his mouth full of pickled egg, threw back his

head, bellowed with laughter. 'Who's getting married, Joanna? Who's the blushing bride?'

'Not *my* daughter, surely, surely. That girl's been ploughed and planted more than once. And the second pod's about to burst!'

'Joanna! Mixed company,' Chuza hissed. 'Women's ears are here.'

'Women's? Oh, but it's men's we have to worry about.' Joanna poked her finger into the whorls of her husband's ear and giggled as brightly as bells. 'On account of, O man: who knows the point of a busy ploughshare *better* than a woman?'

'Haw!' Mary astonished herself with a guffaw as rude as a goat's. But that was funny!

And all the women gave voice to the strange gaiety that had been growing in them all day long. They laughed. They covered their faces at the raw pleasure of their laughter. They sniggered and cackled and wiped their eyes.

The men stared at the women, bewildered smiles upon their faces. The men: they looked like boys in a swimming hole, stripped bare and caught by their mothers. It drove Mary to greater heights of hilarity.

And then Jesus was laughing too. *Oh, Yeshi! Yeshi!* Her son delivered himself wholly to joy, arching his eyebrows, turning his narrow mouth down, snorting. He cough-laughed, producing a strangled sound, like a fawn's dam sneezing.

Mary's laughter died in a dear and perfect delight.

Then there was a stentorian boom. Simon Peter, a bull ox collapsing in mirth. It was predictable. Whenever he heard the ridiculous choke-laughing of his Master, the big man was knocked over by the anomaly. He roared. He beat his thigh. The other men joined in, abandoning themselves to the moment, until both men and women, the young and the old, high-born and low-born, Jews and the lone Nabatean, *all* were united, and the entire family knew a pure and sacred communion for the last time.

'Maryam from Magdala.'

'What? What did you say?'

Gathering rose petals from the table before her, Mary spoke into the sighs that follow laughter: 'It's Maryam from Magdala, Simon' – she blew the petals high into the air – 'the one you asked about. She is the blushing bride.'

Everyone looked to the manger-side of the courtyard.

Indeed! That poor lily was burning red as a rose. And so flustered was she that her mouth kept popping like a sardine's in clear water. She was, as Mary knew with a certainty – Maryam from Magdala was pointedly *not* looking at Yeshi.

And then, to everyone's astonishment, the sober Matthew, still unsmiling, sang in a sweet, liquid tenor the answering stanza to Joanna's wedding song:

I'll come into the garden, bride,
And eat my golden honey;
I'll gather myrrh and every spice
When all the winds are ready
And all your portals open.

'Hoooo,' little Maryam murmured, her ears aflame, enchanting the entire company. None did not love her. And mother Mary was moved to see how the crushable child did trust them all in return, how she was in no wise offended – and yet how desperately she hoped that no one knew her more precious secret: her ineffable love for Jesus. It was this which had brought the mad woman to life again. It was he who had brought her even to the *willingness* to live again.

Old Mary covered for the younger Maryam. She stretched out her arms and led everyone in the chorus that must always follow the stanza Matthew had sung:

And now we eat!
And now we drink!
And all grow drunk on loving!

They sang it several times over, then fell, as they said, to eating again.

While they ate Jesus began to speak, and the mood turned lovely, almost romantic, the food and his sentiments taken together. Nor were his words unrelated to the merriment of the evening; but he moved their thoughts from humour to something far more personal.

'This is what the prophet says,' said Jesus, glancing at Maryam from Magdala (*he knows, Yeshi knows! – but of course he would know*). 'Don't be afraid. Don't be ashamed,' he said. 'You must forget the shame of your youth. For your Maker is your husband; the Holy One of Israel is your Redeemer, the God of all the earth. He has called you like a wife forsaken and grieving in her spirit. For one brief moment I forsook you; but now, with great compassion, bride, I bring you back. In a surge of anger I hid my face from you. For just a moment. And now, with an everlasting love, I have compassion for you, says the Lord, who is to you what no one else can be: your Redeemer.'

In a gesture which Mary had grown to know as Maryam's manner of speaking deep things – and which this evening was more telling than it had ever been before – the pale, spectral woman ascended from her place by the manger and moved smoothly towards Jesus, where he was reclining on his left arm. There she settled herself cross-legged at his back. She folded her hands beneath her robe. She bowed her head. Mary the mother of Jesus began to cry. Jesus didn't turn.

He continued speaking, embracing everyone with a new story. 'I compare the kingdom of heaven to the coming of a bridegroom,' he said. 'Ten virgins take their lamps and go out to meet him. Five of the virgins are wise: besides their lamps they bring jars of extra oil. Five are foolish: they bring their lamps alone.

'But the bridegroom is a long time coming. The day passes into evening. The virgins grow drowsy and fall asleep. And who could blame them? Surely not my rock-man. Surely not the dauntless sons of thunder, who will drink the cup I am to drink.'

All the diners in Martha's house were thoughtful now. Some chewing, some sipping the wine the women had mixed with water. Jesus seemed to be making the story up as he went, pausing for thought, pausing as well, Mary knew, to let its picture form in everyone's mind.

He rubbed his bewhiskered chin with the back of his right hand. His long lashes had taken a lustrous colour in the lamplight, each a nimbus over its eye. *Oh, how I love you, Yeshi, your eyes, your heart, the words of your mouth. O God, how I love you!*

Jesus drew a breath and began again: 'In the very middle of the night someone runs through the city, shouting, "Here he comes!

Get up and come! Come meet the bridegroom and rejoice!"

'All the virgins wake. Immediately they begin to trim their lamps.

'But the foolish discover a problem. They go to the wise. "Give us some of your oil," they beg. "Our lamps are going out."

'The wise ones answer, "If we did what you want, there wouldn't be enough for both of us. Go to the shops. Buy your own."

'Ah, but while the foolish five are gone, the bridegroom arrives, and those who were ready go with him into the wedding banquet, and the door is shut.

'So, when later the other five run to the door, they have to pound on it, crying: "Lord! Please! Open the banquet hall to us!"

'But he will say, "I do not know you." And what then? What then for the foolish?

'Watch,' Jesus said very, very quietly. 'Be ready, my friends. Make yourselves ready for the *real* wedding banquet. Tonight is a pretty pretence – '

O Yeshi, don't! Don't blame our little party!

' – but the real banquet, the kingdom banquet, is coming. You don't want to be caught outside. But, as I told you before, you do not know the hour. You don't even know the day.'

All he said he'd said in gentleness. But Mary's chest had begun to suffer pressures, and her bowels were shifting within. This harmless, playful day – *not yet, there still is time yet* – it didn't *have* to sink into gloom already, did it?

Then Mary saw that other Mary, Martha's sister, striding queenlike among the table-boards towards Jesus. In her hands the sister bore an alabaster flask. And something else: yes, she had unbound the customary braid! All adown her shoulders fell the long black hair, as thick and beautiful as a shawl upon her, her back and bosom both.

A diversion? Mary wondered. *A gift to renew the evening?*

Maryam from Magdala no longer maintained her far-off gazing. She tilted her head and watched while the taller sister approached the place of Jesus' feet, then knelt with a billowing grace. Holding the flask in both hands, the sister pulled the wooden stopper with her teeth from the opening.

Maryam gasped.

A diversion, indeed! thought Mary.

For Martha's sister, Mary's namesake, was pouring the entire flask of oil (it was nard, by the scent of it) over Jesus' feet, his ankles, the lower portion of his legs. She set the flask aside and rubbed the ointment under her two palms into his skin. And then, her hair so heavy it seemed to be wet, with a nod of her head as great as a mare's, she threw it forward. The sable hair formed a veil that covered her countenance. Nevertheless, no one did not see how with that hair the regal sister was wiping the perfume from Jesus' feet.

Judas Iscariot leaped up and clapped his hands. Clapped them again in frightful derision – exactly as Jesus had clapped his yesterday.

'Woman, be hanged!' Judas cried, clapping sharply again and again.

It wasn't as if Mary understood what Martha's darker sister was doing. Nor could she approve of the act – a little too intimate for her taste. Be frank: a little too sexual. But Judas's nasty intrusion was simply intolerable. He, now: *he* was the true destroyer of their 'pretty pretence'.

'No!' Mary shrieked. '*You* be hanged! You go straight to the Devil, Judas Iscariot! Who are you to find fault with what she's doing?'

'A three-hundred-silver-denarii fault!' he shouted back. 'She's wasting treasure! It'd take me a *year* to earn that much! The whole house stinks of her stupidity.'

Simon Peter said, 'I'm going to hit you, fool! Lord, please, let me go over and hit him.'

'Treasure?' James was shouting. 'Foxes have holes. Birds have nests, but we have chosen this life, and nowhere to lay our heads!'

Joanna murmured, nearly brokenhearted, 'We gave our wealth away. Who wants money now?'

'You want me to gather taxes again?' Matthew spoke more openly. 'You want money any way you can get it? You've got something in mind you need to buy?'

'"All she had."' The voice of Jesus cut with articulate precision through the noise. '"Everything she had to live on." Can you have forgotten in a single day?'

'No, no, no!' Judas's eyes were wide. He was flicking them from person to person, fearful, seeking an ally. 'No one understands me! I *meant* that we should give it to the poor, didn't I? That's what I *meant*! No one – Listen, no one anoints somebody's *feet*!'

'Judas, shut up!' Jesus commanded. 'Let the woman alone.'

Jesus turned, sitting, to confront his anointress. With his thumbs he divided her hair at the brow, revealing her tragic face, the eyes cast down.

'The poor are with you always.' Though he was looking at the darker sister, he surely was not addressing her. 'Me you will not always have. And you, boy: you have more to learn than you know. This woman has ministered to me and prophesied at the same time. Learn this: those who anoint the dead anoint the feet. She saved her ointment, Judas, against the day of my burial.'

When he fell silent all were silent. Soon the women arose and began to take the wooden tables with the dishes and the leftover food away.

But Judas could not contain himself.

Looking at no one, twitching his eyebrows up and down as though to keep from crying, he went to Jesus and whispered in his ear: 'I'm the only one who knows what you're going to do. Peter and them, they don't have a clue. But you avoid me all day long. And you pick on me like I was a kid – '

'Judas? *How* do you know what I am about to do?'

'You said it! You said it yourself, and I read the meanings under the words!'

'"Going up to Jerusalem," you mean? Those words?'

'Yes!'

'But there was no secret there. "To be delivered to the chief priests"?'

'Yes! Yes!'

'"To be condemned. To be killed – "'

'No! See? There's the cover. That's the way you talk to cover things. But "those who have ears to hear", you know, they're the ones who get it. I mean, I *get* it, Master.'

'Get what?'

'"Sell your cloak and go buy swords," you say, and look around. Who bought one? Even *before* you said to? "Wars", you say. "Rumours of wars." Well, of course!'

'You are a disciple,' Jesus said, withdrawing a bit, rubbing his ear of the blowing and spitting. 'Judas, you are as much a disciple of mine as anyone here. But you *are* younger and you haven't spent time in serious study and you don't pay attention. You've been very slow to learn – '

'Oh, I disagree! "Jerusalem, your house is desolate!" What is that? Did you think no one was paying attention on Sunday? "House is desolate!" Sounds like a righteous threat to me.'

'A threat? A truth. And the cause of grief in me.'

'And I'd've figured Sunday was the day! Perfect day for the wonders of God. Making a mess of the Temple, scaring the Levites. But then you didn't take advantage of it. Surprised me! So maybe you were looking for a better time.'

'Judas, boy – '

'I'm not a boy!'

'You are sadly callow – '

'I'm not a *boy*!'

'Listen to me. Please. My time will be nothing like the time which any itching insurrectionist is looking for. There'll be no fighting, no mighty hand and an outstretched arm, no marvels, no national victory – are you listening to me? And only one man will spill his blood for the people – '

'Whosever blood! Whose-*ever*, Master! Doesn't matter! What matters is that the time should be soon! Nothing on Monday. Nothing on Tuesday. We did nothing today.'

'I have loved you, Judas, every one of these days. It is not nothing.'

'Talk's weak. Action changes the world. All you need's a reason.'

'I have every reason.'

'Right! All you need's an opportunity. A little nudge.'

'I've put myself in the way of opportunity since the day we came to Jerusalem.'

'Right. A little nudge. A little skirmish to get you going. Push you past talk in the wonders God's given you. Tomorrow night. Passover. Yes, yes, I see that you've been right all along. Master with a master plan, hey? Ha ha. You bet. No day's better than *that* day. Right.'

'Judas Iscariot: do not do this thing.'

'Right! Right.'

Jesus paused and gazed at him with a piercing, steadfast gaze.

The freckles on his eyelid gave a nearly maternal weight to Jesus' expression. Then, quietly, he drew the young man to himself and embraced him. It surprised Judas, whose arms hung straight at his sides, clasped in the arms of his Master. The bare, unwhiskered face – like a moon above the skull of the Lord – ran through a series of emotions, suspicion, discomfort, a dawning knowledge, the satisfied smile of someone chosen, someone elected and commended. But then the hugging went on too long, and his smiling withered at the corners.

'Judas, Judas,' Jesus finally murmured. His words sank like moisture into the cloth that covered the breast of the callow disciple. 'If you love me you will keep my commandments. But I, my child? Whatever you *think* is coming, and whatever is coming indeed, remember this: I will love you even unto the end.'

Judas managed to bend his right elbow. He raised his hand and patted Jesus consolingly at the small of his back. He said, 'I got it, Master. Really. Don't worry. I know exactly what to do.'

The plates and the bowls were clean. All the leaven in Martha's house had been consumed, both eaten and burned. The lamps had been extinguished. In less than an hour it would be midnight. The women had gathered in a single room at the back of the house, and had laid their sad, worn bodies side by side on the clay-hard floor – all save Mary, who sat in shadow near Judas and her Yeshi.

Some kind of conclusion had occurred in that conversation, though she didn't know what. She'd understood the language well enough, at least the cluckings of Judas; and she would have dismissed everything the beak-nosed popinjay had said – except that when he slipped out of the courtyard and into the Judean night, Yeshi did not move. *Ah, God.* The man whom once she had, by the mercies of heaven, suckled, now stood in the darkness alone, his hands drooping, his knees enfeebled and trembling enough to punch the front of his robe.

Be strong! Be fearless! Behold, your God is coming! He will come with vengeance. He will bring a terrible recompense! He will save you.

WEDNESDAY NIGHT

There is a discreet metallic tapping on the bars of the gate that protects the courtyard of the high priest.

A guard goes to the gate, a slave of Caiaphas on watch till midnight. Outside there hunches, impossibly, the shadow of a walking stick. The slave lifts a torch. The shadow resolves itself into a fellow with a youngish face. He's been tapping with the tip of a sword.

'Let me see that sword.'

'What?'

'Let me see your sword.'

'No.'

'Show it, you bloody bandit!'

'I'm not a bandit. Why do you call me a bandit?'

But the young fellow lifts the sword with one hand, holding it back from the bars and attempting a soldier's pose, but poorly, unfamiliar with weaponry. That sword, on the other hand: it's not iron or Roman, but bronze and Greek, remarkably well tooled at the haft, and sharper than bronze has a right to be. Must be Corinthian. Sometimes in Corinth they strike swords of their celebrated bronze, though not often.

'OK,' the slave says. 'What do you want?'

The fellow fits the blade through a loop under his robe. No sheath. Not even a sheath.

'I want to see Caiaphas.'

'Impossible.'

'I have information.'

'You have a name?'

'None you've heard of.'

'Ha! A nameless bandit. Sneaks through the night. And thinks he might, by the mere asking for it, see the chief. If you're not a bandit, you're an idiot. Go away.'

'Wait! I'm serious! I've got very important information.'

'You got money?'

'We're poor. Maybe I can find a silver coin.'

'Not enough for bearing messages. Not even enough for chitchat.'

'Watch out, slave!' Lo, how the puppy snarls! 'Caiaphas wants to know what I know.'

'And he wants my britches too.'

'No, but he *asked* for this. The high priest himself! Officially, publicly, *demanded* it.'

'Of *you*, pup?' The slave elevates his torch and peers elaborately through the bars.

'Of everyone. I *said* "publicly". He sent Levites and messengers everywhere. Don't you know what your master does? But I'm the only one that knows! No one knows the stuff he wants but me.'

'You got cousins and buddies behind you, boy? Hiding?'

'No! I came alone.'

'So what is it the chief says he wants to know?'

'The hiding place of Jesus of Nazareth.'

'Ahhh. Finally. The meat in the nut – not altogether bitter, either. And I s'pose you know this Jesus of Nazareth.'

'Yes. I'm a friend. A very close friend.'

'Couldn't prove it to me.'

'Look, slave! If the high priest finds out you ignored the man with the path to Jesus, it's you on the outside after that, not me. It's you gets sold or whipped or crucified.'

'Good. Good. There's spunk in the puddler. Give me the sword.'

'What?'

'I'll take your sword, *then* I'll take your message to Caiaphas. He's sleeping. I run a risk.'

'No.'

'Sorry, pup. Forget it.'

The guard turns and walks back to the fire he keeps in the courtyard. He tosses the torch on the coals and sits.

The young fellow out in the darkness croaks: 'OK, OK! But I better get money for my information.' The slave looks up. The lad is sliding the weapon from its loop. He pokes it blade-first through the metal bars. 'Money enough for another sword, I better,' he yammers as the guard returns, reaches through the bars and takes the sword by the haft. 'And if I don't,' the hairless caterpillar threatens, 'I'll cut you! What's your name?'

The guard lifts the bar and pulls the slow gate inward.

'Come in. Come in,' he says. The kid walks in, tall as Saul beside the slave. 'Over there,' he commands as he pushes the gate closed and drops the bar in place, 'by the fire. Wait while I go and make the high priest angry by waking him.' And then, walking towards an interior door, lightly swinging the sword in order to find its balance, the slave says, 'Malchus. What's yours?'

THURSDAY: THE BELOVED

In the forenoon of the day of preparation, the women asked Jesus where he planned to eat the Passover meal, once the sun had set.

'Not here, of course,' they said. 'Somewhere inside the city limits – though they widen those limits for Passover. We could celebrate on the west side of the Mount of Olives.'

'No,' Jesus said to them. 'It's fitting for us to fulfil all righteousness – even to eating within the walls of Jerusalem. So then, you go. You choose. I want you to find a room for the men and me.'

'Us? Oh, Lord, by now there isn't a room not spoken for. And who do we know in Jerusalem?'

'Shhhh. The time has come. Everything will happen exactly as it must.' He put his hand as if in blessing on Maryam's head. 'How often,' he said, 'do you see a man hauling water?'

Maryam grew crimson and couldn't talk.

But Joanna was giggling. 'Never,' she said. 'Or almost never.'

'Precisely. Go into the city where you will, in fact, notice a well-dressed man balancing on his head a tall jar of water. Follow him. He'll enter a house two stories high. Find the owner of that house and say to her, "The Teacher asks, 'Where is my guest room that I might eat the Passover with my disciples?'" She will show you a large upper room already furnished and ready. Make preparations there. The men and I will arrive with the lamb after sunset.'

And so it was that Jesus returned to the Temple for the last time.

He with all the rest of us – the men, I mean, and Judas, and the money box – purchased a yearling lamb, unspotted and unblemished.

At three in the afternoon a Levite stood on the pinnacle of the Temple and blew his trumpet. Thrice. Declarative blasts to the men of Israel: *Bring your sacrifices! Let the lambs be slaughtered!*

We bathed. We joined the great river of pilgrims ascending and descending the steps of the Temple Mount. In the Court of the Priests and the Israelites, under the shadow of the great cloud that rose from the broiling, spitting sacrifices, we killed the lamb, whose blood was caught on a silver tray and flung against the altar.

O Lord, I am thy servant, sang a choir of Levites arranged in rows on the steps of the Nikanor Gate. Pipes blew a sinuous, linen-smooth beauty under the song: *I am thy servant, the son of thy handmaid; thou has loosed my bonds! I will offer thee the sacrifice of thanksgiving –*

Then, our animal dressed and flayed, the legs unbroken, the head attached and the whole of it wrapped inside the pelt, we went out of the Temple.

Chuza carried the lamb off to the women, that they might roast it in time for the meal.

And when it was evening, Jesus and the twelve tramped up an outside staircase to the second-storey room, and entered. There were three long tables arranged in the shape of a three-sided square, the fourth side open to accommodate the serving. We moved to our places around the tables and sank down to the carpets and the cushions on the floor.

Jesus, choosing to host this feast, reclined in the middle of the middle table, settling his left side over the bolster and leaning on the elbow of his left arm. I reclined nearest him, on my own left side with my back to his breathing.

From the walls and the tabletops, lamplight enlivened the robes and the faces of everyone gathered here and gazing inward, the close-cropped beard and the well-formed head of the Lord, his thin lips, his dazzling, rust-brown eyes.

Jesus saw to the first pouring of the wine, rose up, went round into the centre of the square, and one by one distributed the cups till each one had one, except himself. 'Blessed be the Lord our

God, king of the universe, who chose us from every people,' Jesus said, 'who exalted us among every tongue and sanctified us by his commandments. And blessed are you, O Lord our God, for creating the fruit of the vine.'

When he had finished that blessing, he said, 'Go ahead. Drink. As for me, I won't drink the fruit of the vine before the kingdom of heaven has come.'

With ceremony, then, we drained our cups. Not Jesus. He had no cup.

Next he lifted before us a round, flat bread and gave utterance to the familiar formula: 'Blessed are you, O Lord our God, king of the universe, who brings forth bread from the earth.' As ever before, he broke the bread into pieces and gave each of us a portion, saying, 'Take it. Eat it.' But just as we put the bread into our mouths, he whispered, 'This is my body which is broken for you. Do this in remembrance of me.'

Unleavened bread by nature is dry. But this bread sucked all moisture from my mouth. I had trouble swallowing it. Suddenly the tenor of the meal had changed. Familiar formulas twisted into a breathless unfamiliarity.

Though the rest fell to eating now, I could but pick at the food. Jesus ate nothing at all. He watched us closely, narrowing his eye.

Then he rose and stripped himself of his robe. He tied a towel around the waist of his seamless tunic and walked to a sideboard where he poured water from a pitcher into a basin. Carefully, Jesus carried the basin to the outside of the tables where our legs lay extended. He kneeled down, and he began to wash our feet. Patiently, attendant to every particular from ankle to toes, he washed Nathanael's feet, and James's and Judas's and Andrew's. He wiped them with the towel.

He washed mine.

Oh, I shuddered under his touch. My heels so hardened, his palms as pliant and as unashamed as lilies. The towel so silken, it felt like hair to me. And I, in my soul, was weeping.

Quietness had settled on the room. No one chewed. We watched our Lord move from one to the other – until, at the last, he came to Simon.

I don't know whether that Rock-man had studied his next move. Likely it was spontaneous. For in the instant Jesus' fingers brushed his feet, Simon snatched them back and locked his arms around his knees.

'Why would you even think to wash my feet?' he fairly whined.

'If I don't,' said Jesus, 'you have no part in me.'

'Whoa!' cried Simon Peter, thrusting his legs straight out and hiking both his robe and his tunic to his thighs: 'Then wash me all over, Lord, hands and head and feet!'

'Those who have bathed are wholly clean,' Jesus said while taking into his hands the horny soles of the fisherman. 'They need but only their feet to be washed.'

When he had finished his peculiar ritual, Jesus returned the basin and the towel to the sideboard. He shook out his robe and put it on.

'You call me Teacher; you call me Lord,' he said as he reclined again at the host's position. 'And you are right; I am. So if I, your Teacher and your Lord, have washed your feet,' he said, catching, every one of us, our eyes, 'then you should do as I have done. You must, my friends, lower yourselves – even to the lowliness of slavery. Each of you must, when I am no longer here, wash the feet of the others.'

Jesus' eyes glittered in the lamplight. I thought it was because he kept shifting them significantly from face to face around the room. 'But go on now,' he said. 'There is food still before you. Eat.'

Most of the disciples obeyed. I put a small bite of lamb in my mouth, but held it there like a pebble on which, if I chewed it, I would break my teeth. I stole a glance at Jesus.

No – the glittering was not some sort of motion in his eyes. It was water, brimming to the lid, making a radiance of his lashes. I looked away, breathing very deeply. The weeping within me threatened to rise up in sobs.

Simon Peter never, never would chew with his mouth closed! He made a noxious show of eating. He rolled the food around with his tongue and drooped his eyelids and smacked his lips and dribbled sauce on his whiskers and enjoyed the cookery all too much.

Then Jesus was speaking. Hoarsely. A mucous thickening in his throat.

'One of you,' he said. He bowed his head and coughed. 'One

of you,' he said, only slowly raising his face again, 'is just about to hand me over. One of you plans to give me away.'

That shut Simon's mouth. And mine. And my wretched pettiness.

It never occurred to us to doubt his word. But in the bewilderment of that announcement we stared at one another: who was he talking about?

Simon started to pop his eyes and to cock his head from me to Jesus. He wanted me to ask. So I did.

I leaned and laid the back of my head on the bosom of the Lord and looked up: his neat chin, the dark, whistling recesses of his nostrils, the cheeks projecting under his eyes, two sad lines dividing his eyebrows...

'Who, Lord? Who is it?'

In that moment, asking that question and at the same time hearing the deep bellows of his breathing, my love for my Lord was complete and pure.

'The one,' he said, reaching for a flat loaf of unleavened bread, 'to whom I give – ' he broke off a morsel ' – this piece.' Dipping the piece in bitter sauce, he handed it to Judas Iscariot.

Immediately two things happened: a wind outside suddenly struck the door hard enough to flutter the flames inside, throwing shadows like ashes around; and in the ghastly shadow it seemed that Judas smiled. As he took the morsel from Jesus' hand, Judas nodded and winked and seemed to smile a conspiratorial smile.

Jesus said, 'What you are about to do, go: do it quickly.'

Judas unfolded his leggy body and stood and went to the door and opened it – and the night came in as black as a raven and took hold of Judas and drew him out as though it had talons and a terrible will, and the door shut, and Judas was gone, and the lamp flames righted themselves again, and the room grew bright.

No: this was like no other Passover meal any of us had eaten before. No youngest lad asked the question, *Why is this night different?* – for our night was different indeed. And if it were to be asked at all, it should have been Judas asking it. But Judas. Well.

And no one told the story: *Israel in slavery. The land of Egypt benighted, covered in thick darkness. The killing of the firstborn sons. The water crossing. Redemption.*

It seemed to me that at one point Jesus murmured, 'I bear you out on eagle's wings to bring you to. Myself.'

When the meal was ended, the Lord took up a large cup filled with wine. This, too, he lifted towards heaven. The sleeves of his robe fell back to his biceps, revealing the banded muscles and the graceful strength of his forearms. He uttered the familiar thanksgiving: 'We will bless him of whose bounty we have partaken,' and the rest of us murmured, 'Blessed be he of whose bounty we have partaken, and through whose goodness we live.'

'We give you thanks, O Lord our God, for giving us this good land for our heritage,' he said as he had said so often, so often before, 'that we may eat of its fruit and be satisfied with its goodness.'

But when he gave us to drink, the great rush of the unfamiliarity nearly took my breath away, for he whispered, 'What you drink, all of you, is my blood of the new covenant, poured out for many for the forgiveness of sins.'

Blood. His blood.

We drank.

I drank looking at him over the rim of the cup, even as he gazed back into my eyes, his lashes forming a radiance around his gentle attentions. His *blood*.

When we were done drinking, Jesus said, 'Little children, I will be here with you only a little while longer. You will look for me. But where I'm going, you cannot come. Listen to me: I give you a new commandment. Love one another. Exactly as I love you, you must love one another. By this will all the world see me in you – if you have love for one another.

'Sing something,' he said.

We did. Matthew's sweet tenor led us into a portion of the *Hallel* psalms, and during the verses it felt like a normal Passover again – until we all went outside:

Why is it, O sea, that you flee?
O Jordan, that you turn back?
Mountains, why do you tumble like rams?
And hills, like little lambs?

Earth, tremble before the Lord!
Quake in the presence of God,
Whose rivers gush from solid rock,
And bread from heaven drops!

In silence, in the dark of the Jerusalem night, we went down from Zion by a long flight of steps into the lower city, which we crossed towards the Fountain Gate. We bore no torches, no light at all, nothing by which to draw attention to ourselves. And though pilgrims had stayed up late, milling outside the houses, visiting after their meals, we went later than all. Streets and alleys were deserted. Now and then we heard squads of legionnaires marching somewhere among the buildings, but they were easily avoidable. I felt safe. I trusted Jesus. He knew what he was doing.

We crossed the Kidron Valley and began to climb the Mount of Olives. Jesus, going before us, leaning rather more than usual on his staff, spoke a sentence without looking around; half the language, then, was lost to the disciples at the back of our group.

'Tonight, on account of me,' Jesus said, 'you will all turn tail and run.'

'What? What?' This was Simon Peter, pushing forward, bumping and touching us all because of the darkness. 'What did you say?'

Jesus slowed his progress and, still facing forward, said, 'It has been prophesied: *I will strike the shepherd, and the sheep of the flock will be scattered.* So it will be. But after I'm raised up, I'll come and go before you into Galilee.'

'No, no, no, no, *no!*' Simon Peter must have passed Jesus and got in front of him. 'Not me! Even if everyone else runs away on account of you, I won't! I never will!'

We came to a full stop. 'Rocky, I'm going to tell you the truth,' Jesus said not unkindly nor in caution, but as a simple fact: 'Before the rooster crows an end to this very night, you will deny any knowledge of me. You'll deny me, Simon, not once, but three separate times.'

'No!' the stricken disciple howled. 'Even if I have to die with you, I'll never deny you!'

But Jesus was climbing at speed again. And so was I, though Simon wasn't. As I passed him he grabbed my robe and hissed,

'What is this? What's he talking about? What's supposed to *happen* tonight?'

I knew where Jesus intended to go. As soon as we began to climb the mount, I knew, and so experienced less difficulty than the others on the darksome path. There was no moon. Stars there were, but cold and distant, turning the world below into shapes, not faces. And if once the stars were the warrior hosts who, from their courses, came down to fight the Canaanite, tonight they were maidens afraid, and *All the stars*, I thought to myself, looking up into the forceless sky: *See? – all the stars throw down their spears, and water heaven with their tears.*

We were going to Gethsemane.

Just as we arrived at the edge of the garden, Jesus said, 'Sit here while I go inside to pray.'

But before the disciples had lowered and composed themselves on their robes on the ground, Jesus did what he had done two times before: touched Simon and James and John on their arms and motioned them to follow.

Step by step his breathing grew thicker, more laboured. It issued forth in moanings. 'I'm sick with sorrow,' he whispered. 'I am sick to death with grieving.'

The four of them came to that oak tree with the horizontal branch which had been smoothed on its topside by sitting. But Jesus remained standing. 'Stay here,' he whispered. He set his staff against the outstretched branch. 'Keep watch with me.'

The three disciples sat down among the roots of the tree. They leaned their backs against the trunk and tuned their ears and frowned and glowered like men on guard. Simon laid his sword across his thighs.

The shuffling sound of the Master's footsteps diminished as he went farther into the garden.

There came a cry, then the thump of a human body hitting the ground. The disciples tensed, but before they actually got up or ran to help, they heard a run of desperate words: praying. Jesus was praying. Wailing. He didn't want company.

'Abba! Abba! Abba, Father! You can do anything. There's nothing you can't do. Take this cup away from meeeee!'

Away from meeeee! It rang in the trees on the mount and into the sky. Some of the disciples outside the garden, horrified, did not feel safe any more.

Then, in a muffled voice, as if he were puffing the words through the dust of the earth: 'Yet not my will. Your will be done.'

Soon the shuffling sound of his footsteps began again and increased, signifying an approach.

Then Jesus was standing and looking down in the powdery light on three disciples, brave, collapsed and sleeping against the tree.

'Simon, Simon, couldn't you watch with me but one bare hour? You'd best wake up and pray that you do not come into the time of trial. The spirit is so willing. The flesh. Is weak.'

Jesus receded into darkness again, and he prayed again, but with control and a greater dignity: 'My Father, if none of this can pass unless I drink the cup – well. So. Let it be. Your will be done.'

Once more he found his rugged fishermen slumped and sleeping; once more he went and prayed, this time with a murmurous, wordless groaning; once more he returned to the unconscious three.

'There's no more time. There's no more resting,' he said. Then in sharp command, clapping his hands: 'Get up! Let's go! My betrayer is right over there!' He snatched his staff and went.

Simon Peter woofed and jumped up, pitching his sword to the ground. He dropped to his knees to retrieve it, while the other two ran after Jesus, who was already at the garden's edge –

– where the rest of the disciples were on their feet, eyes wide in an arriving torchlight, their faces slack with terror, staring at a gang of Temple policemen, more than a hundred Levites and servants and slaves of the high priest, all of them weaponed, swords and battle-hammers and armour and torches that boiled forth a pitch-black smoke; and at the head of this multitudinous gang, Judas Iscariot! – his long white person framed, strangely, in a laminar darkness.

The skinny fellow was grinning. Sweating, panting, happy: *gawky* with happiness! His eyes darted over the whole band of disciples, until he saw Jesus emerging from the garden behind them. And then, I swear, he winked – and I was overcome with understanding: Judas Iscariot had come to his great adventure.

Flapping his arms, puffing his feathers, strutting grandly up to Jesus, Judas affected a greeting. 'Rabbi!' he said as if surprised. 'Hi!' Then he bent his neck and slouched his knees – not to bow before his Master, but to kiss him.

He kissed him.

'That's the one!' shouted a slave. He drew a bronze sword from its scabbard and led the whole gang forward.

But just as they were laying hands on Jesus, Simon Peter burst from the garden, swinging his own sword recklessly. He roared and lunged and sliced an ear clean off the side of the slave's head. Blood blossomed at the wound, and in spite of the fighters all around him, Simon prepared to deliver another cut, when Jesus –

It was Jesus who stopped him. No one else, neither friend nor foe.

It was Jesus who grabbed his staff like a long-handled axe and whacked Simon at the back of his knees, dropping the man like timber to the ground.

And then it was Jesus who, in the midst of a stunned multitude, reached down for the ear and approached the slave. That slave! I recognized him. I knew his daughter. His name was Malchus.

'Put your sword away,' Jesus said while he blotted the slave's blood with the hem of his robe, then touched the ear to its perfect wound. 'I've said it before, Simon, but you weren't listening: all those who take the sword will die by the sword.' When he removed his hand, the ear stayed where it belonged. Healed.

The Lord then lifted his voice, even as he had done throughout the land, even as the Teacher had done throughout the entire time of his service. 'Why have you come out with swords and hammers to arrest me like a bandit?' He spoke without fear. They listened without menace. 'You've seen me before. You know my face and my manner. I've taught in the Temple while you marched by and listened and didn't arrest me. Even so. Even so,' he said, his tone now changing, 'let the Scriptures be fulfilled.'

He held his staff in both hands before him, horizontally, like an offering. Suddenly the armed police came to their senses. They rushed forward with shouts, with the fury of men embarrassed. They jerked the staff from Jesus' hands and pressed it against his back and forced his elbows around it and yanked the wrists forward and began to bind them at his belly with leather cords.

When the police roused up, so did the disciples. The snarlings of the soldiers scared them. But the self-righteous savagery of men with something to prove — that terrified them altogether. They turned and ran as fast as they could. They all ran away, though Simon limped and was last to vanish.

I knew Malchus to recognize him and to call him by name; I didn't know him personally. He was an Arab by birth. As a lad he had been sold into the house of Caiaphas, was circumcised like any Judean boy, and had been working for years to purchase his freedom. It was his daughter whom I knew best, from whom I learned confidences like these, his heritage, his private designs — and like this: that her father, secretly to signify his contempt for every people he had served so far, had given his daughter a Greekish name, the word that signifies the *Rose*: Rhoda.

Whether she still did or not, I hadn't had time to discover; but some years ago Rhoda kept a camel for its milk. I noticed her once as she was leading her charge to a watering pool outside the city, a swart Arabian child of luminous eyes and massy black hair, marching forward under the neck of the beast which, at its shoulder, was twice her height. To me she seemed a daring little demoiselle. So I fell in step with the child and struck up a conversation and found that she was bright and talkative, and we got on together. I would walk often with my laughing rose thereafter, she leading her camel out of the city by the Gate of the Essenes and past their latrines (ever concerned for purity, the Essenes) down to the Serpent's Pool in the Valley of Hinnom.

Did Rhoda seek freedom as did her father?

She laughed at that. If Papa couldn't be free as a slave, he'd never be free.

And was she, then, free?

Look at her! Look at her: what did *I* think?

A child who commanded both wit and a camel and a full-grown man, himself a seeker?

I thought, Yes.

I said, 'Yes.'

After they arrested him, the many-headed horde of policemen took Jesus back into Jerusalem and up Zion to the house of the high priest. I followed. Every room was lit. Torches lined the courtyard. No one was sleeping. All the household, slaves and servants and family alike, were up and busy – and even as I neared it, I recognized the maid at the gate. It was Rhoda, no longer little, but lean, enlarging, a leopard-like slant to her eyes, a smooth swart forehead, fourteen years at least.

I came and stood outside the bars.

'Do you remember me?' I asked.

She scanned my face. 'Ha ha! Ha ha ha!' she laughed with a bright, immediate pleasure. 'You're the man who never milked a camel!'

I smiled and I nodded, though wanly. On any other day, this would have been a delightful renewal.

'You do remember,' I said.

'Of course,' she said. 'You went off to follow that man they call the Baptizer.' A quick apology darkened her face. 'Oh, no! Forgive me. I heard what happened – '

The words flew out of my mouth of their own accord: 'It's happening again.'

'What – '

'No. I'm sorry I said that. I shouldn't have said that.'

I spent a moment to gather myself. There was a great deal of commotion in the courtyard – so many Temple policemen milling about, some warming themselves at a fire, all of them, I supposed, waiting to hear what Caiaphas might want them next to do.

Rhoda saw my expression and the direction of my looking.

'Big doings tonight,' she whispered. It was as if no time had passed between our previous friendship and now. 'They brought some sort of an outlaw in. Bad enough to make the chief priests put their britches on.'

I said, 'Rhoda – '

'You remember *too*!' she sang out. She reached through the bars as if to hug me. 'You didn't forget my name!'

'I – Yes. I do – remember,' I stammered before this cheerful assault. 'I'd never forget the name of the Arabian rose.'

'Awww. My friend.'

'Rhoda, please. Would you do me a kindness and open the gate? I should be inside. I need to be inside.'

'Well,' she glanced behind her. 'Why?'

'The man they brought here? – bound like an outlaw? His name is Jesus of Nazareth – '

'*That* one? Really? But we – we had such a party when he – I mean, we *like* that man. Why would anyone want to capture him?'

'Why, indeed. It's their want that drives them,' I said, 'not his crime. I know him, Rhoda. Very well. I'm one of his followers. I need to know what's happening at his trial. Whether they'll set him free. I need to be near him.'

'Yes,' Rhoda was whispering again. 'You love him, don't you?'

She lifted the bar that locked the gate.

I heard a wet, urgent hissing behind me.

Even as Rhoda began to pull the heavy gate inwards, Simon Peter, moving painfully and in an awkward crouch, crept to my side. 'Me, too,' he hissed.

'I don't think it's a problem,' I said. 'Rhoda will let the both of us in – won't you, Rhoda?'

Still whispering, loving the collusion, she smiled at Simon and said, 'Of course. Come in.' And as he skulked past her: 'You must be a follower too,' she whispered, 'of that man Jesus, right?'

Simon astonished me. Crouching, holding his fist at his forehead as if to shield his eyes, he answered with a snappish, stiff conviction, 'I don't know what you're talking about' – and off he went towards the fire, where he kept his shoulders hunched and his face concealed beneath his fist.

I myself, after touching the rose on the tip of her chin, slipped into the vestibule of Caiaphas's house, whence I could look through one of two doors into a large reception hall.

The house was palatial, high on Zion, one of those mansions a traveller could see even over the city walls. The floor of the vestibule was a mosaic, a rosette beneath my feet, so brilliantly coloured that lamplight set it afire. The room behind me seemed to offer sunlit scenes at night; in fact, its windows were not windows at all, but frescoes painted in reds and yellows: false. But the most treacherous of ironies: the room before me, the room in which they had arraigned my Lord, was gorgeous. We slept on our robes in summer nights, under them in the winters. The roofs we knew were thatch and mud, our faces as dark as the farmer's, our feet as hard as donkey's hooves. We had never, never seen so elegant a room as this before. The walls were stuccoed in broad panels shaped like bossed ashlars. The ceiling had been plastered in triangles, squares, hexagons, octagons, a Greekish arabesque; it was fully twelve feet high – and from it, bestowing everywhere a shadowless light, hung candelabra of countless branches fitted with candles of beeswax, scented, smokeless.

Like the bees' hive that room hummed with low voices: twenty, thirty men in there, not our people, not our friends, men self-satisfied and menacing. I gripped the doorframe in the vestibule and rose to my toes. I peered left and right, searching some sign of my Lord. Then someone began a loud, uncultured yammer, and the assembly arranged itself to face the east wall, at the same time creating a semicircle of formal attention. There, then, his back to the wall, I saw the profile of the high priest Caiaphas seated behind a stone table, and Jesus on the other side of the table, bound and gazing steadfastly down on him, guards and weapons in the offing. The priest was oiled, resplendent; he wore his hair in the 'Julian' style, cut very short. Jesus held his thin mouth closed, his head slightly aslant as if he were curious.

' – I swear it, said he would destroy the Temple – '

The loud voice issued from a man obscenely small, standing in the place of witnesses between the judge and the indicted. Beside him stood another witness, as gross in proportion as the little man was little.

These, O Lord? *These* are your accusers?

' – with my own ears!' the first witness yelled. 'With my own ears, right after he trashed the Temple – everybody knows he trashed the Temple, that ain't news is it? – I heard him threaten this terrible thing!'

The high priest lifted his chin and nodded to the little witness: 'Step back,' he said.

It was only as the man minced back to the larger assembly that I began to recognize the priestly families gathered in this room. *O my God, what justice can be here?* The House of Boethus sent its slaves to the very winnowing floors of the farmers to snatch the tithe at its source. The sharp-tongued House of Hanan uttered curses and killing incantations against its enemies. The House of Kathros, whose members I'd seen already across the Jordan, oppressed the poor with a bitter pen. The House of Ishmael, whose sons were treasurers of the Temple, whose sons-in-law were trustees, commanded its slaves to beat the people with staves and fists.

And all of these in fine robes! Fresh, unwrinkled! Well-combed, not a one of them blinking sleep from his eyes. *O my Lord, they knew they were meeting tonight! They prepared for your arraignment!*

The grosser witness suddenly spoke: 'On the other hand,' he said importantly. He paused. He smiled. He squinted upward and scratched the flesh beneath his chin. He spoke again: 'Well. Not to contradict my brother. But – I don't think this Galilean actually said he *would* destroy the Temple, you see. What he said was that he was *able* to destroy it, and, ha ha ha – ' the witness covered his mouth with a delicate strip of cloth ' – ha ha, then he said that he was able to build it *up* again, *construct* it, you understand, in, ha ha, three days.'

'Go.'

The large man looked nonplussed. He raised his eyebrows. 'Sir? Excuse me?'

'Go! Get back. Your testimony is ludicrous.'

Gross in proportion, blotched scarlet in mortification, the witness went – while Caiaphas turned a bland gaze towards Jesus. 'Well?' he said, then waited.

Jesus neither spoke nor altered his expression. With close attention, it seemed, he studied the oiled face in front of him. Jesus was altogether motionless – except for that muscle. No one but me could see what only a friend might see: that muscle below his ear, at the corner of his jaw, pulsing.

Caiaphas said, 'How do you answer your accusers?'

No one moved. No one murmured a word to his neighbour. Every man watched the drama at the stone table, awaiting some kind of response, denials, pleadings, rhetoric.

But Jesus did not satisfy them. Jesus said nothing.

'Oh, come, sir.' The high priest folded his arms and leaned away from the table. 'No defendant does not speak on his own behalf. It's only natural. And you have the right. We acknowledge the right. So: what do you have to say for yourself?'

Nothing. Jesus stood as erect as he might with his elbows drawn back around his staff, his chest strained outwards like the turtledove's before the beasts. He looked at Caiaphas, neither anger nor pleading in his face, but a quiet regarding only. And he said nothing.

'Look,' said Caiaphas, raising his arms to the room at large. 'We've got the man, right? The man is here. Alone. Isolated from his noisome, fanatical multitudes. That was the hardest part. This is the easiest! Give me a witness and a charge that will stick, and we'll hurl the matter straightway into Pilate's court. The governor knows. The governor's prepared.'

Finally someone began to move through the grand reception hall. Someone was working his way among the chief priests towards to the stone table.

And then he appeared, and my heart failed, and justice died at his appearing. Rather than taking his stand in the place of the witnesses, that man, that Pharisee – his hand against the phylactery box upon his forehead, never glancing in the direction of the accused – moved to Caiaphas's side and knelt down and began to whisper in the high priest's ear.

This was Eleazar the gap-toothed Pharisee that had followed us through Galilee, apparently burdened with much sad news. He spent a long time imparting confidences to Caiaphas, nodding, gesticulation. Then, when he was done, they both stood up, Eleazar and Caiaphas, in an unusual complicity.

Eleazar the Pharisee, having known Jesus for twenty-one years and having brought to conclusion, finally, his purpose in the life of my Lord, bowed himself backwards into the assembled men of the court and lost himself forever.

Caiaphas raised an accusing finger to the criminal before him. 'By God,' he began, allowing his voice the resonance of outrage.

'I charge you under oath by the living God to tell the truth! Are you the Messiah? Do you declare yourself to be the Son of God?'

Jesus took one more moment before opening his mouth – a brief space in which the high priest's posture seemed slightly awkward. Then, quietly, he spoke: 'You have said so,' he said. 'But now I say to you that in the future you will see the Son of man sitting at the right hand of power, coming on the clouds of heaven.'

'Blasphemy!' the high priest bellowed. He took hold of his translucent linen robe, found a tiny cut at the neck of the cloth, and tore it smoothly top to bottom, indicating thereby the depth of his shock and his grief. Stepping around the accused, he addressed the entire room. 'The man has blasphemed,' he announced. 'I see no need for another witness. What's the verdict?'

And, 'Death,' the various priests in the room responded. 'He deserves no less than death!'

Immediately two guardsmen moved forward and started to play a silly children's game with Jesus, one of them blindfolding him, the other slapping him across his face, and both demanding in kiddish voices: 'Who was that? Prophesy, you bloody prophet: which of us hit you?'

But Jesus had stumbled at the slap. He caught himself on one knee and slowly strove to rise again, when a second slap knocked him to the floor.

My Lord, on his face on the floor, twisting his knees, unable to stand –

I withdrew. I left the vestibule. I went into the courtyard. I was sick to my stomach. There was no other ending now. Whatever Judas Iscariot had imagined his kiss would accomplish, however I might beg for it, plead for it, there would be no descent of the warrior stars. No angels with flaming swords. No saving him. No help for it now. My Lord, my Jesus was going to die.

Rhoda grabbed my robe.

I was stumbling through the courtyard, past people warming themselves around a fire. She grabbed the robe, tugged at it and said, 'I'm not wrong, am I? You said it yourself!'

'Rhoda! What?'

293

'That he's a follower.'

'What? What are you saying?'

She took my arm and pulled me towards the fire and pointed. 'Him!' she declared, triumph already slanting in her eye. She meant Simon Peter, who, seeing her, jumped up and began to edge from the firelight. 'That one!' Rhoda cried. 'He's a follower of Jesus, isn't he?'

'The Devil, woman!' Simon growled. 'I don't know the man!'

But this woman was completely free. She knew no restraints, whether on her voice or her person. She let me go and started after Simon.

This caused the policemen to laugh and cheer. One of them drew a sword. ' "Doh-an even gnaw da man," ' he mimicked Simon. 'Listen to him,' he hooted, whacking Simon's leg with the side of his weapon. 'Blighter's got an accent as gummy as the Galilean inside! He's a disciple, all right!'

'Damnation!' Simon thundered, whirling around. 'Hellfire and damnation, I do not *know* your Galilean inside!'

Somewhere on the courtyard wall a rooster started crowing, crowed and crowed and would not quit.

And in that same moment they brought Jesus out from the vestibule into the courtyard. As with sunbeams through the muddle, Jesus looked directly at Simon.

The big man gaped. His face shattered, and he began to wail, 'Oh, *no, no-oooo* – '

I hissed in Rhoda's ear, 'Get the gate!'

She ran forward. I grabbed Simon beneath his shoulders. We both followed Rhoda, though I bore as much of his weight as he did walking. And when she'd drawn the gate wide enough, I forced Simon through.

We took five steps into the night. Then, suddenly, he found strength and threw me aside. He lumbered awkwardly around a corner and down an alley, and then he fell. I heard the fall. I heard a kind of writhing thereafter. And I heard how bitterly the big man wept.

FRIDAY: MARY AND THE BELOVED

##

Mary

She has been in this place before, crossed it at a dead run — twice — though now she stands in the back and waits. It was just after the Passover then; it is very Passover now; daylight then, the dawning now. And she was young, and her husband was with her, and she knew nothing of deliberate pain, though she thought she did, and hope stretched out before her happy as the heart is long. Yes, and they were looking for Jesus on that day, even as she strains her neck to look for her same son now. But it's still an hour before the sun's rise, and the heavens are the colour of charcoal, and she can't see anything clearly. Servants have lit lamps in the high apartments of the praetorium, whose windows are visible over the protecting wall. Pontius Pilate is awake.

Yeshi was twelve. After dashing through the public square and crossing the valley, they found him in the Temple among a group of Pharisees, impressing his teachers. In that place and on that day he astonished his parents with what he had come to know. Not of Torah, as wonderful as that knowledge was. But of his heritage; for Jesus had somehow divined the nature and the identity of his real Father.

Dear Joseph has died betimes. Mary misses him more than she can say, even to herself. The man was plain and simple, his hands like shovels, his heart forever faithful. He smelled of fresh wood and ploughed earth. Nothing celestial about him, and no division between the two of them. Mary doesn't hate the holy mysteries; but they shut her out; and if they are capable of love, it is a love too noble and composed to care about white hairs or the flab above a woman's elbow or the insufficiencies of her soul.

Herod has come to town for the Passover. The city is thick with authorities. And every ruler brings his forces, his servants, his gaudy retinue.

But Chuza, that completely inoffensive man, can still talk with those who serve Herod and know the news. A half hour ago, shortly after cockcrow, he found Mary and Joanna together. Quietly, to the older woman in particular, he reported that the Lord has been condemned to death by the chief priests and that they are bringing both formal charges and their prisoner here, to the praetorium and the governor, for sentencing.

They stand at the back of the wide, paved public square which fronts the gates of the praetorium, she and Joanna, Maryam from Magdala, and nearly no one else –

– *and there, now. There. I see torches and lamps approaching by a winding street uphill. A group of men in tight formation. The shadows of some individuals following behind. Ah, God! – why do they need weapons? Yeshi must be among them. I can't see him. I can't see my Yeshi.*

The Beloved

It is a small band that takes Jesus through the chill of the predawn morning up to the praetorium: guards, representatives of the priestly families, Caiaphas's Temple police, Caiaphas himself, flanked by several of his personal servants, each of them armed. The day requires his attendance at the Temple soon, but he knows the governor. He intends to expedite this sentence personally, and then to assume his Passover duties.

The frame of my Lord must be concealed inside that circle of torchlit, human flesh.

Appearing suddenly out of the night and plucking at my arm with ineffectual pinches, Judas Iscariot is whining, 'What did they do? What are they doing? Where are they going?'

I look at him, his face ghastly in the shadow of the torches ahead of us. I would keep walking, but he winds his fingers together and nearly goes down on his knees. 'Stop!' he pleads. 'Tell me, didn't he do *anything?*'

My Lord will die before this day is done. That catastrophe, together with my cold knowing that it shall be, has given me a preternatural awareness. I understand what Judas is asking. More than that, I understand with a morbid clarity what he believed would happen when his Master was placed (by his, Judas's, clever designs) into an impossible position: Jesus would reveal his own impossible powers. Jesus would perform the wonders that had saved so many lives before. Jesus would abolish an evil leadership and replace it with his own more generous, more kindly command. Piteous, piteous Judas Iscariot.

'No,' I say. 'Jesus did nothing.'

'Why not?' The child is thunderstruck, shattered by his misery. 'Why wouldn't he save himself? The Master *said* he knew what I was going to do! Oh, God! – he could've called twelve legions of angels! To fight for him! Nobody withstands angels! They only had to *be* there!'

'The Sanhedrin has found him guilty,' I say to the wretch and begin again to follow the band of police, which has turned corners, leaving us in darkness. 'Jesus is going before us now – '

'I know! I saw!'

I don't pause when he interrupts me. I keep talking and walk the faster. ' – to the praetorium. The chief priests are taking him to the governor – '

'They paid me in silver.' This is stark confession. Judas is striving not to despise himself. 'The chief priests. For information – '

'Pontius Pilate will seat himself on the *bema* and agree with the verdict of the Sanhedrin – ' We turn a corner. I see the torchlight ahead at the eastern edge of the public square. ' – will agree with the verdict and pass sentence, and then it will take nothing like your legion – '

'*That's* when he'll act, right? In front of Caesar?'

' – nothing like your legion, Judas. A minor detachment of Roman soldiers will lead him to his execution – '

'No! Don't say that! Why do you say that?'

'And he is – ' My heart is very hard. I will indeed say it: 'Jesus is going to die.'

Mary

In the east, like bright coals on the shoulders of the Mount of Olives, a red glow rises. On the pavement in front of the *bema* – that high stone platform from which the governor issues formal judgments – old torches are being extinguished. Soldiers and the unarmed priests stand waiting. And Yeshi, it must surely be, stands among them. She hears the easy laughter of the working men. It flows thoughtlessly back from the *bema*. Well, and that's what the soldiers are, after all, aren't they? At least in their own minds? Working men?

'Mary? Is that you? The widow Mary from Nazareth?'

The grey form of a woman moves uncertainly across the square. Her accent is familiar. She speaks with a hometown hesitation. Only Nazarenes lengthen 'Nazareth' that way.

'Yes?' Mary, too, is uncertain. 'I'm that one.'

As she nears, the woman seems to be Mary's age, though her tread is halting. She leans on a hard-knobbed stick.

Ah, it's the walking stick that was confusing! The dawn light illuminates the wrinkled face:

'Anna!' Mary cries. 'It's you! Oh, Anna!'

The two women fly together and fall on one another's neck and embrace and burst into tears.

'It's been so long!'

'So long. Too long.'

Mary holds her friend at arm's length. 'How are you, Anna?'

'Oh. You know. Sick.'

'I see that. I'm sorry. Does it hurt to walk?'

'I thought the cane would make the journey possible.'

'It didn't?'

'My feet are crooked, Mary. Walking has broken them.'

'But you could have celebrated the Passover at home. Why did you come so far?'

'Because I am sick.'

'You came for healing?'

Anna bows her head. She hides her eyes in the crook of her arm and shakes. She's crying again.

'Mary, Mary, it is not my feet. I am sick at heart. My son is here.'

'Here? In Jerusalem?'

'Here. There.' She points to the praetorium. 'In prison.'

'Oh, Anna!'

'He had gone into the hills south of Gerezim. The Romans found him. They say he – his band, his... I don't know. They say that he attacked them. They killed his friends and brought him here and published the charges: *Jesus the son of Abbas, an insurgent and a murderer, did ambush the forces of Rome...* I had to come. What else could I do?'

Mary's eyes are stinging with tears much angrier than Anna's. She covers her breasts with the palms of her hands and presses hard enough to hurt. 'What else,' she agrees, 'can any mother do?'

The Beloved

Caiaphas has sent word to Pontius Pilate that he's unable to attend the governor inside the rooms of the praetorium. It is the Passover; to enter a Gentile's quarters would render the high priest unfit for his office. Would, then, the governor be so gracious as to complete their brief business here, outside the gates, at the *bema* in the square?

In fact, Pilate neither emerges nor chooses to be 'so gracious'. He sends instead a messenger. An official messenger, to be sure; but a messenger nonetheless, which pricks the high priest's pride.

'I've been advised,' Pilate says through the messenger, 'that the man you bring is a Galilean from the tetrarchy of Herod Antipas. Herod's in residence. Take him to Herod. Let him be troubled with his own.'

As the messenger retreats – and as Roman soldiers now appear to take the place of the Temple police, to see to the prisoner, and to prosecute Pilate's wishes themselves – the well-oiled face of Caiaphas loses all its grace. His eyes narrow. I read the sentiment there: *I thought we had an agreement! Well: I think we'll see to agreements my way now.*

Caiaphas, looking thievish in his torn robe and soiled hems, signals servants, police and priests to follow him, and sweeps eastwards into the city.

At the changing of the guard I am granted a quick, unhappy vision of my Jesus. He is tired. He cannot keep his head erect. Blood has crusted on the rims of his lips and in the whorls of his right ear. His eyes stare dead ahead. They aren't blank. They see. But they see nothing I can find. Yet he walks with the lightness that has always characterized his slender strength. He is Jesus. He remains my Lord.

The Roman soldiers – actually they are Syrian recruits with less love for Jews than the priests for Jesus – yank my Lord and drive him forward with the butts of their spears.

I turn. The square is, for the moment, quiet. Very few people. Women standing in a lonely knot at the back of the pavement. Judas, of course, has vanished. Neither Simon nor any other male disciple is here.

Then, as pure as a long note blown on the golden trumpet, sunbeams break over the Mount of Olives and strike vermilion the stones of the praetorium wall. My own person is outlined as a shadow on the face of the *bema*. I do not know that man. Should I pray? I love Jesus. This is not a protestation. Nor is it the expression of a mere feeling. There is no passion in it, nor even the peace I knew last night while lying on his bosom. It is a fact as demonstrable as that I have arms. I love this Jesus of Nazareth. But love in me now is the desolation of perfect knowledge. I see everything. Nothing can surprise me. I am omniscient.

I know what Caiaphas has gone to do. I anticipate the crowds even before they start arriving here. Even Herod cannot order an execution outside his territory, in provinces under Roman jurisdiction.

By sunrise Jerusalem is stirring. Pilgrims are singing morning songs; the air is scented with fires blown hot again; breakfasts prepared before the Passover are eaten on rooftops, in tents and small rooms and courtyards and lanes.

And then, of course, the people: small groups, larger groups, individuals. The people: day-labourers, shopkeepers, artisans, country priests, pilgrims, women as well as men, farmers and herders uncomfortable in the city. The people: merchants on mules, the wealthy preceded each by a train of their clients, the chief priests especially formidable for the number of servants, officers and slaves surrounding them. The people, I say, come and fill the square before the praetorium.

A goodly number have been sent: those that make a fine display of rulership; lawyers; the first men of the city. Caiaphas intends to deal with the Nazarene right here, to conclude an incendiary matter right now, with death. As insignificant as this Jesus must finally be, Caiaphas is raising the level of political and religious participation because the event itself has become important. Agreements are agreements, after all, and keeping them keeps order. Pilate cannot refuse a delegation such as this one: no.

But Caiaphas, himself arriving now with the guard that brings my Lord from Herod, is astonished, then angry, then frightened.

Fully three quarters of the people in the square are not his! They are the hordes that welcomed, as they screamed it, the *son of David* to Jerusalem last Sunday! Word has spread. Many of the country priests, hearing the word from Caiaphas, passed the word to pilgrims, and pilgrims to pilgrims, and beggars to the poor: *The king who comes in the name of the Lord* was tried last night! By the chief priests! Found guilty! Is about to be sentenced by Pontius Pilate in the public square!

Mary

There he is! There's Yeshi, standing on the left side of the *bema*, higher than the heads of the multitudes.

It should be glory. He should be glorious there on high. He should be teaching, telling the story that stuns this congregation with wonder and love. But he's tied up. And silent.

Oh, God! Mary knows what it means when he sets his jaw that way: *Yeshi, you bullheaded – Oh, Yeshi, your stubbornness is going to get you killed.*

His wrists are tied. His hands are relaxed in front of him. Mary sees his nostrils flare – Ah! It's a sign that Jesus is sighing, not visibly nor loudly, not so much as a parting of his lips; but the mortal gesture drives a sword into her soul.

Mary's head goes light. Her knees buckle.

To steady herself she grabs blindly for hands on either side of her and hangs on. One belongs to Anna. The other belongs to the slender wraith, Maryam from Magdala, whose returning grip is very, very strong.

The Beloved

In the centre of the *bema* the governor has seated himself in a great wooden chair beside a slanted canopy supported by four poles held by four slaves. Pontius Pilate has arrogated to himself the trappings of eastern kings: he'll never be too much in the sun.

I have remained close enough to see the crossed gaiters of his sandals from the instep to the knee; the flesh is pressed into the whiteness and the shapes of bulbs of peeled garlic.

The high priest Caiaphas stands on the right side of the *bema*. Fresh clothes. A magnificent turban atop his skull, though one can see the sides and the back of the head, where he has caused his hair to be cut as close as Pilate's.

Caiaphas, holding the turban tight to his head and shaking his jowls, is spouting charges against the Lord, who stands silently opposite him: ' – declaring that he, he himself, is the Messiah already come! The anointed one! Anointed, you understand, as king!'

Every word Caiaphas says is immediately echoed by a brass-throated servant who stands before the *bema* and booms so that all the people might hear: ' – ANOINTED, YOU UNDERSTAND, AS KING!'

Pilate raises a hand. The high priest takes the cue and closes his mouth.

Pilate turns his entire body towards Jesus and studies him: a slender, even-featured Galilean; tight, curly hair and beard, an unthreatened expression, almost benign in the rust-coloured eyes.

Jesus tilts his head and returns the look.

Pilate smiles and says, 'Well, then: *are* you the king of the Jews?'

'WELL, THEN: *ARE* YOU THE KING OF THE JEWS!'

There is a moment of quiet scrutiny between the two. Finally, Jesus says, 'So you say.'

'SO YOU SAY!'

Suddenly Pilate crouches forward and hisses at the bellowing servant, 'Hey, you *aselle*! Shut up!'

'I AM THE HIGH PRIEST'S MAN!'

Pilate whirls towards Caiaphas. 'Shut the hole on your *asello*!'

'But the people should hear – '

'BUT THE PEOPLE SHOULD – '

'Shut it, sir, or that guard there' – pointing – 'will *open* it with a length of sword forever!'

Caiaphas, the more discountenanced, signals his servant to desist.

The people should hear: in fact, Pilate is scanning the huge crowd that packs the square from side to side and then back even into the streets. 'Why, Caiaphas, *are* so many here?' he asks. 'I was given to believe this would be an easy business quickly finished.'

'It might have been quick and easy, Governor, at a much earlier hour, say, before the sunrise, when first we brought the man to you. Word got out.'

Pilate contemplates the crowd a little longer. At Passover the influx of more than a hundred thousand pilgrims triples the population of the city, all of them religious, more than a few angry and fanatical. Abruptly Pilate declares, 'I find no basis for the charges against this man.'

Caiaphas blinks. Then straightway renews his accusations: 'Governor! He's been busy perverting the nation! I've heard directly from Eleazar, a Pharisee of the house of Gamaliel, that he forbids the common folk to pay taxes to Caesar!' Caiaphas spreads his arms: 'And you think this crowd's a problem? Everywhere he goes that Nazarene stirs up crowds like this! How can you find no basis – '

Pilate raises his hand again and turns to Jesus.

'Your turn,' he says. 'What's your defence?'

But Jesus says nothing.

The crowd is shifting, shuffling behind me.

Someone yells, 'Speak up!'

Someone else: 'Gov'nah? Gov'nah? What'd you say?'

Pilate, still to Jesus: 'Haven't you an answer? I count at least five charges levelled against you.'

Jesus continues to hold his peace. He seems to be paying no attention at all to the governor. He's gazing at the people. *Do you take offence at this?* his eyes ask: *But blessed is everyone who takes no offence at me.*

'Jesus the son of Joseph.' Pilate applies the formal name, now, and speaks with the disinterested tones of a judge: 'By our law, silence declares the accused to be guilty. You don't talk, this court is over.'

'Now! Now!' someone shrieks. The wail goes up and falls like a bird shot dead – 'For God's sake, do it now!' – and then is heard no more.

Jesus, lean, his posture as straight and limpid as a wax candle, has closed his eyes. He does not open his mouth. He does not talk.

Pilate breathes a low curse and squints again at the crowd. Heads and opinions are blowing about like wheat in the first winds of storm. Some of the people are annoyed by Jesus' silences. They seek theatre. Others care for the outcome – whether for or against the accused – and are growing more and more anxious in their ignorance. All sense the tensions of the various authorities and soldiers everywhere: something significant seems to be happening!

And I myself can feel how the very size of the multitude whipsaws its individual members. They are frightened in the grip of so great and tameless a beast. Yet they are electrified by the tensions surging through it: *something significant!*

And I recognize the calculation in the squint of the governor. He's taking the measure of the crowd. How ungovernable is it? How potentially riotous? But it's the *crowd* he wants to know, not Caiaphas's interpretation of it nor his cynical hopes or fears for it. The high priest's importance is swiftly diminishing.

'Get that crier back,' Pilate orders him as if he were a servant.

'What?' Caiaphas is mortified. 'You're talking to – ?'

'Get him, sir. Get him now. And you,' Pilate jabs a finger at the centurion behind the *bema*, a middle-aged man with an old scar across his cheek and upper lip, 'go down and bring me the most depraved prisoner in custody.'

There is a space of time when nothing happens. The several figures on the *bema* wait, two of them uneasily, a third with his eyes closed, his jaw muscle pulsing, the wings of his nostrils spreading when he breathes.

The crowd, far from dispersing during the interlude, only grows more agitated.

As soon as the brass-throated crier appears, Pontius Pilate stands up and addresses the people directly: 'We have a custom together,' he announces.

'CUSTOM TOGETHER!'

Simply to understand what's being spoken on the *bema* quiets the greater part of the people.

'A Passover amnesty – '

'AMNESTY!'

' – that at the festival I set one prisoner free and clear him of all charges. What do you say? Shall I attend to that custom now?'

A scattering of voices holler, 'Yes.' And then, more volubly, 'Yes!'

The centurion comes out through the praetorium gates, followed by four guards dragging a wild-looking, powerfully built prisoner. He is magnificently chained, each guard wrapping loops of chain around his own arms.

'Up here!' Pilate commands, and the prisoner is forced to mount the *bema* steps and then, with a great clanking, to take a stand on the left side, near Jesus. This man's hair is as black and lustrous as obsidian. If he wore a headband, it's gone now, allowing the hair, caught beneath the chains, to reach down to his waist. He looks familiar.

Pilate asks the guards a murmured question. One answers right clearly: 'Jesus the son of Abbas, sir.'

There are pockets of nearly violent motion among the multitude. As soon as he saw the prisoner emerge, Caiaphas fairly vaulted from the *bema*. He rushed to the chief priests hissing commands, and they and their armed servants are now dashing like dogs farther and farther through the multitude, hissing orders, glowering, threatening the people.

But I know more than Caiaphas knows. These tactics are unnecessary. It isn't that Pilate seeks to free the Lord but rather to test the resolve of the mob, whether or not it could riot on behalf of the one it once called *king* and *the son of David*, Pilate, unencumbered by righteousness or ridiculous religions, is twice the ruler Caiaphas is.

Mary

The women, the only disciples save two who followed Jesus to this place, watch as the Roman governor raises his arms as if in blessing. He utters a word. An instant later they hear that word break above them: 'SILENCE!'

With that instant's separation between sight and sound, Pilate speaks: 'Even so shall it be. An amnesty. Citizens, tell me which of these men you choose for freedom? Which one do you love the more? Will you choose this man, Jesus the son of Abbas, who is, I'm told, a murderer, an insurrectionist? Or that man, Jesus of Nazareth, the king of the Jews?'

Anna gasps. 'It's him!' she squeaks. 'It's my son!'

Mary scarcely notices. It is *her* son who is enduring the hatred of the rulers of her Temple, of the Jews. It is Yeshi who infuriates her now, refusing to use his God-given skills for argument and persuasion.

But Pontius Pilate called him 'the king of the Jews'. Can she find some hope in that? And immediately the chief priests are howling outrage at the title. Can she find some hope in *that*? Mary believes it's the priests and the powerful of her nation who want to destroy him. Maybe this Roman is truly impartial. Maybe he'll choose to free her Yeshi after all. Maybe there's hope in –

Oh!

Suddenly Mary realizes that Anna is staring at her; that she has pulled her hand from Mary's; that Anna is dry-scrubbing her hands one with the other. Oh, no. Mary starts panting. This is terrible! Terrible! She doesn't know *what* to think any more. Or how to pray, and the dizziness darkens her seeing again: one of their sons is going to live. And one of their sons is going to die – precisely because the other will live!

Mary's heart is screaming: *Jesus! Choose Jesus!*

She suffers a spasm of hatred for Anna – and then a rush of apology and compassion. They are women broken on the very same wheel. And what if Mary *did* scream, 'Jesus, choose Jesus'?

Which Jesus would anyone think she was pleading for, when both of the prisoners are 'Jesus'?

Mary goes a little crazy. She sits down on the smooth stones and starts to cry. And to laugh. It is her mouth and her rib cage convulsed with laughing. It's her eyes and her bowels that cry. All her emotions have come loose.

But Anna slumps down beside her, and for the second time that morning the women fall on one another's necks, and each receives the helpless embrace of the other. They lean together sobbing with anguish and laughter. What else is a mother to do?

The Beloved

'There is no help for it,' Pontius Pilate continues. 'The one unchosen must be put to death.'

'DEATH!'

'And perhaps you already understand the reality – '

'THE REALITY.'

' – where goes the leader, there go the followers too.'

'FOLLOWERS TOO!'

In fact, the first voices to answer Pilate's 'Which man?' named the Nazarene. Then one or two more cultured voices cried, 'The son of Abbas!' But that epithet *the king of the Jews* seems to have been potent, and the common folk were gaining courage and volume, 'Release the Nazarene!' – until just now, and the governor's caution: 'Where the leader, there the followers.'

It doesn't matter to him which man will finally be chosen. Simply, he wants to gauge how attached the people might be to this particular charismatic, whether they're willing to bleed on his behalf. If not, Pilate has solved his problem. He needn't send swords and arrows and spears against the mob. He need only cancel one life, and all will be peaceful again.

'The son of Abbas!'

Greater and greater grows the chorus in favour of the black-haired brigand. In fact, the animal crowd, stamping, tearing at its tethers, is developing one huge voice: 'Release the son of Abbas!'

This, then, is the handiwork of Caiaphas and the chief priests and all their minions; this is *their* choice. And in our language the mob is shouting, 'Bar-abbas! Bar-abbas! Release to us Bar-abbas!'

'Then what – '

'THEN WHAT!'

Pilate cries above the bull-roar of the multitudes: 'Then what shall I do with the one you call the king of the Jews?'

There are no longer pleas for the release of Jesus.

The House of Kathros cries, 'Crucify!' The Houses of Boethus and Hanan and Ishmael cry, 'Crucify!' And soon, in a brutal, singsong pealing, it is the multitude crying: 'Crucify him! Crucify! *Crucify him!*'

'Why?' demands the sovereignty of Rome: 'What evil has he done?'

'*Crucify him!*'

Then here comes Caiaphas, leaping in triumph up to the *bema*. 'If you set that man free,' he huffs. He is hoarse.

But his brazen servant booms forth the sentences like breakers pounding the sea: 'IF YOU SET THAT MAN FREE, YOU ARE NO FRIEND OF CAESAR. FOR THE MAN WHO CALLS HIMSELF A KING IS AN ENEMY OF CAESAR!'

Pontius Pilate smiles. He nods. He has fathomed this crowd to the very seabed of its souls, and has his measurement.

'Fine,' the governor says right quietly. 'That one,' referring to Jesus Bar-abbas: 'unchain him. He's free to go. That one,' referring to Jesus, the Lord, 'will be flogged. Then he will be crucified.'

Mary

Now a marvellous gesture takes place.

'Look,' says Maryam from Magdala. 'Oh, please, you must get up and see this.'

Mary and Anna help each other. They stand and look where Maryam is looking, towards the *bema*. In speechless gratitude they watch, and are ever thereafter cleansed of enmity, sisters even to the end.

They cannot hear which son is chosen to live and which to die.

The mob is brutal in its bellowing. Pilate points. He points again. He has pointed at both. But then comes that heavenly, transforming gesture: Jesus the son of Anna, the Jesus in chains, who once had warned the other to flee Galilee for his life, goes down on his knees before the son of Mary. He bends his great head to the stones. And he kisses Yeshi's feet.

Mary covers her mouth with both hands. 'Oh!'

Then Yeshi bows at the waist and runs his fingers into the hair – and lays his palms upon the neck – of his darker namesake. It is a blessing, intense and private. Which will live? Which will die? Mary does not know; but she has fallen in love with Anna's boy. She will hold him in the highest regard, forever.

The multitudes whistle and hoot with contempt.

The Beloved

In all the time I've lived with Jesus, I have never heard him react to physical pain. That he felt it I saw in his face. His lips would pinch and whiten. His brow would knot. His eyes had a trick of cutting left, the eyelids fluttering. But the line of his tightly curled hair never broke, causing him, even in his severest injuries, to seem neat, unruffled. And he never made a mumbling sound.

Today he maunders and gargles in pain.

There is no natural pillar or standing post in the upper square. So the Romans have hauled out a ponderous transport wagon and set the wheels with stones and bound the Lord, stripped of all but his loincloth, to the boards at its back.

Once he stood candle-like in the stern of a storm-tossed boat, his robe snapping like a banner, and raised his arms; and the sea went still.

Often he raised his arms and whole populations of people fell quiet, and they were taught, and thousands were fed with fish and bread.

On hilltops in the twilight he raised his arms like flagstaffs, and he prayed.

Now his arms have been raised for him. They are tied to the corners of the wagon's high boards; his cheek has been driven against the rough wood.

The legionnaire standing at angles behind my Lord grips the haft of a flagellum in his right hand. He snaps his wrist. He makes its tails and their metal claws seethe through the air, a serpent sound. Then, suddenly running, the legionnaire swings his full arm up over his head and leaps and, flying by Jesus, doubles himself so fiercely down the metal claws rake the back of the prisoner, slicing his flesh from shoulder to waist; Jesus twists; the skin widens; his wounds are opening smiles, white bone appearing like teeth inside, as dry as limestone – but then blood races through the long wounds and tumbles over.

The first strike draws no sound from Jesus. Only that twisting flinch. His cheek is rubbed raw on the wood. He frowns. He does not so much as whimper.

The fifth strike causes his eyelids to flutter as soon as the flagellum seethes through the air, and at the strike he grunts.

By the twentieth strike his eyes stream tears and his mouth is locked open on a guttural, uninterrupted groaning, and his back has become a ploughed field, bloody chunks dropping off and sticking to his buttocks.

After the twenty-fifth pass, the poor legionnaire has become so weary he must give place to another, fresher man, this one a Syrian excited by racial hatreds.

The crowd is dissolving. The chief priests left a while ago to perform their Passover duties. Some people were too horrified (I *want* to believe this) to stay. Most have simply lost interest.

A toothless old beggar, watching beside the wagon even to the last slap of the flagellum, snaps his fingers and croaks, 'Salt! Salt!' He thinks the criminal still hasn't felt sufficient pain.

'King of the Jews,' muses one guard to another; they've been reclining on the pavement. Jesus has soiled the loincloth front and back. He hangs from his bound arms, his head rocked backwards, his mouth open, his Adam's apple prominent, his eyes blind, unconscious.

'Right!' commands the centurion who first brought Jesus Barabbas out of the praetorium gates. 'Enough. Return the transport!'

The great wagon is hauled back through the gates. They haven't chosen to cut my Lord away from it. His bare feet drag over stones, the toes turned inwards, his back glistering in sunlight. It is nearly nine in the morning.

Ten yards inside the gates the wagon slows and stops. 'King of the Jews!' I hear the guards guffawing. From my stance outside, I can see only Jesus, stretched, bent, unconscious.

Then a guard comes into view with a robe of royal purple. He ties its cords around Jesus' neck and pulls the fabric wide behind him, then lets it fall.

'Ha ha ha!'

Another guard appears with a woven circle of thorny brambles. He tips Jesus' head forward and jams this odd crown onto it, then produces a stout reed and begins to swat Jesus about the face and ears.

'Hail, king of the Jews! Ha ha ha!'

Jesus coughs. He rolls his head away from the irritating reed. He's waking up.

Down go the guards on their knees. They deserve a little diversion. They bow in obeisance, spluttering *hails* and *kyrie eleisons* to this sorry excuse for a king.

'Right, boys!' the centurion renews his authority. 'Let's get this business done.'

It will be. Yes. They will finish the business. I know.

Mary

Yeshi's robe is bloodstained through and through. They dressed him after the scourging, though not thoughtfully. Not well. The robe isn't cinched. It hangs open. Mary sees that they replaced his tunic too. At least for now, for his slow procession northwards through the city. Before he will be –

They're prodding Yeshi towards the Garden Gate. They're going outside the walls. Executions cannot be done inside the walls. Jerusalem would be rendered impure. God save Jerusalem from impurity.

But being dressed, even in his own clothes, gives her son no dignity.

He's bending over a thick length of oak, holding it by circling both his arms around one end of it. The other end scrapes over the road-stones. He tugs it foot by foot, throwing his head forward to get some purchase. As the scourging is customary, so is this, that he must carry to Golgotha the wood that will carry him to death.

My joy is gone! Grief is upon me! My heart is sick!

Oh, listen to the groaning of my son, like lamentation throughout the land –

'Look out!'

Ha! Jesus has dropped his crossbeam!

No, he's fallen down with it. His arms come apart. He rolls to his back – then immediately howls and cringes over onto his side.

Oh, Yeshi!

Behind him there follow two more men condemned and carrying their crosspieces too. They are forced to stop. The small deployment of guards also stops.

A centurion behind them shouts, 'What's the hold-up?'

He butts his way forward, grimaces at Yeshi, kicks Mary's poor boy twice, but to no effect, then shrugs and points at the nearest full-grown male. 'Pick it up, mate. Poor sod's done in. You carry the splinter, hey?'

For the wound of my son is my heart wounded!

Horror is destroying me.

The centurion grunts, 'Get up, you.' He crouches in front of Yeshi, grabs his tunic and pulls him to his feet. 'Go on, now. Walk. I took the burden off you. Go!'

Yeshi sways a moment.

His pretty mouth is open, his tongue thickish, his eyes rolled up, O God! O God!

But the pupils descend. Sight returns. He obeys. He goes.

The little column lurches forward behind him.

Mary mashes her lips into the same bloodless white as did her son, once. She rips the shawl from her head and whirls it down beneath the feet of strangers. She will go bareheaded. Her hair explodes a wolfish grey, but tangled and fretted and wild as briars.

Is there no balm in Gilead?

Is there no physician here?

Great God! – why is there no healing for my son?

Oh, that my head were a rolling ocean of water, that my eyes could spout tears day and night for the sorrows of my son!

Oh, that I had a hut in the desert, where I could escape this people and

hide from them! They go from evil to evil to evil –
Oh!

Nameless

Solid hits of the iron hammer.

Bang, bang: iron spikes drive bit by bit into the oak beam. At first its points went through flesh and cartilage like that living tissue was nothing more than porridge; but this wood, now: wood takes a harder bite. *Bang!*

The convict's stripped naked.

This sort of execution's meant to shame him every which way it can. That's why it's done on a hill by a highway – and on the other side of that highway, look: tombs! Stone tombs. Get it? And all the folks that pass between can get a good look. And the corpse'll hang a month here anyway, drying up, shrinking. And we'll know when he's dead on account of the ravens; they'll perch on his shoulders and start to peck the gobby eyeballs out.

Somebody tried to give the fellow a slug of myrrh-laced wine. Dulls the pain. Beggar refused.

All right: and now that we got his hands and wrists secured to the crosspiece – to the *patibulum* in Romish – two of us heave that beam with its loopy, swinging body to the top of a stout post. Top's within our reach. This fellow won't hang all that high from the ground. (Though I've heard where they hung a Roman twelve feet high at the toe: wanted *everyone* to laugh at that Optimas; even painted the whole cross white. Ha!) There's a peg-hole drilled in the back of this beam, and a peg sticking out of the post. One slips (bump!) onto the other. See? And see how the ends of the crossbeam waggle up and down? Poor beggar leans left, the right cranks up. Same thing *ipso verso*. Makes his shoulder-sockets stretch and tighten opposite each other.

All right: so now we crouch low on the ground and pound the last spike through the heel-bones (this job wants some hard hitting and a little finesse, two of us working together). And now the solid hits; *bang, bang;* the spike bites into the rucked wood of the post.

They gave us a shingle. We slip it into a slot on top of the post. I figure it tells this fellow's crime. But the centurion reads it out loud: *Jesus of Nazareth, the king of the Jews.* Somebody's having a good joke.

OK, so now we repeat the process two more times, two more crooks, two more executions this morning, one going up on the right, one on the left, and that makes three, and finally we catch a break.

The only one with clothes worth having is that king-crook in the middle. We cut his robe into four even parts, a swatch for each of us. But the tunic's something fine. Honestly. It's woven with the tiniest weaves and all of a single piece, not a seam from neck to knee. I never saw the like, not even in Damascus. If we tore the cloth we'd ruin it. So we do a bit of gambling.

Bos wins it.

He's a blue-eyed Gaul and a cross-eyed fool. He rolls the tunic up into something like a pillow and lies down on the dirt and crams it under his greasy head and goes to sleep.

Mary and the Beloved

Jesus is awake. Alert.

Who will believe my report hereafter? He who hadn't the strength to carry the crosspiece, who was beaten unconscious, whose wrist-bones are grinding on rusted spikes, whose ribs like hoops are straining through the flesh, whose stomach is scooped hollow, whose – who –

His eyes are open! Between the flying wings of his arms, his head twists this way and that, looking, observing: alert.

Jesus sees the centurion and the four guards slouched at the feet of the crosses. When passers-by point and snort their scorn, he sees it.

Someone shouts, 'Hey, you! Temple-destroyer!' Jesus hears the taunt. 'Destroy that cross and save yourself!' He lifts his eyes and confronts a priest who shoots out his bottom lip and shakes his head.

'Pass a law, your majesty!' Another traveller. A Levite. 'All kings come off their crosses today! Ha ha ha!'

The petty scorn is normal. Everyone's glad it's someone else who's cursed and crushed and hanging on the awful tree. Even the mourners who come to pray outside the tombs of their relatives across the road – even those bereaved deride the crucified: 'Pretty boy, pretty boy, get Daddy to deliver you, you precious son of the Almighty!'

By degrees I realize that during some outrage of the morning Jesus has bitten off the end of his tongue. He parts his lips and blood spills forth, soaking his chin whiskers, streaking his chest like a red rain. He tries to talk and it's a kind of pulp that searches his teeth. His breath sprays a pink mist. But he *sees* right sharply. There is no blood in his seeing. The rust-brown eyes of my Lord dart here and there with a terrible comprehension.

'Father.'

That's Jesus! I hear the word as much by love as by my ears. It sounds like *Faedir*, but I know that he's saying, 'Father.'

He thrusts his jaw forward as if to yawn. He gags, swallows, works his mouth, opens it – oh, that ruined, bloody stump of a tongue! He draws breath into the splayed cage of his chest, then:

'Father, forgive them!'

Draws breath, wretchedly.

'They do not know!' – spitting blood.

Another breath.

'What they are doing!'

His knees buckle. His body drops. The arms catch the weight. How can that small frame be so suddenly heavy? Sinews pop. His chest closes. Air is forced out of his lungs in sighing.

There is no wind. The sky is everywhere cloudless and blue, but not bright. Not a fresh cerulean. It is ancient and as dark as indigo. The sun lurks in the south-east like a beggar at the window.

'Messiah? They call you, heee. Messiah. Right?'

I'm halfway down this killing hill, this 'Golgotha'. I am kneeling in one of the depressions which give it the aspect of a jawless skull. I am in one of the eyesockets. There are two; from the round brow of the hill the crosses sprout; and a rock-lined mouth at the bottom bites the earth. In the stillness I hear the man who hangs to the left of my Lord: 'Messiah, heee. Right?' He addresses Jesus with violent wheezings. It takes me a moment to recognize these wheezings as a painful laughter. If he's low, there's one still lower.

'Why the hell. Heee. Don't you save yourself? Heee. And save us into the bargain. Heee.'

Whether the bystanders notice the criminal's *huspah* or not, the criminal to the right of Jesus does, and gathers the spittle to scold him: 'You're on your way. To your Maker, Nachash. And you don't fear? The meeting? Fool.'

There is a pause. Neither talks. All three of the crucified breathe in pain, hoisting their torsos by the strength of their arms, pressing wrist-bones on the iron spikes, then gulping air while their chests can expand – before their bodies drop and the hard yank at their shoulders narrows the chest again. They will live so long as they breathe. They will breathe so long as they have the strength to lift their weight upon the nails. But when they lift themselves, the crosspiece seesaws: the failure of either arm is failure finally.

The man who hangs at Jesus' right side speaks.

'Jesus?'

Jesus turns his head. Those darting eyes find the eyes of the criminal.

The criminal says, 'Remember me. When you come. Into your kingdom.'

Jesus holds the gaze. He opens his mouth: 'Ahhh.'

Oh, what effort my teacher requires to make his words!

'Listen,' he says, 'to me' – and though the language is mashed, it's profoundly familiar. My heart jumps. I go rigid and start to pant. These words: my dear Lord used these same words for matters most important, when he was most intense. But look at him now! I am taken by surprise. I sob.

'Today.' Jesus heaves himself up to breathe. He says, 'Today. You will be with me. In paradise.'

My eyes gape upwards at my Lord. They stream tears. I have folded my hands at my throat, but I cannot stop sobbing. *Paradise*, he says, and I think I feel the fine spray of blood that issues from his mouth. I think it falls on my forehead. I think it cools the skin there. I can't control my sobbing.

And then Jesus is looking directly at me. I, my miserable self – I am seen! Such terrible reversals: I see me as he must see me, vile, awkward, blubbering –

But I hear, or I seem to hear, a quiet command. 'Bring my

mother,' Jesus whispers.

His eyes rise and gaze a little way behind me. I turn, and there is Mary, bareheaded, gaunt, caught as if in amber, caught and fixed as if in the midst of a fall.

I obey. I get up to my feet and walk down the hill and put my arm around his mother and press the soft flesh of her shoulder and bring her with me up this hill, to the central cross. She comes mechanically. Her expression doesn't change. She stares at Jesus. Neither does my expression change. I'm hiccuping with my sobs. Mary is dry as leather. I am moisture.

We stand before Jesus, sharing my arm. And Mary whispers, 'Yeshi.'

She's unwashed. I can smell her. Why, when I am myself so detestable?

She whispers, 'Yeshi,' and I swear that Jesus contrives to smile. His head is but a half foot higher than mine. His rust-coloured eyes study his mother, moving from portion to portion up to her face; and I can *feel* which part of Mary's flesh comes under his gaze, for it shivers.

Jesus speaks to Mary.

'Woman.'

He breathes. He flicks his eyes to me, then back to her: 'Behold your son.'

She does. She glances at me. In a flash I'm seen again and not aggrieved. Mary looks back at Jesus. He offers a slow nod, and just as slowly she allows her weight to shift against my own. I take it, gratefully. My Lord has granted his mother another child. Though her womb will ever remember him, her weight and her age have me.

Nor does he intend to leave me an orphan.

'Son,' he says. He lifts his small body in order to suck the air. He is speaking to me. 'Behold your mother.'

And Mary's arm comes up and embraces my waist. We, neither of us, say a thing. I was wrong about her scent. It isn't offensive. It's homely in my nose, bread-dough and herbs and the close odour of a bedroom. I haven't stopped sobbing, but my expression is changing. We are family. It is noon, and we are not alone.

All day I've known his dying. I saw that future with a sober dread. But I did not anticipate this, such loveliness, such grace upon grace –

Then suddenly Mary and I are clinging to each other like children, horrified, sliding down to the ground together.

For the earth groans. Loudly. As if it were pulling apart. The ground begins to tremble and hiss, and it seems that dust spurts up from a million worm-holes. Dust shoots up from gaps and caverns and cracks in the ground; no, but it *isn't* dust; it has no substance; it is darkness itself. Darkness spews into the day from the eyesockets of Golgotha, from the seams of the tombs across the road, from the stones of the sepulchres, from *Sheol* and all the regions under the earth; and like a vast shadow, the darkness arises, swallowing Jerusalem, rushing towards every horizon, covering the seas, blacking the middle air and the sun and the firmament. Black!

And out of the blackness, a voice of the most indulgent and merciful sympathy speaks: *If you are.*

Do I, blinking upward, imagine the figure of a man? Blacker than the darkness? Filling the sky? In form more noble than the angels?

But where is Jesus? When I draw my looking down and close, I can see nothing; I lose orientation.

That voice! That damnable, smiling, earnest, urbane, sourceless, soundless voice! The wind, if there were a wind: *If you are the Son of God*, it says.

And suddenly I hear Jesus.

He's screaming! He shrieks like another wind altogether, hollow, hateful, inarticulate, the wind through winter reeds –

Oh, Jesus, Jesus, my Lord!

If you are the Son of God, the consoling voice persists, *fear nothing. Prove everything. Pitch your body headlong down. His angels ought to catch you and bear you up –*

'Begone!' Jesus shrieks as if tempests are tearing him apart: 'Begone, Satan!'

But the black air scarcely stirs. The physical world is dead-still, cloying as a cave. But these are not physical. These are spirits in defiance, fighting.

No! The voice casts off consolation. It thunders over the earth like wild horses charging: *This is MY hour and the power of darkness!*

'You are.'

Oh, my Jesus, hold your peace! Save your strength.

'You are,' he struggles on. 'A murderer. From the beginning. You are. A liar.'

But there are no angels to catch you, are there? No lie, no lie, abandoned child. Because there is no Father anywhere to claim you now.

'You are. The father of. Lies – '

LISTEN! The draconic voice shakes the foundations of creation, commanding: LOOK AROUND! WHAT CAN YOU FIND? WHERE IS YOUR FATHER NOW?

Now comes the quiet that lies at the bed of the sea. Dead men rot in such a quietness; and the bones of Abraham, which turned to powder an aeon after he died, the bones of Abraham are gone altogether.

Mary shivers. Mary is here! In my arms! Ha: I had forgotten her. The blackness so consumed me that it took from me my very sensations.

And then there ascends a sound we both can hear. Mary gasps to hear it and claws my skin with her fingernails.

'*Eli! Eli!*' Jesus is wailing. '*Lama sabachthani?*'

My God, my God, Jesus is pleading: *Why have you forsaken me?*

And no one answers.

No one.

The earth inhales. The darkness returns into the earth. There is suddenly a stark sunlight. It is nearly three in the afternoon.

'Eli?' one of the soldiers says. 'You think he's calling the prophet? The one the Jews say flew to heaven on a fire-spout?'

Another soldier soaks a sponge in the sour wine he's brought for himself, and raises it to Jesus' face and mashes it against his mouth. Some of the liquid must go in; his Adam's apple bucks; but most of it runs down his scabrous beard and onto his chest, pooling in the separations between his ribs.

Jesus no longer lifts his torso in order to breathe. He hangs farther and farther from the post, like winged victory pitching forward. His shoulders are out of joint, the arm-bones attached by ligaments and tendons only. They've stretched. The sweat has dried. The blood has dried. His eyes are closed, the lashes turned back and sticking to the lids like tiny darts. His jaw falls loose. The riven tongue inside is so swollen it almost closes the hole. A little air whistles from his lungs. It makes fricative sounds like *Ffff* and *Shhh*. It sounds like a battle cry muted by distance, a shout from a thousand miles away.

Then, distinctly, Jesus utters a word, *Faedir*, and then another, *Into*.

Mary lets go of my arm. She stands up. She faces Jesus, and speaks those same words herself, out loud: 'Father, into.'

Jesus manages to open one eye. But he cannot focus. Nor is he able to talk any more. Nevertheless, he moves his lips soundlessly while Mary speaks aloud the words he forms. It is his sentiment; it is her voice.

They are praying:

'Father. Into your hands. I commend my spirit.

'Amen.'

But Jesus' *Amen* is really only *Ahhhhhhhh*; for it is his final breath, expiring; and his head descends the length of his neck, and he dies.

There isn't a cloud in all the sky above us. Not one cloud.

My Lord and Mary's full-grown boy: he is dead.

SATURDAY: MISCELLANEA

═══

The Women

Martha said, 'You didn't wash him?'

'We didn't have the chance to wash him.'

The women lay quiet in the night.

Abruptly, someone shifted: turned onto her side and drew her knees up to her chest – or so it seemed by the sliding of her fabric.

In the distance a jackal yapped.

Martha said, 'I'd have found the time.' Her breathing had the wheeze of the heavyset, whose flesh constricts their windpipes.

'Yeah, and you'd've yanked the spikes yourself? And you'd've got the corpse down all by yourself?'

' "The corpse"?' A third woman. Her voice trembled with unhappiness. 'How can you speak of the Lord that way?'

'He's dead!'

'Please. Please. Please.'

'Well, I'm sorry – but Martha doesn't know what she's talking about. We didn't have time to find jars and water – or *soap*, for that matter. Didn't even know if the governor would let us bury Jesus till Joseph came running from the praetorium with the permission. By the time the Lord's poor body lay aground on the linen shroud (he so small, he so slight) it was sundown. Sabbath had started. And when the men rolled that flat stone over the entrance to the tomb, well, it was night. We came to Bethany through the night. We. The two of us. Not Mary. She stayed.'

For a long moment no one spoke.

Then, Maryam from Magdala uttered her regret: 'We didn't even bind his chin up.' Hers was a wistful, diminutive bleating: 'The winding sheet, a veil to cover his face, but his mouth kept falling open.'

The jackal began snarling and grunting – feeding, it seemed on old flesh.

The women lay on the floor of a single room in Martha's house. Side by side, in fetid air, listening to the predatory sounds of the night. No one had slept. No one was sleeping now. Dawn was at least an hour away.

All of the women but one had been in Jerusalem the previous day. Not Martha. Martha had insisted on optimism. When word of Jesus' arrest had wakened them before the cockcrow yesterday, she refused to give in to despair. When everyone else dressed and rushed from Bethany, Martha promised to prepare a supper against their returning. They should, she called, preserving the ordinary in her tone and her priorities, they should 'bring the men back with you, OK?'

But the men had not come back. Only the women. In sad, ragged groups the whole day through.

Already by nine, two of them were standing in the mulberry grove behind Martha's house. They'd left the praetorium as soon as the governor had sentenced Jesus to death, their hopes and their futures shattered.

Others could not stomach his scourging. Faces cold and prickling with sweat, their breathing shallow, their vision tinged with red, they stumbled away from Jerusalem.

A handful followed Jesus even to Golgotha, beating their breasts and wailing among a host of other women.

Daughters of Jerusalem, Jesus managed to say; he'd been relieved of the crosspiece; he'd become aware of the piteous band behind him: *do not weep for me. Weep for yourselves and for your children.*

The handful of discipling women saw the spikes, heard them clank on rock as the guardsmen threw them down. They saw the Lord crucified. But only five of these endured unto his death. And then there were but three remaining to see the place where Jesus was buried. One was Maryam from Magdala. Another was his mother. Mary. Who still had not come back to Bethany. She alone of all the women.

'We didn't wash his hair,' Maryam was murmuring. 'We didn't trim his hair or his beard. We didn't minister to Jesus at all. We didn't – we couldn't – anoint his beautiful body.'

'Now, stop right there!' Martha barked. 'You're forgetting my sister!' The woman sounded angry. Right! And she would agree. She thought herself righteously galled by the incompetence surrounding her. Yes, and by the lie the Master told her – he, the 'resurrection and the life'. Right!

In fact, the poor woman's soul was torn asunder by a guilt too terrible to be named. She alone, Martha alone of all the women who loved and followed Jesus, had not gone into Jerusalem to see her Lord, to suffer the horrors, to sit vigil unto the end. If his body had not been properly honoured, she'd been the first to neglect it – and she the worst of all for having busied herself with household matters and singing pretty songs while –

And this is how the hard, pragmatic Martha handled guilt, by striking out. By finding fault and stinging it with criticism.

'Don't forget my sister Mary!' she barked in the direction of gentle Maryam, her voice husky with her weight and her emotion. 'Mary anointed him! Anointed his "beautiful body"! She anointed him three days ago, and Jesus told us the meaning of that, didn't he? *She saved her ointment*, he said to Judas. *She saved her ointment against the day of my burial.* So don't go moping, Maryam. Jesus was anointed!'

There followed a very long pause in the women's room.

The jackal set up a sharp, plaintive yapping, as if something bigger had driven it from its food.

Then Joanna – who had turned away from the sight of the spikes and had *run* away at the sound of the hammering – spoke quietly, repentantly, like Maryam from Magdala: 'We didn't lament outside the tomb,' she said. 'Mary and Martha lamented for Lazarus. We lamented a full day for a boy in the village of Nain whose name we did not know.'

A strengthless grey light showed at the high windows. Joanna got up on her hands and knees and crept towards Maryam, then lay down beside that diaphanous child. In the manner of privacy she said, 'We haven't yet honoured him with our tears, have we?'

Susanna asked, 'Did anyone think to set his sandals inside? Beside his head?'

'No one knows where his sandals are.'

'Nothing of his was left. Nothing. His staff was broken and thrown in the fire at the high priest's house.'

Now Joanna spoke in the manner of leadership: 'Tomorrow,' she said, 'after the sabbath. As soon as we can. We will carry embalming spices and precious perfumes back to the tomb of the Lord. Today we'll prepare them; tomorrow we'll bear them thither and accomplish our final tasks. And we will lament. We will start to weep inside the tomb at the side of his stone bed; nor will we cease our weeping until his flesh is dust and his bones are pure and we lay them in a box to await the time when his Father will knit new skin upon those bones and breathe and grant them life again.'

Martha nearly writhed in vexation and in shame. She was the householder. She had been mistress. Leadership had been hers before.

A Levitical Report

On the day of the Passover, while legionnaires were preparing Jesus of Nazareth for crucifixion by means of a public whipping, a young disciple of that same prisoner, Judas Iscariot, accosted certain chief priests in the Court of the Israelites outside the Temple sanctuary.

He harangued them there, demanding that they take back some monies which they had in good faith paid him for services rendered. The young disciple laboured under the impression that these dedicated men could influence the governor, causing him to soften the sentence already placed upon his Master.

The chief priests, of course, honoured their transaction with the young man and refused his monies.

It was then that Judas Iscariot offended against our laws, against our sacred place, and against our God.

Showing every sign of demon possession, Judas Iscariot threw himself into the court reserved for priests alone; he ran past the Altar of Holocausts and up the very steps of the sanctuary, halting only at the doorposts of the dwelling place of God. Then, as if that weren't profanation enough, he next flung his monies through the doors! He hurled his silver monies across the holy floor, where it rang like the bells on the skirts of Satan!

The chief priests were, understandably, horrified.

It took them a moment, therefore, to gather their senses and send for us.

By the time we arrived to arrest the offender, he had vanished amongst the pilgrim crowd.

I myself, having received a fairly accurate description of the offender, took a detachment of Temple police and set forth to find either this Judas himself or another man known to have followed the Nazarene, Simon the son of John, a Galilean who might lead us to the God-offender.

We would have interrogated Jesus of Nazareth, but that he was crucified by then.

We didn't find either disciple that day.

Nevertheless, my report does not recount a failure. Rather, it concludes with praise for our faithful God, who, as he himself declares to Moses, 'will by no means clear the guilty'. And even as the Lord God promises, 'I will punish you according to the fruit of your doings,' so has he done to Judas Iscariot.

We found that young man – nineteen years of age, according to our investigations – dead, hanging from a large oak tree in a garden on the western slopes of the Mount of Olives. Clearly, it was at the promptings of heavenly justice that he brought himself to his own conclusion; for he climbed onto a low, smoothed, horizontal branch of the oak and, standing there, tossed a leather cord with a plumb at the end of it over a stout limb still higher in the tree; that cord, braided for strength and soaked in water to cause it to shrink thereafter, he tied around his own neck.

Judas Iscariot leaped out into the empty air.

The garden in which we found the young man's corpse is called Gethsemane.

The Beloved

The mother of Jesus spent Saturday among the hewn tombs. I watched her. I watched with her.

I watched over her.

Mary's lips moved continually but soundlessly. Sometimes I bowed my head to honour the piety, believing she was praying. Sometimes I shivered, convinced by the flash in her eye that she was cursing.

She stayed the whole day through, never leaving the place, not even to relieve herself.

I went into the city and brought her food she didn't eat.

I brought water which, finally, late in the day, I did persuade her to accept. But she drank from the goat-skin for three minutes without stopping for a breath, then staggered and gasped for air and, leaning against fresh limestone, threw it all up again, in great rhythmic gushes.

She dropped to her knees. Mary collapsed to the ground. I knelt down beside her. With clean linen and a laving of my fresh water, I washed her face, her poor old face, Mary's riven, ruined, tired face. She has a widow's peak at the hairline when one can brush back the maniacal hair in order to see it.

When she was clean I offered the water again. This time she took small sips and then rested her head upon my thigh.

'What shall I call you?' I asked while we were still together. 'Do you want me to call you "Mother"?'

'Not Mother,' she said.

I felt the warmth of her breathing through my tunic. The air was cooling. The sun stood but two hands over the western horizon. The limestone ridge into which the Lord's tomb had been carved now cast its shadow over us and halfway up the crosses, two of which still held men's bodies, their legs in shade, their hollowed faces ruddy in the sunlight. There were vultures circling on their lazy wings above. There were black ravens perched at the ends of the crosspieces, waiting. The men were not yet dead. They could keep their eyes a little while longer.

'Marah,' Mary said. 'Call me Marah.'

'Bitter.' Call me 'Bitter'.

I made no comment. I would ask her the same question again, but later.

By sunset I could have sworn that Mary had fallen asleep; a light sweat beaded the skin below her nose, and this despite the evening's chill. Yet the woman was moving her lips. Just slightly. And frowning. Dreaming? I whispered her name. I whispered, 'Marah?' There was no response. Her incisors kept clicking together, her jaw making the tiniest bites, her lips moving, moving, moving –

Mary

Cursed be the day on which I was born.

That day on which my mother bore me: let it be shorn of every blessing.

Cursed be the man who carried the news to my father, saying, 'A daughter is born to you!' and thinking he'd make my father happy. Let that man be like the cities which God Almighty overthrew without a ripple of pity. Let him hear shriekings in the morning and alarums at noon, because he did not kill me in the womb!

I wish my mother had been my grave, her womb forever swollen.

Why was I torn out of the womb to witness so much toil and sorrow? To suffer such. Unceasing. Shame?

SUNDAY II

Maryam from Magdala

None has awoken as early as she.

For fear of distressing the other women, she gathers her robe and pulls it over her shoulders as quietly as clouds do gather in the midnight sky. Shoeless, she sneaks out from the house and into the dewy orchards on the eastern slopes of the Mount of Olives. These are the wee hours of the morning, and this is the first day of the week.

Already Maryam feels the heat of weeping behind her eyes. Lamenting comes unbidden. It is not a formality; it has become a way of life. Since Friday night she's drawn her breath in sorrow; she's released it in sighing. And the stew that Martha served the sad company of women yesterday: in spite of the chicory root and pickled capers, it caught in her throat like boiled grass. Maryam hasn't eaten. She's wrapped her head and her face to the eyes in a rough scarf. Neither has she washed or cared for her body in any way.

The others will follow soon enough with spices and candles and water, cloth, perfumes. Maybe the men will come and roll the stone away so that the embalmers can enter his tomb. And Maryam will serve then with the rest of the women, burn incense inside the sepulchre, oil the Lord's body, wash it, perfume it, wrap it properly, caress it – caress his beautiful face for the first time since ever she had begun to love him.

But now, right now in the dark before the family wakes, Maryam has to cry. She can't wait for the family. She can't wait for a more suitable time. Sorrow has swelled so hugely within her, she'll burst if she does not hurry to the tomb and fall on her knees and cry.

Maryam runs outside the city, along its northern wall. She sprints between the pool of Bethesda on her right and the Sheep Gate on her left. For several hundred yards she skirts the campground of pilgrims' tents erected on flatland north of Jerusalem; then she passes the Fish Gate (closed till morning) and rounds the north-west corner of the wall, turning south towards Golgotha and the garden of tombs.

This woman is light as the lacewing; and grief, rather than dulling her, has charged her with a fretful energy. The running is easy. All her sinews are taut for the running, her senses hectic. She does not stumble in darkness. She doesn't fear obstructions. She is a swallow on the stiff wing. Her cry is a trifling, *Twit, twit, twit*. Maryam from Magdala: she is in distressful flight.

The Beloved

There's a knocking on the door.

Someone's come up the outer steps (but we heard nothing of that) and knocks rapidly on the door to our room – with anger? Authority? Urgency? No, but the knocks lack authority; it seems to me a small hand rapping.

We stir. Some keep sleeping. Who knows what time of the night it is. No one gets up or moves towards the door. No one cries out an answer.

Knock, knock, knock!

Simon Peter hisses: 'Could be Caiaphas's men.'

'In the night?' I wonder.

'They took Jesus in the night.' He lies beside me. He whispers as if the door were made of paper and not of thick cypress wood. 'Could be they followed you from the sepulchre to this place.'

Knock, knock!

I suppose that Simon could be right. In this season of evil

anything at all could happen between 'the sepulchre and this place.' But would Levites be so… polite?

The knocking stops.

The latch rattles. That chills me. But the door is well bolted and the latch ineffectual. It drops in its slot and is still.

This place: we are in the upper room where Jesus ate his last meal with us. While Mary and I were keeping a midnight watch at his tomb, the men were gathering here. Philip, Andrew, Thomas. One by one. Nathanael, James. No plan to it: horror drove them. Simon. Matthew. After the Lord was crucified, after the Lord Jesus slumped into his death, and hatreds prowled the world like roaring lions, and the bones of my brothers went soft as rotting fruit, they just showed up. Thaddaeus. Simon the Cananaean. Grim-faced, stunned, one by one. And then they didn't leave. They bolted the door. They spent yesterday, the sabbath day, secluded in this room. Well, Martha's house seemed too obvious a hideout. The enemies surely know by now that Jesus had been staying over there. And though the women must have gathered in Bethany, they were no threat to the authorities. Jesus' men, however; the men of the pretender-king, however –

Judas had talked, hadn't he? Judas had snatched their walls away, their protections, their privacy, their Master, their lives!

But even the disciples hadn't known of this upper room until three days ago. And the people of the house, both mother and son, had served them so kindly on Thursday night and were truly welcoming every day thereafter, late and soon –

The fellow the women had followed in order to find a room for our Passover, the man carrying a jar of water on his head, is the son of this house, John Mark. His mother, Mary, is the householder. She it is who found Mary and me late this night by the tomb of the Lord; she wrapped a blanket around the poor, weary mother of my Lord and brought us home, to this house. She kept Mary in rooms below, while I took my place here with the rest of the men.

Bang! Bang!

The knocking begins with greater force; someone is swinging a hammer against the wood. Or battering it with the butt-end of a spear.

'They're back!' Simon woofs, immediately tensing.

Bang! Bang! Bang!

I roll to my stomach and start to rise. 'I'm going out there.'

All the men are moving now. 'Is that safe?' they mutter. 'It's the witching hour. The Devil's casting lots.'

Simon: 'What d'you plan on saying?' He sounds superior, like an officer questioning a subordinate.

'I don't know. But if it's soldiers, then Mary's in danger.'

I am on my feet, picking my way around living bodies.

Bang! Bang! Bang! Bang!

Simon: 'It's us they want! Not Mary. The men! They expect vengeance.'

'Are you telling me to stay put?'

Simon: 'What d'you plan on doing out there?'

'I don't know, Simon! I have no idea. But I will not cower in here!'

Bang! Bang!

Simon: 'I have the sword. I'm coming with you. Andrew, open the door for us, then shut it and bolt it behind.'

Through the windows the southern sky shows as a dirty wash, houses and hilltops black against it.

I place myself against the doorjamb. I'll leap out the instant it opens.

Bang! Bang –

I slip the bolt. Andrew yanks the door. Almost I plunge through it –

But there is no weapon on the other side. Nor soldiers nor enemies. It's a woman, wailing. It's Maryam! – the fragile Maryam from Magdala, whose bones I would have crushed if I'd leaped on her.

'Oh, oh, oh, oh!' she cries in a high, trilling voice, scarcely audible even now. She is striking her chest with a large stone – ah, child! – hard enough to bruise it.

'Maryam, what's the matter?' I take the stone from her hand.

The woman's as white as a dove's egg, as scant as the shell. Her feet are bare, her face scarf-wrapped up to the eyes. Anguish contorts her spine.

'They've stolen his body!' she wails. 'They've taken the Lord! I don't know where they put him.'

'Show me.' I don't turn back for my robe. The tunic's enough.
'Let's go.'

Maryam flits down the steps then sprints up Zion towards the Garden Gate.

I run as fast as I can.

By the time I reach the Garden Gate, the coming sunrise ignites a golden fire behind the trees on the Mount of Olives. Soon Jerusalem will be milling with pilgrims, and shops will open, and herdsmen will be driving their livestock to the slaughterings, and the streets will smell of breakfast, the streets will smell of wood fires and dung fires and the roasting fat of the sacrifice.

Maryam is kneeling directly in front of Jesus' tomb when I arrive. The flat stone that had covered the entrance has toppled to the ground some two yards away. I go to Maryam and likewise kneel and peer inside. There's just enough light to see the scrawl of a linen shroud, collapsed, ridged and wrinkled on the stone shelf where the body of the Lord should be lying.

She's right, this piteous child. His body isn't here.

Just then we both hear the heavy clumpings of another runner. Simon Peter comes down the road from the city and drops to his hands and knees. Without pause or comment, but with the point of his sword dragging the dirt beside him, he crawls into the tomb:

'What the – ?'

I crawl in after him.

More than the shroud, now, I can see the cloth that covered Jesus' head; but that cloth is neatly folded on the farthest corner of the burial shelf.

'If it's not grave robbers,' Simon growls, 'it's Caiaphas took the body. He what? He thought we'd *worship* the remains?'

But no robber would have folded the head-cloth like that. Thieves and vandals don't think of neatness. And wouldn't they have kept the body wrapped to take it away? Something. Something deliberate. Something (oh, heaven, let me think it!), something divine has happened here.

Simon Peter slaps the stone with the flats of both hands. He growls. He tears at his hair and beard.

'By God! By God!' he swears before me in the hollow cavern.

'There *must* be a vengeance!' And in this moment, watching his contortions, I am suddenly filled with the knowledge of Simon Peter.

He is monumentally disappointed. He fears thought; he hates inaction; and meditations feed like maggots on his bowels. Simon was *hoping* for soldiers outside the door of the upper room. Maryam's appearing caused him to stumble. And then he ran here wanting the grave to be empty: *Oh, give me reason for my rages!* Truly, the brutal execution of the Lord Jesus has driven Simon to his rages; but his impotence in the event, his cowardice at the high priest's house, his failures – these have made him mad. He yearns to murder; he yearns at the same time to throw himself in harm's way, a sort of putting things right again. His sword, that short *machaira*, is really little better than a dagger. It's nothing against spears and javelins and arrows and maces and armour. Some part of Simon knows that a righteous fight, however powerful his body and his angers, must lay him low. Three soldiers, armed, would kill him. And then the women will have one more corpse to bury.

When he crawls out of the sepulchre, therefore, so do I. And when he returns to Jerusalem through the Garden Gate, so do I. I cannot leave my brother, sick with self-hatred, alone.

Maryam from Magdala

She hasn't moved. Still she kneels in front of the tomb. And she is weeping. Not in lamentation; not in remembrance and honour for her Lord, which would have been her final act of love; but in loss. The body of Jesus is lost. Therefore, Maryam has lost her life. She has lost her way. There is absolutely nowhere to go from here. She will lie down and die before the Feast of Weeks.

A roseate light falls on Maryam's small back, which shakes with her silent sobbing. She is a slender damsel bending groundwards. She is a stalk of sweet grass, bent by the jackal's paw in its passage. Her face swells; her hands are wringing themselves into a bloodless white.

A voice says, *Woman?* Two voices, echoing as if in a stone basilica, say: *Woman? Why are you crying?*

Her eyes shut tight, it seems to Maryam that the sun is bright against her face. But when she opens her eyes she finds no sun. The sun has not arisen – and when it does it will rise behind her. No, the light is playing her false: it comes from the clothing and the countenances of two men sitting inside the sepulchre, one at the head and one at the foot of Jesus' shroud. They are the ones who have spoken to her.

Slowly, Maryam rises to her feet. 'O sirs,' she whispers in a voice destroyed by sorrow, 'because they've taken my Lord, and I don't know where they've put him.'

Her eyes ache. Her sight is stunned by the angelic brilliance. Instinctively, she turns away, rubbing the water that pools in her vision – and there, in the road, she makes out the blurred figure of a man.

'Woman, why are you crying?' asks the figure, walking towards her. 'Tell me: what are you looking for?'

'Him,' Maryam answers. 'My Lord.' She begins to babble: 'Are you an intendant of cemeteries? Did someone ask you to take the body out of this tomb? Did you? Did you take the body, I mean? If so, could you tell me where you put him? I'll go, and I will get him – '

But the watery figure continues to approach her until he stands but an arm's length away. He, too, is growing bright. But not like the men in the tomb. Like the morning. He *is* the morning itself, splendid, filling the space between heaven and earth, sparkling like stars ascending and descending on the open tomb!

O good and holy God! – who? –

Then the figure clothed in white, this man composed completely of light, speaks. He utters a single word. But in that word Maryam knows everything. She knows him; she knows herself; she knows the grace of the Father and the glory of his only begotten Son.

The Light says, *Maryam.*

Jesus! It's Jesus!

He calls her by name, saying, 'Maryam from Magdala.'

She leaps straight up and cries, 'Rabboni!'

Oh, how beautiful the planes of his face! He stands with his head in the heavens, and yet he is only just her size; and he is –

his rust-bright eyes and the freckles that emblazon them are – deft and dazzling and full of life.

Bolder than she has ever been, Maryam spreads her arms. She will embrace the Lord whom she loves! She will throw herself upon the neck of him for whom her face and her throat are flaming: 'O my darling Teacher!'

But: 'Hush,' the Lord commands her. 'Don't take hold of me,' he says, 'I haven't returned to my Father yet.'

Such impetuosity, Maryam! You've never acted like this in front of Jesus! And on any day before she would have been terrified by such emotion; she'd have feared it was her devils returning again. But on this day, at this daybreak hour, nothing at all can trouble Maryam from Magdala. Not even the *Hush!* of her Lord.

Because he is alive!

And so is she: alive.

And more than that, he has a job for her to do. See? Maryam has become the first servant of the newly risen Jesus. Maryam, that once bore evil spirits here and there, now bears the good news of the Lord!

For 'Go to my brothers,' he says. 'Tell them that I am returning to my Father and your Father, to my God and your God.'

Fleet afoot is our pale, our wraithlike child! And she has torn the veil from round her face; it streams behind her as she runs. Her ankles flash like lambs on the hillside, her feet like ibexes high on the mountains. And her mouth is open. And she is singing. And the song precedes her where she goes.

I have seen, sings Maryam from Magdala.

She is greater and more beautiful than the swallow now. She is the osprey, white at the throat, her bosom and abdomen snowy white: *I have seen the Lord!*

She is the osprey who skims the seas to wash her feet in their salty waters. And high above her, soaring on the mighty thermals, on those invisible pillars of the dome of the universe, flies the eagle.

I've seen the Lord!
I've heard his voice!
Attend his word, O nations,
And rejoice!

The Beloved

If, after the Passover meal on Thursday, John Mark hadn't taken the tables out of this room, we'd be standing on the tables. We are a crowd now. We are men and women together, a good number of the disciples of our Lord, the crucified. But we are not altogether in agreement. And the fussing makes an almighty noise in so close a space.

Maryam from Magdala says she's seen the Lord Jesus alive. Simon disputes her more coarsely than is necessary. He's angry at her. He's angry at everyone. But she stands her ground. I'm surprised by the spunk. This is Maryam, after all.

The other women believe Maryam. More than that, they chatter forth arguments of their own. Joanna and Susanna and James' mother and Salome all say that when they brought water and towels and unguents to the tomb this morning, they too didn't find the body of the Lord. Instead, they were met by angels, bright and frightening. The angels declared that Jesus is risen from the dead, and so, of course, there'd be no body anywhere. And the women swear that the angels sent them to us – 'to Simon Peter in particular!' they repeat pointedly, three times over – to announce that Jesus will go before us into Galilee.

'A silly story,' Philip insists.

Philip's by the door. He has bolted it after every person who's entered here.

James likewise has argued that, even if the Lord *is* roaming somewhere, hale and hearty, it's prudent to keep the door shut tight. 'Let him knock,' James offers up a pallid joke: 'We'll let him in.'

Nobody laughs. We are a contentious congregation, more goatish than sheepish.

John Mark stands on a stool and watches at the window. For what? For whom? It's evening, dreary, passing into night.

Simon Peter can't keep still. He paces. He prowls around the room frowning like a thunderhead, rumbling at anyone who doesn't make a way for him.

Now Joanna raises her voice above the others: 'Well, don't we make a fine, united synagogue!' she cries.

She pushes John Mark from the stool and gets up on it herself. Now she has a vantage for her scolding: 'You know us! You men have known us since we gave ourselves to the Lord in the first place, since we started serving both him and you in Galilee. So here we come with the best news a body can imagine, news straight from the angels – and all at once you will not trust us! "A vision"? What's the matter with you? You call what we saw – saw with our own eyes – "a *vision*"! Idiots! Jackals! Blowflies! You know how to spoil the loveliest, most beautiful gifts of God. We might as well go down to sit with Mary and leave you to yourselves. You... men!

'Philip!' Joanna commands, 'open the door!'

But Philip doesn't move. He has been chastened. The door stays bolted.

The room generally has gone quiet. Men shuffle their feet and hang their heads. It's a real threat, the women's leaving the men alone. They missed the women all last night and would miss them doubly now.

But Simon stalks the borders of our community.

'A vision, a vision!' he snarls. 'Didn't I myself go to the tomb? Didn't I myself go *into* the tomb? After Maryam and before you all? I saw nothing there! I – '

Suddenly Simon is silenced. He shrinks. He seems to be sucked into himself, gaping towards a corner of the room.

Everyone turns to that corner and looks.

'Oh, my God,' Joanna whispers.

There, regarding us with level eyes, easy in his well-knit frame, athletic, light and smiling, is Jesus.

He opens his mouth and speaks with articulate precision. 'Peace be with you,' he says.

But the men have turned to stone. Mortality is cold upon them, and some are plain afraid. *It can't be Jesus. Scourged. Tormented. Broken on a cross –*

Jesus removes his hands from beneath his robe and raises them up, palms forward. It would be a blessing, and perhaps it is a blessing, but he means mostly to show us the deep, unbloody holes the nails have made. Next he gathers back his robe and shows us the place where a sword pierced between his ribs and through his lung and into his heart while still he hung ɔss and a soldier wished to prove him dead.

s I.'

Yes!

Jesus!

It is Jesus indeed.

And this time when he says, 'Peace be with you,' the men and the women, the old and the young, every disciple is cut free from every kind of binding. They – we! – begin to laugh and to weep for joy. It is Jesus!

And now I do unbolt the door. I rush down the outside stairs and dash into the rooms below.

'Mary!' I cry to his mother – his mother and mine. 'Mary, come and see! He isn't dead! He's alive!'

And when we enter the upper room again, Jesus is moving among the disciples, taking their faces between his wounded hands, and breathing upon them a visible breath.

'Receive the Holy Spirit,' he says to this one and to that one.

He turns to Simon Peter, and the big man, gaping still, almost mews with emotion. No longer angry, he cringes. At the touch of the Lord, he shivers. And though Jesus speaks no differently to him nor handles him any differently from the others, the Master's breathing seems to scorch him like fire: tears stream from Simon's eyes. To a guilty man, the purest love is a punishing thing.

Jesus says, 'Receive the Holy Spirit.'

We are Adam. We are a dull, lumpish clay. Jesus is the Lord God, the Creator in the Garden of Eden, breathing life into the first man's nostrils, and we're becoming living beings – all over again.

'Receive the Holy Spirit.'

Finally, my Lord: you say it also unto me.

'As my Father has sent me,' you say, 'even so do I send you.'

Your hands are firm, giving shape to my face. Your breath is warm, with the fragrance of balm. Golden anthers fleck the irises of your steadfast eyes, and I can hear the clickings of spittle when you speak, so close is your mouth to mine: 'Whosesoever sins you forgive, they are forgiven.' This you say to me, my Lord. This you give to all whom you've commanded to love as you have loved. 'Whosesoever sins you retain, they are retained.'

338

And when, one week later, you grant Thomas as the last of all to see your wounds and to receive his peace, he falls to the floor and utters the confession I have never since ceased to sing unto you:

My Lord, my Lord and my God!

PART NINE

THE BELOVED

MIM

=

'Mim,' Mary called to me.

I was leading the donkey that pulled the pretty little carriage Jesus had built before our final trip to Jerusalem. Mary sat in the carriage. Cross-legged. On a cushion. Queen-like, save for her clothing and the toy-like quality of her transport.

Mim: I heard her voice but didn't understand the word she spoke – if it was a word.

'What? Did you say something?'

'I said "Mim",' she said.

So it was a word after all. I turned to look at her, frowning: 'What is a "Mim"?'

'A name. It's a name.'

Her hair had gone grey. Not silvery, not snowy, neither pretty nor handsome, her hair was the grey of weathered wood and still as thorny as a briar patch. Her cheeks were plump. Her arms and her breasts were likewise plump, giving the woman the appearance of grandmotherly benevolence. Hers was the lap that invited babies – even as a small, continual nodding of her head invited the confidences of young men and young women. But the nod was an affliction of advancing age, and that grandmotherly ampleness cloaked a critic most acidic and thin as a blade. Many a young man, seeking assurances, got knocks instead. Once, when she was very young, Mary had outrun boys bigger than herself; now that she had grown old, the mother of the Messiah held strong opinions and a mind to speak them and a tongue to make them sting.

I had heard the woman at her prayers: she scolded the Lord God Almighty!

And that the Lord had made his mother also mine was not, I came to realize, an unqualified favour. If men on crosses can joke, Jesus joked – and ever since has grinned about it in his glory. Mary cut and stitched my clothes; but she cut them according to measurements she believed I *ought* to have. They fitted painfully. She saw to my meals; but the what and the when and the how of our eating was always controlled by her own decidings. If I came late to supper, I ate my bread in a boyish shame.

Soon after the Lord Jesus had ascended to his Father, we – whom, at his leave-taking, he had called 'apostles' – became witnesses to his loving, to his life, his death, his resurrection. We spread through the provinces of Palestine and then through the lands of the Gentiles, proclaiming the words and the deeds of Jesus, making disciples in every nation, striving for the salvation of the world: *Let every knee bow; let every tongue confess that Jesus the Messiah is Lord, to the glory of God the Father!*

Maryam from Magdala travelled with us awhile, her face flushed with high colour, her narrow nostrils widening as if alert to every scent, as if to find and delight in every new waft of delicious air. Her joy was robust, constant, larger than she was – and, to me, somewhat alarming. Well, her body was slender, her fingers long, uncallused. She had a beautiful little foot, its arch so curved she seemed to walk on tiptoe. When she sought to run, she drove her shoulders up to her ears, pressed her arms to her sides and swept her hands back and forth on the axis of her elbows. In other words, the child was not constructed for strong exertions. But joy in Maryam required strength. It was a consuming fire. It required muscle, a powerful heart, a broad body to dissipate the heat, good sleep, sustenance, endurance. Yet the bones of our diaphanous child were light as birdwing, as thin as a whistle is hollow. And her reserves had never been full.

Maryam's joy could kill her. Could kill 'my body', she said when we spoke of it late one night, 'but never stop my heart. I'm half in love with death,' she said, 'because I wholly love my Lord.

I'll go to him. I'll fly to him, and he will meet me in the air.'

Even so. Even so did that prescient woman give expression to the *anagnorisis*, the recognition, slowly growing within my own heart. Therefore I record it here: death had lost its sting. Death itself had died in the dying of our Lord. This woman knew right well the effects of her wild happiness, and she did not fear them.

The crimson Maryam travelled with Mary and me for a year and a half. They sang, the two of them, a killing music wherever I preached, weaving their voices in new songs and hymns, Maryam the high notes, Mary the low. We uttered our songs in those days. They were not written down, neither in composing nor in remembering. They leaped from our lips, as it were; and though I could not myself sing a steady note, I could endeavour words:

> He is the image of God invisible.
>> The firstborn of creation,
>> Before its suspiration.

> By him and for him was made the world and all –
>> Dominions, thrones and powers,
>> He holds it all together.

> He is the head of the body, he its soul;
>> He: the firstborn from the dead;
>> He: in all pre-eminent.

> In him the fullness of God was pleased to dwell,
>> Through him to reconcile
>> The world unto himself.

>> And what is he to us?
>> Why, bleeding on the cross
> Jesus incarnadined earth and sky with… peace.

Maryam from Magdala left us in the winter of our second year together. We woke in the morning, and the flaming child was gone.

It had snowed in the night. Lightly. Laying a pale dust on everything. But there were no tracks away from our small cover under an overhanging rock. When we exhaled, Mary and I, we blew plumes of a pale steam, like spirits, into the air. Maryam had left before the snowfall, but after our lying down the night before. And I've never discovered where she went; nor have I heard from the woman since; nor have I talked with the person who talked with her after that. She vanished. But I have no doubt that her expectations were fulfilled, and her joy was granted its fullest expression. No: she *became* her joy. For she met the Lord in the air. He welcomed her there.

Both during our travels with Maryam and long, long thereafter, my closest, most motherly companion was the mother of my Lord (to the glory of God – and so forth). When I preached, the knowledgeable Mary, widow of Joseph, mother of her 'Yeshi,' would take up a position to my left and slightly behind me. This afforded her opportunity to participate in the proclamation of the good news:

'It was at Jericho of Judea,' I would say in the house, for example, of an Ephesian, his whole family assembled before me, 'that Jesus restored the sight of a blind man named Bartimaeus – '

And Mary would interrupt. The thin critic inside of her would whisper loud enough for the horses to hear: 'No, not Jericho. He did that near the pool of Siloam. And the man's name wasn't Bartimaeus.'

Or I would introduce some of Jesus' most incisive sayings this way: 'Once when he was teaching the crowds on a mountain, Jesus delivered a series of striking beatitudes. "Blessed are those," he called, "who are poor in spirit, for theirs is the kingdom – "'

'No,' Mary hissed. 'It was on a plain! And he blessed the poor: just *poor*. Never softened his word for the rich! Never said anything *like* "in spirit".'

On the other hand, my dear, adopted mother was the most engaged of all my listeners. She lost herself in the story of Jesus' temptations by Satan in the wilderness; and, seeing the girlish wonder in her round face, I thought her lovely, truly. Whenever I spoke of the crucifixion, she lamented quietly; then she delivered up round guffaws when I spoke of his rising again. Her knowledge, her sorrow and her maternal love were a mighty force, albeit a spiritual one, in the congregations of the Gentiles. And when I announced the purpose of all the work of the Son of God with these words: *For God so loved the world that he gave his only Son, that whoever believes in him shall not perish but have eternal life. For God did not send his Son into the world to condemn the world, but that the world might through him be saved*, Mary wept.

'Mim,' she said, riding in the carriage behind our little donkey. 'It's a name.'

'Ah. Yes. And what's the importance? What's your meaning? Why are you telling me about it?'

Mary laid her eyes lightly on my face. She wasn't so much looking at me as looking inside herself and remembering.

'You asked me once,' she said, 'what you should call me.'

'I remember. You told me to call you "Marah".'

'You never have, have you? – called me Marah.'

'Because you've never been bitter to me. Tough, forthright, bossy. But never bitter.' I drew the donkey to a stop. Mary was grave. This was not a casual conversation.

'Oh, I have been bitter. Often. And angry for the lot that God saw fit to give me for most my life. But, though it never sweetens – life can never be green and sweet again – the bitterness passes. And a measure of wisdom takes its place. Now I know that it *had* to be so, my life, my lot. I had to suffer the outrages of my son. Because Yeshi had to suffer the outrages of wickedness and then to enter into his glory.

'But in these later days,' Mary mused, her eyebrows rising, 'I keep recalling the past, my earliest past, times that were young and green and truly sweet. I remember the morning of my life.'

She tugged at the soft flesh beneath her chin. There was a fine spray of whiskers above the corners of her mouth.

'I had a husband then,' Mary said. 'Joseph. His name was Joseph. A shambling bear of a man. Tender, protective, not always obedient to my demands, you know – but there, as thick as the walls protecting Jerusalem. He loved me, and I felt beautiful, and my fingers were nimble, weaving cloth that the rich desired, and he made the cradle that carried our baby, and he was proud of little Yeshi; he taught him the craft of his own good hands, though he said the boy would make a name far greater than "carpenter" when he grew up, and he was right, though he never knew it, for he died betimes, did Joseph. My husband. He died. Yet, while he was with me, he called me "Mim".'

She sighed. Then, as if I had suddenly appeared by the side of the cart, she focused her eyes on me and cleared her throat.

'Miriam,' she said. 'He favoured the Hebrew of my name. And in our friendliest moments he nicked it to "Mim". Please. Call me "Mim". I think I'd like to have that old feeling back again. Mim.'

In extremest old age, Mary died.

During the date harvest five months ago, my Miriam left me.

She fell and broke her hip. Shortly thereafter she slipped into a brutal, thrashing sleep which lasted nearly a week. I watched over her. I washed her face and throat and flesh with sponges cooled in springwater. Remembering something of her own medicines, I gathered the polished, whitish seeds of the colchicum and crushed them to powder and steeped that in a sweetened wine. It makes a sedative, which I spurted from my mouth into hers. In the same way I gave her water to drink. I chewed bread and kissed its paste into her mouth. For several days I could, by stroking her throat, cause her to swallow the food; but then she stopped swallowing, and I, too, sadly, stopped.

Mary, Miriam, never regained her consciousness. Near noon on Rosh Hashanah, the first day of the New Year, she gasped three times distinctly – and then the breath escaped her lungs, and she breathed no more.

I lit candles and placed them two at her head and two at her feet. Though I am a man and she a woman, I claimed my right as her only kinsman, and therefore it was I who gave her a final bath, I who trimmed her pugnacious hair and wrapped her body in a linen shroud and covered her eyes and placed the myrtle branches by her – and I myself became her piper. I sat on her bed and blew a doleful music, and then I buried her.

She lies, as did Yeshi once, in a stone sepulchre; but she will lie there longer than he: almost a year. And then, by Rosh Hashanah this coming year, I will have carried her dry bones to Nazareth. I'll bury them beside the bones of her husband, Joseph, where they two shall sleep until the coming of her son, the king of glory, when we all shall jump from our tombs and see his radiant face.

During these last five months, living without her companionship and conscious of the brevity of my bodily life, I've been busy about a single thing: the preparation of an account of the life of Jesus, the book which lies before you now.

The witnesses are all falling asleep. James was the first of us to die: martyred thirty years ago in Jerusalem at the hands of King Herod Agrippa, who thought to make his synagogues happy thereby. The Romans crucified Simon Peter in their capital. That was a decade ago. I've heard stories of the ends of other apostles, that Thomas was speared near the Indus, in India, that Philip died and was buried in Hierapolis, that Andrew was bound to a cross in Patras of Achaia, lingering two days upon that engine and preaching the name of Jesus until he died. There are many stories these days, but few apostles to confirm them. Perhaps none are left but me. And so I write.

Mary made our long years together rich by means of her talk, her memory of things she'd kept in her heart and pondered even from the beginning. She told me stories I would never otherwise have known. From her I learned of the birth of the Lord, of his youth, of his first pilgrimage to Jerusalem. By her willing, round, unvarnished honesty I entered the grand theatre of this woman's interior world and was granted to know her dramatic emotions through the lifetime of her son.

And to the best of my ability, I have been recording the combined spirits, observations, insights, griefs and joys of the mother of Jesus and of the disciple whom he loved.

And if you cannot hear it in the tone of my telling, I'll state it here as plainly as I might: I admired Mary. The diminutive woman whom angels and enemies accosted, who herself accosted God, was a lion. I loved her deeply. I love her still.

What Mary didn't see, I saw. And much we saw together.

I am the disciple who testifies to these events. My testimony is true. There are, I confess, many other things that Jesus did; but if all his works were written down I don't think the world itself could contain the number of the books that would be written.

But *these* are written that you may come to believe that Jesus is the Messiah, the Son of God, and that, by believing, you may have life in his name.

REVIVAL

═

There was for us, it must be recorded (confessed), a time of confusion. Following that first, dazzling week when the risen Lord Jesus met us in the upper room and sent us as he'd been sent by the Father, we experienced almost a month of irresolution during which we, disciples, followers, the young and the old, both men and women, lost hold of the unity we'd known when he still walked among us.

Some wandered from Jerusalem towards the north, fetching up in their hometowns, or by the Sea of Galilee.

Some of the women stayed in John Mark's mother's house. Others repaired to Bethany. Joanna and Chuza went back to Cana and occupied a room in the house of their son-in-law.

Some went down to Jericho and the Jordan; others spent their days in the Temple, praying.

Simon Peter was not wholly responsible for this malaise. The changes had been radical; we'd been whipsawed, toppled by our emotions; the future, and the work required for the future, were nearly beyond our comprehension. I think our dissolution was something like a bodily convalescence – and we the body. We had to rest, to eat, to contemplate.

But neither is Simon without fault.

On account of his natural boisterousness, folks had followed him ever since we started in Capernaum. The size of his body, the size of his voice, his supreme self-confidence, even the bravura that picked up Jesus and began to tickle him – all these had caused the disciples to defer to him, granting him (second to Jesus) the role of a leader.

But after the Lord had clasped his face and breathed on him in the upper room, Simon had fallen into black despair. No longer critical of sisters and brothers, but seeming wounded by their very gladness, he withdrew into a puling sickness and extinguished the gladness, heart by heart. Like sticks into a whirlpool, anyone who swam too near the big man's self-pitiful vortex was sucked into the same consuming gloom. The family grew confused. Its members wandered away. We dispersed.

I know that Simon didn't intend to confuse us. Moreover, I believe he was oblivious to the effect he had on the others. Self-centred in joy, self-centred in guilt – this is the paradox of leadership: it attends so publicly, so compellingly to the self, and so scantily to the feelings of its followers, that they tend to discredit their selves as well.

Simon went north. Thomas went with him, dark clouds trailing behind the both of them.

Nathanael went to Cana. The sons of Zebedee had already repaired to their father's home in Capernaum.

Mary and I invited Maryam to walk with us. It was natural not to leave her alone, though she was no longer the ephemeral, night-like thing of pale uncertainties. The woman had taken into herself something of substance. Something of weight. Surely, she would have found her way alone. But our incidental kindness, inviting her to walk with us – and even choosing her birthplace as the destination – made Maryam our companion for years thereafter, the three of us forming the core of a community that shall continue long after I, too – the last of the three – am gone.

Yes. In several days we had made our way to Magdala, the village that deadens one's nose with the reeking stink of fish.

'Fish!' said Mary the mother of Jesus, laying a finger against her nose. 'Does anyone else think it's time to go fishing?'

Well, so I equipped myself and went and looked and soon found Simon sitting like a cormorant on a rock by the Sea of Galilee. I walked up and stood beside him and asked after his wife ('Fine') and after himself.

'Fine. Go away.'

I walked out on a stone jetty – maybe ten yards from Simon ashore. I dropped a line into the water and in a few minutes hooked a little tilapia. I withdrew the hook and threw the fish at

Simon. It slipped under his robe and set up a fearful flipping in his lower parts.

'What the – ?'

'Your lunch,' I called merrily.

I baited my hook and repeated the process. I had to wait awhile longer this time, but soon enough I caught another fish. This one too I pitched at Simon. It hit him a good slap on the forehead.

He rose up, yelling, 'Now, look here!'

'*My* lunch,' I said. And, having gained his attention, I jabbered on, approaching him, winking, challenging, finally turning him by the shoulders and pushing him in the direction of the village: 'Simon, are your hands still hard to the ropes and the oars? Do you remember the play of the winds? The run of the currents below? When was the last time you went fishing? Why don't we go fishing tonight? For old time's sake. Get one of Zebedee's boats. And bring Thomas back. I saw Nathanael in town.'

You will have realized, surely, how unnatural this sort of behaviour is for me. It was Mary who conceived the idea, Mary who sent me to test it, and Mary who joined the fishermen in order to see it through.

The night was moon-struck and, after the evening breezes, altogether still. We, pale as salt in one another's eyes, spent the first half of the night casting in various shallows which Simon and James both swore had been thick with fish in the past.

But we hauled our nets back light and empty.

'Perhaps you've forgotten your trade,' Mary said. She sat primly on the foremost thwart. Every time she said something like that, ever in tones of helpfulness, we rowed to another place and Simon cast his net with a greater intensity and a braver flourish.

His blood was coming up. Competition can waken certain men even from the dead.

'Simon,' Mary called by way of encouragement, 'let's go back and get your wife. Let's ask her how it's done.'

If it had been me taunting him, it would have been me in the water next. But Mary was a woman. Simon ground his teeth and hung a lantern over the gunnel and cast his net.

The more she talked, the longer we fished. All through the rest of the night we fished, casting and casting and catching nothing.

Finally, at daybreak on glassy seas, we heard the voice of someone ashore, calling: 'Children!'

It was a man about a hundred yards off, veiled by the dawn mist over quiet water. Whether or not he could have seen us, he can't have helped but hear the fulminations of these unsatisfied fishermen.

'So, children!' he called 'Haven't caught so much as a single keeper, have you?'

Simon hissed like grease in a fire: 'Children!'

But I cupped my hands to my mouth and shouted back, 'No! Not a thing the whole night through.'

Then, suddenly, the morning fairly hummed with familiarity. This – or something like it – had happened before.

The man called: 'Cast the net on the right side of the boat, and you will find your fish!'

Well, we did as the man had suggested, and immediately the net was so heavy we could scarcely keep hold of it, let alone haul it aboard.

And I knew him. I knew that man!

'Simon,' I said, 'it's the Lord!'

And Simon Peter, caught completely by surprise, snatched up his garment and leaped into the lake and began swimming for shore.

We came only slowly behind him, rowing hard against the drag of our remarkable catch. Mary was standing in the bow, facing the shore with her hands upon her mouth.

'Yeshi.'

Simon, raining water all around him, pulled himself out of the sea. I could see now that Jesus had a fire going among the stones, two fish and some barley bread roasting over it.

'Bring meat enough for all of you,' he said, and Simon straightway jumped back into the boat and grappled the net and, all by himself, brought it up on the pebbled beach, a wonderful, flashing heap of large fish.

Jesus said, 'Come, then. Let's eat breakfast.'

'Simon, son of John,' Jesus said, 'do you love me more than these?'

Breakfast was finished. The crumbs and the leftover bits of

fish had been tossed into the sea, where small fry nipped and fed in the freshening water. We lay here and there on the grassy shore, enjoying a period of rest in the presence of the risen Jesus – something as rare as the sun at midnight and more wonderful than any miracle he performed before his crucifixion – when I noticed that the Lord had set his rust-radiant eyes on Simon Peter.

Then he spoke – 'Do you love me more than these?' – and Simon, who had been so solicitous for the comfort of the Lord, jumping up to serve him, asking after his every need, now began to pull his whiskers with a wary, mistrustful grin.

'Yes,' he said, 'Lord,' he said. He frowned. 'You know that I do, don't you?'

Jesus didn't answer that question. Rather, he gave the disciple a job to do. He said, 'Feed my lambs.'

If I were Simon, I think I would've rejoiced to be given a shepherd's role by the good shepherd himself. But Simon resorted to that wary grin again, as if trying to read all the meanings behind Jesus' simple request to *Feed*.

On second thoughts, I might have felt Simon's misgivings indeed, because Jesus did not take his eyes from him. He kept studying the big man with such a glittering incisiveness, that Simon dropped his own eyes and lost the grin. He seemed to be counting his fingers, one through five.

Jesus said, 'Simon, son of John, do you truly?'

Simon shuddered then gaped at Jesus with a silent, pitiful appeal, as if to say: *Do I what?*

'Do you love me?' Jesus said.

I thought I saw that gloom again, darkening the edges of Simon's expression: 'Yes, Lord,' he said with emphasis: 'you *know* that I love you!'

Jesus said, 'Tend my sheep.'

It seemed that Simon was about to utter some sort of acceptance, but Jesus spoke immediately a third time, 'Simon! Son of John!' Jesus stood up and asked: 'Do you love me?'

And Simon Peter began to cry. He wept as bitterly as once he had wept in an alley at night.

No, this wasn't gloom after all, or a return to his despairing. It was something more terrible and more hopeful. I had just watched as the big man was broken into pieces. Jesus had brought him to an open shame and a deathly contrition. Thrice Simon had denied his Lord. Three times in a difficult situation he had refused the opportunity to demonstrate love for his Lord, and so he despised himself. *This* is what had been eating at Simon's bowels and destroying his joy and dissolving the blessed fellowship of the disciples.

But now, visibly present and calling it all to mind again by asking three times, *Do you love me?*, the Lord Jesus revived his blustering rock-apostle by loving him with a killing love.

In the midst of sobbing, bowed to the ground, Simon managed to answer, 'Lord, you know everything. You know that I love you.'

Jesus slipped his hands under Simon's shoulders and lifted the big man to his feet as if he weighed next to nothing. He kissed him. With the sleeve of his robe, he wiped the tears from Simon's eyes. He caught that bearded face between his two hands and gripped it tightly.

'Then do the work I've given you to do,' Jesus said. 'Thou bully shepherd, feed my sheep.'

Simon Peter tried to nod, but the hands still held him. As tall as he was, now Jesus seemed the taller. As heavy as he was, now Jesus seemed the more majestic, for light spilled from him and fountained from his person.

'Truly,' said Jesus, 'when you were younger, you tied your belt around yourself and went where you chose to go. But when your years have all ripened and you are much older, you will stretch out your hands, and someone else will tie the belt around you and lead you where you do not want to go. I tell you this in order to show you the kind of death by which you will glorify your Father in heaven.

'Simon! Follow me!'

DEPARTURE

━━

And then it was that all the disciples gathered on the mountain to which the Lord had told us to go.

And we saw Jesus coming from afar.

And there was not one of us sad any more, nor any one of us who did not raise up hands of love and devotion in order to worship him.

The tread of his bare foot, lightsome: but whether on the ground or somewhat above it, I do not know. His hair and his beard, close and woolly and well defined: but in colour, passing ever between the rust of iron and the whiteness of snow. The eyes of the Lord were marvellous. His eyes were all-encompassing. His eyes arrived before the rest of him, as the light arrives before the lantern, and they gazed without equivocation at each one of us, steadfastly; and I said thereafter that they were yellow with the lofty slant of the eagle's; but others said they were tawny with the roaring glory of a lion; and still others, black and rolling, the eyeballs flashing white at the sides like the eyes of an ox; but Maryam from Magdala, she said, 'A man's. He never had ought but a man's eyes.'

And when he had come among us, the Lord Jesus began to speak.

And these are the words he said:

All authority is given me in heaven and on earth. Go, therefore, and make disciples of all nations, baptizing them in the name of the Father and of the Son and of the Holy Spirit, and teaching them to obey everything that I have commanded you.

And lo: I am with you always, even unto the end of the world.

He blessed us then.

And while he was blessing us, he was parted from us.

While he was being carried upward, the hosts of heaven broke into singing. Angels and angels gave voice to their joy. The legions of Jesus, ten thousand thousand, voices in a skyborne choir sang:

Glory!

And we felt the mountain tremble beneath our feet. Pack animals in the villages of Galilee, donkeys, mules, the bullocks stabled in courtyards and caves, stamped backwards from their mangers. They raised their heads against their tethers, and they bewildered the peasants by bawling, and horses bewildered their riders and camels their caravans by refusing to go.

Glory to God in the highest!

Even so did the hosts of heaven thunder.

It was an angelic fire sheeting the sky. And Jesus walked on twelve million stars as one would walk on sand. And we kept peering up above us, though soon we were seeing nothing, no thing – no *one*, for even Jesus had been caught away into the unseeable light of paradise.

Glory to God in the highest, proclaimed the cosmic storm of the Lord: *and on earth, peace!*

I alone – one beloved of my Lord – I lingered on that holy mountain under a vacant sky, in the silence defined by the booms of that previous chorus.

In solitude.

I waited upon the more normal breezes of the evening, when the wind turns and blows from the east towards the sea. I waited for the loamy scent, the verdure of early summer. I thought I might cry to him. Or pray. Yes, it would be prayer now, wouldn't it? – and prayer as never we prayed to heaven before.

I thought that I might pray to him: *O Jesus! bequeath us peace!*

But as the sun descended behind me and I lifted my eyes again towards the east of all our beginnings, above me, afire in the light of the dying sun, there circled the eagle.

EPILOGUE

##

WORD

Who has not read and heard and considered the first words of Torah, *In the beginning, God...*?

Whose mouth has not been shut, whose mind not stopped, whose frame not turned to ash at the grandeur of the thing, a beginning? A first? And God?

In the beginning God created the heavens and the earth.

But I have seen the Son of God, who also called himself 'the Son of man'.

I've walked with him. I was his beloved and bore no other name but that. I span his scant earth-time by thrice as many years as his. And I know he knew the beginning as closely as did the Creator – and knew the Creator closely too, more intimately than any parent and child by blood connected, know each other.

Well, then: I cannot lay my pen aside until I've given expression to the mystery inexpressible, the timelessness and the placelessness of the Lord.

What I write here, what I indite as last of all, might be sung, could someone give it a music. Me? I confess, there is no music in me – except insofar as I love it. I can't sing. I growl below the soaring voices of the blessed. I don't make melodies. And all the singers I have ever known have left me to my poor, inglorious means: a way with words, a memory weighty and comprehensive and dagger-sharp with detail, a knowledge of Greek and the Scriptures, and the spirit that drives me to write things down.

Forgive me, those of you who are bound to read what I have written; but it must be written; it must be preserved; and it must be read. No: it shall not be that flocks and the people yet unborn should never hear the story.

Or the truth with which I end my book and my life, both together:

In the beginning
Was the Word.
The Word was with God.
The Word was God.
He was in the beginning with God;
All things were made through him;
Without him was not anything made that was made.
In him was life.

This life was our light.
And this light still shines in the darkness.
Darkness has not devoured it!

The true light approached the world,
Then came into the world,
But the world refused to know him.
He came to his own,
But even his own refused to receive him.
Nevertheless:
To all who did receive him,
To all who believed in his name,
He gave the power to become the children of God:
These have been born anothen*:*
They have been born
Not of a woman's blood
Nor of the will of the flesh
Nor of the whim of a hot-blooded man,
But of God.

The Word. The Word. The Word
Became flesh and dwelt among us,
Full of grace and truth.
I have myself beheld his glory:
Glory as of the only Son of the Father.
And from his fullness have we all received
Grace
Heaped on a greater
Grace.
For the law was given through Moses.
Grace and truth?
These came to us through Jesus Christ.
No one has ever seen God.
The only Son,
Residing in the bosom of the Father —
He has made him known.

Walter Wangerin Jr.
30 May, 2005

The Book of God: The Bible as a Novel
Walter Wangerin

**'Powers along with great stamina for hundreds of pages…
Terse and punchy… it will be read and enjoyed.'**
Time Out

Here is the Bible's story as it has never been told before.

The Bible as an epic novel, with all its sweeping action, its
larger-than-life characters, its universal themes of good and evil,
and always, above everything else, its enduring story of a love
that staggers the imagination: the love of God for his people.

The Book of God unfolds the Bible's story in a clean, continuous
thread, free of repetitions, lists of laws and genealogies. Award-
winning author and storyteller Walter Wangerin draws on his
theological and literary scholarship to add flesh and bones to
biblical characters – exploring their motives, their feelings, their
relationships – and painting the lavish backdrop against which
their story is told.

Extraordinary stories of love and conflict, of the human and
the supernatural, unfold alongside the compelling claims that
have brought millions to this book of books.

Wangerin unravels the Bible text to reveal the entire Bible story
in all its drama. He has created a compulsive, engrossing saga
for all who enjoy an epic story. And he brings a wealth of new
insights to those who already know the story well.

ISBN 0 7459 3983 X (paperback)

Paul: A Novel
Walter Wangerin

'An epic adventure. The dramatic story of one of the most provocative and influential men in history.'
Publishing News

The apostle Paul has been one of the most provocative, outspoken, enigmatic and influential men in history. In this stunning novel, Walter Wangerin recreates Paul the man. Here are rich insights into first-century life: Paul was more travelled than any centurion or merchant; his heritage was both Roman and Jewish. We catch glimpses of Roman lifestyles, rich and poor, at home and abroad. We discover the pagan practices of Corinth; the rage of the disempowered Pharisees. Here is breathtaking drama: attacks, imprisoment and shipwreck. Here too are high emotions, played out in Paul's deep friendship with Timothy and fiery conflict with Peter. Yet we see how Paul's encounter with Christ shaped his life and his character, enabling him to carry the torch of the gospel across the first-century world. Wangerin has meticulously researched Paul's passionate and personal letters to the early church, and retraced Paul's Mediterranean journeys to inform this stunning portrait and powerful adventure story befitting the sequel to his outstanding The Book of God.

ISBN: 0 7459 5055 8 (paperback)

All Lion books are available from your local bookshop, or can be ordered via our website or from Marston Book Services. For a free catalogue, showing the complete list of titles available, please contact:

Customer Services
Marston Book Services
PO Box 269
Abingdon
Oxon
OX14 4YN

Tel: 01235 465500

Fax: 01235 465555

Our website can be found at:
www.lionhudson.com